Angular: Up and Running
Learning Angular, Step by Step

Shyam Seshadri

Beijing · Boston · Farnham · Sebastopol · Tokyo

Angular: Up and Running

By Shyam Seshadri

Copyright © 2018 Shyam Seshadri. All rights reserved.

Published by O'Reilly Media, Inc., 1005 Gravenstein Highway North, Sebastopol, CA 95472.

O'Reilly books may be purchased for educational, business, or sales promotional use. Online editions are also available for most titles (*http://oreilly.com/safari*). For more information, contact our corporate/institutional sales department: 800-998-9938 or *corporate@oreilly.com*.

Acquisitions Editor: Mary Treseler
Developmental Editor: Angela Rufino
Production Editor: Kristen Brown
Copyeditor: Kim Cofer
Proofreader: Jasmine Kwityn

Indexer: Ellen Troutman-Zaig
Interior Designer: David Futato
Cover Designer: Ellie Volckhausen
Illustrator: Rebecca Demarest

June 2018:   First Edition

Revision History for the First Edition
2018-05-31:   First release

See *http://oreilly.com/catalog/errata.csp?isbn=9781491999837* for release details.

The O'Reilly logo is a registered trademark of O'Reilly Media, Inc. *Angular: Up and Running*, the cover image, and related trade dress are trademarks of O'Reilly Media, Inc.

The views expressed in this work are those of the author, and do not represent the publisher's views. While the publisher and the author have used good faith efforts to ensure that the information and instructions contained in this work are accurate, the publisher and the author disclaim all responsibility for errors or omissions, including without limitation responsibility for damages resulting from the use of or reliance on this work. Use of the information and instructions contained in this work is at your own risk. If any code samples or other technology this work contains or describes is subject to open source licenses or the intellectual property rights of others, it is your responsibility to ensure that your use thereof complies with such licenses and/or rights.

978-1-491-99983-7

[LSI]

Table of Contents

Introduction

It's funny that we constantly over- or underestimate the impact of certain events and projects in our lives. I seriously believed that the last project I worked on at Google, Google Feedback, would end up completely changing how the company interacted with its customers. And I believed Angular (AngularJS at the time) would just be another flash-in-the-pan, yet-another-framework that would not outlive the Feedback project's admin interface.

And in hindsight, it was exactly the other way around. While Feedback still exists and is baked into a lot of Google products, it is Angular that has gone from a tiny project used by one internal team at Angular to now being used by thousands of developers and companies worldwide. And a lot of it stems from Misko, Igor, and the entire team around it, and their unerring dedication to improving how we develop web applications.

What started off as a two-member project is now one of the largest open source communities on the web, and the framework has impacted and been a part of thousands of projects across the world. There are dozens of books, hundreds of tutorials, and thousands of articles on Angular, and Angular's adoption and support continues to grow each day.

Some of the major concepts that were ahead of their time during the first version of Angular (like data binding, separation of concerns, dependency injection, etc.) are now common features of new frameworks.

The biggest change to the AngularJS ecosystem has been the release of the new version of Angular (initially called Angular 2.0, now just called Angular). It was a drastic, non-backward-compatible change that almost divided an entire community. But with community engagement and an open, inclusive team, what could have been a disastrous step turned out to be a much needed overhaul of Angular to bring it to the new age of web development.

Truly, what makes Angular a great technology and framework is the community around it—those who contribute to the core framework, or develop plug-ins for it, as well as those who use it on a day-to-day basis.

As part of the community, I am truly excited to present this book, and contribute in my own way to what makes this community great.

Who Should Read This Book

This book is for anyone who is looking to get started with Angular (2.0 and onward), whether as a side project, as an additional tool, or for their main work. It is expected that readers are comfortable with JavaScript and HTML before starting this book, but a basic knowledge of JavaScript should be sufficient to learn Angular. Knowledge of AngularJS 1.0 is not needed or expected.

We will also use TypeScript, which is the recommended way of developing in Angular, but a preliminary knowledge is sufficient to read this book.

We will take it step by step, so relax and have fun learning with me.

Why I Wrote This Book

Angular as a framework has grown immensely, and comes with a large set of features and capabilities. With a large community behind it, it also comes with an influx of helpful content. But the help content, tutorials, and guides are either focused only on particular topics, or sporadic and not necessarily useful for someone getting started.

The aim of this book is to provide a step-by-step guide on getting started with Angular. Each concept is provided in a logical, organized fashion, building on top of the previous one. With so many moving parts and an active community, this book does not intend to cover each and every aspect, but instead focuses on the core building blocks in a detailed fashion while letting readers discover the rest on their own.

At the end of the book, you should be familiar with a majority of the Angular framework, and be able to use Angular to develop your own web applications and use it in your own projects.

A Word on Web Application Development Today

JavaScript has come a long way, to the point where it is one of the most widely used and adopted programming languages. Nowadays, it's rare for web developers to have to worry about browser inconsistencies and the like, which was the primary reason for frameworks like jQuery to have existed.

Frameworks (like Angular and React) are now a very common choice for developing frontend experiences, and it is rare for anyone nowadays to decide to build a frontend application without leveraging one.

The advantages of using frameworks are manifold, from reducing boilerplate code, to providing a consistent structure and layout for developing an application to many more. The primary intent is always to reduce the time spent on cruft, and focus more on the major functionality we want to provide. And if it works across browsers (and platforms, like Android and iOS, in addition to desktop), then more power to it.

Angular (as well as other frameworks) provides this, primarily through some core fundamentals that are at the heart of the framework, including:

- Powerful templating syntax driven by declarative programming
- Modularity and separation of concerns
- Data binding, and through it, data-driven programming
- Testability and awesome testing support
- Routing and navigation
- And a host of other features, from server-side rendering, to the ability to write native mobile applications, and much more!

With the help of Angular, we can focus on building amazing experiences, while managing complexity and maintainability in a seamless fashion.

Navigating This Book

This book aims to walk a developer through each part of Angular, step by step. Each chapter that introduces a new concept will be immediately followed by a chapter on how we can unit test it. The book is roughly organized as follows:

- Chapter 1, *Introducing Angular*, is an introduction to Angular as well as the concepts behind it. It also covers what it takes to start writing an Angular application.
- Chapter 2, *Hello Angular*, walks through creating a very simple Angular application, and diving into how the pieces work together. It also introduces the Angular CLI.
- Chapter 3, *Useful Built-In Angular Directives*, digs into the basic built-in Angular directives (including ngFor, ngIf, etc.) and when and how to use them.
- Chapter 4, *Understanding and Using Angular Components*, covers Angular components in more detail, as well as the various options available when creating them. It also covers the basic lifecycle hooks available with components.

- Chapter 5, *Testing Angular Components*, introduces how to unit test angular components using Karma and Jasmine, along with the Angular testing framework.

- Chapter 6, *Working with Template-Driven Forms*, covers creating and working with forms in Angular, specifically template-driven forms.

- Chapter 7, *Working with Reactive Forms*, covers the other way of defining and working with forms, which is how to create and develop reactive forms.

- Chapter 8, *Angular Services*, covers Angular services, which includes how to use built-in Angular services, as well as how and when to define our own Angular services.

- Chapter 9, *Making HTTP Calls in Angular*, moves into the server communication aspect of Angular, and delves into making HTTP calls, as well as some advanced topics like interceptors and the like.

- Chapter 10, *Unit Testing Services*, takes a step back and covers unit testing again, but this time with a focus on unit testing services. This includes testing simple services and slightly harder cases like asynchronous flows as well as services and components that make HTTP calls.

- Chapter 11, *Routing in Angular*, goes in depth into how we can accomplish routing in an Angular application and covers the Angular routing module in detail as well as a majority of its features.

- Chapter 12, *Productionizing an Angular App*, finally brings together all the concepts and covers taking the developed Angular application to production and the various concerns and techniques involved in the same.

The entire code repository is hosted on GitHub, so if you don't want to type in the code examples from this book, or want to ensure that you are looking at the latest and greatest code examples, visit the repository and grab the contents (*https://github.com/ shyamseshadri/angular-up-and-running*).

This book uses AngularJS version 5.0.0 for all its code examples.

Online Resources

The following resources are a great starting point for any AngularJS developer, and should be always available at your fingertips:

- The Official Angular API Documentation (*https://angular.io/api*)
- The Official Angular Quickstart Guide (*https://angular.io/guide/quickstart*)
- The Angular Heroes Tutorial App (*https://angular.io/tutorial*)

Conventions Used in This Book

The following typographical conventions are used in this book:

Italic
> Indicates new terms, URLs, email addresses, filenames, and file extensions.

`Constant width`
> Used for program listings, as well as within paragraphs to refer to program elements such as variable or function names, databases, data types, environment variables, statements, and keywords.

`Constant width bold`
> Shows commands or other text that should be typed literally by the user.

`Constant width italic`
> Shows text that should be replaced with user-supplied values or by values determined by context.

> This element signifies a tip or suggestion.

> This element signifies a general note.

> This element indicates a warning or caution.

Using Code Examples

Supplemental material (code examples, exercises, etc.) is available for download at *https://github.com/shyamseshadri/angular-up-and-running*.

This book is here to help you get your job done. In general, if example code is offered with this book, you may use it in your programs and documentation. You do not need to contact us for permission unless you're reproducing a significant portion of the code. For example, writing a program that uses several chunks of code from this book does not require permission. Selling or distributing a CD-ROM of examples from O'Reilly books does require permission. Answering a question by citing this book and quoting example code does not require permission. Incorporating a significant amount of example code from this book into your product's documentation does require permission.

We appreciate, but do not require, attribution. An attribution usually includes the title, author, publisher, and ISBN. For example: "*Angular: Up and Running* by Shyam Seshadri (O'Reilly). Copyright 2018 Shyam Seshadri, 978-1-491-99983-7."

If you feel your use of code examples falls outside fair use or the permission given above, feel free to contact us at *permissions@oreilly.com*.

O'Reilly Safari

 Safari (formerly Safari Books Online) is a membership-based training and reference platform for enterprise, government, educators, and individuals.

Members have access to thousands of books, training videos, Learning Paths, interactive tutorials, and curated playlists from over 250 publishers, including O'Reilly Media, Harvard Business Review, Prentice Hall Professional, Addison-Wesley Professional, Microsoft Press, Sams, Que, Peachpit Press, Adobe, Focal Press, Cisco Press, John Wiley & Sons, Syngress, Morgan Kaufmann, IBM Redbooks, Packt, Adobe Press, FT Press, Apress, Manning, New Riders, McGraw-Hill, Jones & Bartlett, and Course Technology, among others.

For more information, please visit *http://oreilly.com/safari*.

How to Contact Us

Please address comments and questions concerning this book to the publisher:

O'Reilly Media, Inc.
1005 Gravenstein Highway North
Sebastopol, CA 95472
800-998-9938 (in the United States or Canada)
707-829-0515 (international or local)
707-829-0104 (fax)

We have a web page for this book, where we list errata, examples, and any additional information. You can access this page at *http://bit.ly/angularUR*.

To comment or ask technical questions about this book, send email to *bookquestions@oreilly.com*.

For more information about our books, courses, conferences, and news, see our website at *http://www.oreilly.com*.

Find us on Facebook: *http://facebook.com/oreilly*

Follow us on Twitter: *http://twitter.com/oreillymedia*

Watch us on YouTube: *http://www.youtube.com/oreillymedia*

Acknowledgments

This book is dedicated to my wife, Sanchita, and my parents and grandmom who were my rock as well as my motivation to write this book in the best manner I could, all the while balancing my own fledgling startup in its most precarious time (the beginning!).

I'd also like to thank my reviewers, Yakov Fain and Victor Mejia, who had to read and review my unedited ramblings and make sure I got my point across in the most succinct and understandable terms.

This book of course wouldn't be possible without the faith and efforts of the awesome team at O'Reilly, especially Angela and Kristen!

And finally, thank you to the amazing Angular community for all their contributions, feedback, and support, and for teaching us how to use and make it better.

CHAPTER 1

Introducing Angular

Our expectations of what we can perform on the web (and by web here, I mean both desktop as well as the mobile web) has increased to the point where what used to be full-fledged native desktop applications are run on the browser. Web applications now resemble desktop native applications in scope and complexity, which also results in added complexity as a developer.

Furthermore, Single-Page Applications (SPAs) have become a very common choice in building out frontend experiences, as they allow for great customer experiences in terms of speed and responsiveness. Once the initial application has loaded into a customer's browser, further interactions only have to worry about loading the additional data needed, without reloading the entire page as was the norm with server-side rendered pages of the past.

AngularJS was started to first bring structure and consistency to single-page web application development, while providing a way to quickly develop scalable and maintainable web applications. In the time since it was released, the web and browsers have moved forward by leaps and bounds, and some of the problems that AngularJS was solving weren't as relevant anymore.

Angular then was basically a completely new rewritten version of the framework, built for the new-age web. It leveraged a lot of the newer advances, from modules to web components, while improving the existing features of AngularJS, like dependency injection and templating.

 From now on, when I say AngularJS, I refer to the original AngularJS framework, the 1.0 version. Whenever I mention Angular, it refers to the newer framework, from 2.0 onward. This is primarily because Angular 2.0 onward does not predicate itself to using only JavaScript, but also supports writing applications in TypeScript.

Why Angular

Angular as a framework provides a few significant advantages while also providing a common structure for developers on a team to work with. It allows us to develop large applications in a maintainable manner. We will dig into each one of these in more detail in the following chapters:

Custom components
> Angular allows you to build your own declarative components that can pack functionality along with its rendering logic into bite-sized, reusable pieces. It also plays well with web components.

Data binding
> Angular allows you to seamlessly move your data from your core JavaScript code to the view, and react to view events without having to write the glue code yourself.

Dependency injection
> Angular allows you to write modular services, and have them injected wherever they are needed. This greatly improves the testability and reusability of the same.

Testing
> Tests are first-class citizens, and Angular has been built from the ground up with testability in mind. You can (and should!) test every part of your application.

Comprehensive
> Angular is a full-fledged framework, and provides out-of-the-box solutions for server communication, routing within your application, and more.

 Angular as a framework has adopted semantic versioning for all new releases. Furthermore, the core team has an aggressive roadmap, with a new major release planned every six months. Thus, what started off as Angular 2 is now referred to as just Angular, since we don't want to call them Angular 2, Angular 4, Angular 5, and so on.

That said, unlike AngularJS to Angular, upgrading between versions of Angular (say 2 to 4, etc.) is an incremental step, and more often than not an almost trivial upgrade. So you don't need to worry about having to do a major upgrade every few months with drastic code changes.

What This Book Will Not Cover

While Angular as a framework is quite large, the community around it is even larger. A lot of great features and options for use with Angular in fact stem from this community. This makes life harder as an author to figure out how to write a book that preps you, the reader, as an Angular developer, while still limiting the scope to what I think are the essentials.

To that extent, while Angular can be extended in so many ways, from writing native mobile apps using Angular (see NativeScript (*https://www.nativescript.org/*)), rendering your Angular application on the server (see Angular Universal (*https://univer sal.angular.io/*)), using Redux as a first-class option in Angular (multiple options; see ngrx (*https://github.com/ngrx*)), and many more, the initial version of the book will only focus on the core Angular platform and all the capabilities it provides. It will also strive to focus on the more common cases rather than cover every single feature and capability of Angular, as such a book would run into thousands of pages.

The intention is to focus on the parts that will be necessary and useful to all Angular developers, rather than focus on bits and parts that would be useful to a subset.

Getting Started with Your Development Environment

Angular expects you to do a fair bit of groundwork to be able to develop seamlessly on your computer. Certain prerequisites need to be installed that we will cover in this section.

Node.js

While you will never be coding in Node.js, Angular uses Node.js as its base for a large part of its build environment. Thus, to get started with Angular, you will need to have Node.js installed on your environment. There are multiple ways to install Node.js, so please refer to the Node.js Download Page (*https://nodejs.org/en/download/*) for more instructions.

 On macOS, installing Node.js through Homebrew has been known to cause some issues. So try installing it directly if you run into any problems.

You need to install version 6.9.0 or above of Node.js, and version 3.0.0 or above of npm. You can confirm your versions after installing by running the following commands:

```
node --version
npm --v
```

TypeScript

TypeScript adds a set of types to the JavaScript code that we write, allowing us to write JavaScript that is easier to understand, reason about, and trace. It ensures that the latest proposed ECMAScript features are also available at the tip of our fingers. At the end of the day, all your TypeScript code compiles down to JavaScript that can run easily in any environment.

TypeScript is not mandatory for developing an Angular application, but it is highly recommended, as it offers some syntactic sugar, as well as makes the codebase easier to understand and maintain. In this book, we will be using TypeScript to develop Angular applications.

TypeScript is installed as an NPM package, and thus can be simply installed with the following command:

```
npm install -g typescript
```

Make sure you install at least version 2.4.0 or above.

While we will be covering most of the basic features/concepts that we use from TypeScript, it is always a good idea to learn more from the official TypeScript documentation (*https://www.typescriptlang.org/docs/home.html*).

Angular CLI

Unlike AngularJS, where it was easy to source one file as a dependency and be up and running, Angular has a slightly more complicated setup. To this extent, the Angular team has created a command-line interface (CLI) tool to make it easier to bootstrap and develop your Angular applications.

As it significantly helps making the process of development easier, I recommend using it at the very least for your initial projects until you get the hang of all the things it does and are comfortable doing it yourself. In this book, we will cover both the CLI command as well as the actions it performs underneath, so that you get a good understanding of all the changes needed.

Installing the latest version (1.7.3 at the time of writing this book) is as simple as running the following command:

```
npm install -g @angular/cli
```

 If you are scratching your head at this newfangled naming convention for Angular packages, the new syntax is a feature of NPM called *scoped packages*. It allows packages to be grouped together within NPM under a single folder. You can read more here (*https://docs.npmjs.com/misc/scope*).

Once installed, you can confirm if it was successful by running the following command:

```
ng --version
```

Getting the Codebase

All the examples from this book, along with the exercises and the final solution, are hosted as a Git repository. While it is not mandatory to download this, you can choose to do so if you want a reference or want to play around with the samples in this book. You can do so by cloning the Git repository by running the following command:

```
git clone https://github.com/shyamseshadri/angular-up-and-running.git
```

This will create a folder called *angular-up-and-running* in your current working directory with all the necessary examples. Within this directory you'll find subfolders containing the examples, organized by chapter.

Conclusion

At this point, we are all set up with our development environment and are ready to start developing Angular applications. We have installed Node.js, TypeScript, as well as the Angular CLI and understand the need and use of each.

In the next chapter, we will finally get our hands dirty building our first Angular application and understanding some of the basic terms and concepts of Angular.

CHAPTER 2

Hello Angular

In the previous chapter, we got a very quick overview of Angular and its features, as well as a step-by-step guide on how to set up our local environment for developing any Angular application. In this chapter, we will go through the various parts of an Angular application by creating a very simple application from scratch. Through the use of this application, we will cover some of the basic terminologies and concepts like modules, components, data and event binding, and passing data to and from components.

We will start with a very simple stock market application, which allows us to see a list of stocks, each with its own name, stock code, and price. During the course of this chapter, we will see how to package rendering a stock into an individual, reusable component, and how to work with Angular event and data binding.

Starting Your First Angular Project

As mentioned in the previous chapter, we will heavily rely on the Angular CLI to help us bootstrap and develop our application. I will assume that you have already followed the initial setup instructions in the previous chapter and have Node.js, TypeScript, and the Angular CLI installed in your development environment.

Creating a new application is as simple as running the following command:

```
ng new stock-market
```

When you run this command, it will automatically generate a skeleton application under the folder *stock-market* with a bunch of files, and install all the necessary dependencies for the Angular application to work. This might take a while, but eventually, you should see the following line in your terminal:

```
Project 'stock-market' successfully created.
```

Congratulations, you have just created your first Angular application!

 While we created our first application with the vanilla Angular CLI command, the `ng new` command takes a few arguments that allow you to customize the application generated to your preference. These include:

- Whether you want to use vanilla CSS or SCSS or any other CSS framework (for example, `ng new --style=scss`)
- Whether you want to generate a routing module (for example, `ng new --routing`); we'll discuss this further in Chapter 11.
- Whether you want inline styles/templates
- Whether you want a common prefix to all components (for example, to prefix `acme` to all components, `ng new --prefix=acme`)

And much more. It's worth exploring these options by running `ng help` once you are a bit more familiar with the Angular framework to decide if you have specific preferences one way or the other.

Understanding the Angular CLI

While we have just created our first Angular application, the Angular CLI does a bit more than just the initial skeleton creation. In fact, it is useful throughout the development process for a variety of tasks, including:

- Bootstrapping your application
- Serving the application
- Running the tests (both unit and end-to-end)
- Creating a build for distribution
- Generating new components, services, routes and more for your application

Each of these corresponds to one or more Angular CLI commands, and we will cover each one as and when we need or encounter them, instead of trying to cover each command and its uses upfront. Each command provides further flexibility with a variety of arguments and options, making the Angular CLI truly diverse and capable for a wide variety of uses.

Running the Application

Now that we have generated our application, the next part is to run it so that we can see our live running application in the browser. There are technically two ways to run it:

- Running it in development mode, where the Angular CLI compiles the changes as it happens and refreshes our UI
- Running it in production mode, with an optimal compiled build, served via static files

For now, we will run it in development mode, which is as simple as running

```
ng serve
```

from the root folder of the generated project, which is the *stock-market* folder in this case. After a little bit of processing and compilation, you should see something like the following in your terminal:

```
** NG Live Development Server is listening on localhost:4200,
   open your browser on http://localhost:4200/ **
Date: 2018-03-26T10:09:18.869Z
Hash: 0b730a52f97909e2d43a
Time: 11086ms
chunk {inline} inline.bundle.js (inline) 3.85 kB [entry] [rendered]
chunk {main} main.bundle.js (main) 17.9 kB [initial] [rendered]
chunk {polyfills} polyfills.bundle.js (polyfills) 549 kB [initial] [rendered]
chunk {styles} styles.bundle.js (styles) 41.5 kB [initial] [rendered]
chunk {vendor} vendor.bundle.js (vendor) 7.42 MB [initial] [rendered]

webpack: Compiled successfully.
```

The preceding output is a snapshot of all the files that the Angular CLI generates in order for your Angular application to be served successfully. It includes the *main.bundle.js*, which is the transpiled code that is specific to your application, and the *vendor.bundle.js*, which includes all the third-party libraries and frameworks you depend on (including Angular). *styles.bundle.js* is a compilation of all the CSS styles that are needed for your application, while *polyfills.bundle.js* includes all the polyfills needed for supporting some capabilities in older browsers (like advanced ECMA-Script features not yet available in all browsers). Finally, *inline.bundle.js* is a tiny file with webpack utilities and loaders that is needed for bootstrapping the application.

ng serve starts a local development server on port 4200 for you to hit from your browser. Opening *http://localhost:4200* in your browser should result in you seeing the live running Angular application, which should look like Figure 2-1.

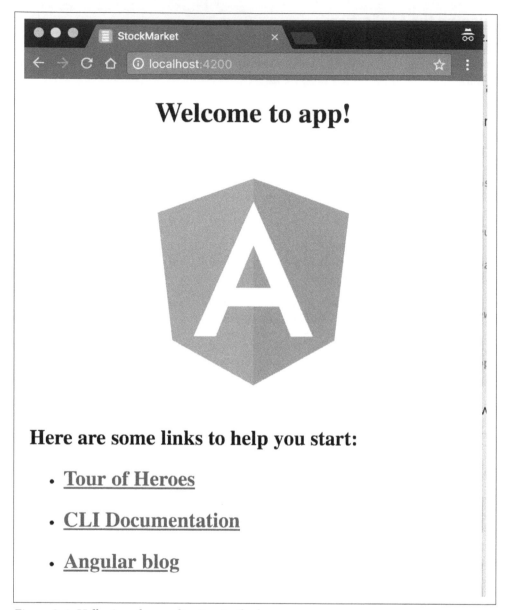

Figure 2-1. Hello Angular application in the browser

You can actually leave the `ng serve` command running in the terminal, and continue making changes. If you have the application opened in your browser, it will automatically refresh each time you save your changes. This makes the development quick and iterative.

In the following section, we will go into a bit more detail about what exactly happened under the covers to see how the generated Angular application works and what the various pieces are.

Basics of an Angular Application

At its core, any Angular application is still a Single-Page Application (SPA), and thus its loading is triggered by a main request to the server. When we open any URL in our browser, the very first request is made to our server (which is running within `ng serve` in this case). This initial request is satisfied by an HTML page, which then loads the necessary JavaScript files to load both Angular as well as our application code and templates.

One thing to note is that although we develop our Angular application in TypeScript, the web application works with transpiled JavaScript. The `ng serve` command is responsible for translating our TypeScript code into JavaScript for the browser to load.

If we look at the structure the Angular CLI has generated, it is something like this:

```
stock-market
+----e2e
+----src
    +----app
        +----app.component.css
        +----app.component.html
        +----app.component.spec.ts
        +----app.component.ts              ❶
        +----app.module.ts                 ❷
    +----assets
    +----environments
    +----index.html                        ❸
    +----main.ts                           ❹
    +----.angular-cli.json                 ❺
```

❶ Root component

❷ Main module

❸ Root HTML

❹ Entry point

❺ Angular CLI config

There are a few more files than listed here in the *stock-market* folder, but these are the major ones we are going to focus on in this chapter. In addition, there are unit tests, end-to-end (e2e) tests, the assets that support our application, configuration specific to various environments (dev, prod, etc.), and other general configuration that we will touch upon in Chapters 5, 10, and 12.

Root HTML—index.html

If you take a look at the *index.html* file, which is in the *src* folder, you will notice that it looks very clean and pristine, with no references to any scripts or dependencies:

```
<!doctype html>
<html lang="en">
<head>
  <meta charset="utf-8">
  <title>StockMarket</title>
  <base href="/">

  <meta name="viewport" content="width=device-width, initial-scale=1">
  <link rel="icon" type="image/x-icon" href="favicon.ico">
</head>
<body>
  <app-root></app-root>                    ❶
</body>
</html>
```

❶ Root component for our Angular application

The only thing of note in the preceding code is the `<app-root>` element in the HTML, which is the marker for loading our application code.

What about the part that loads the core Angular scripts and our application code? That is inserted dynamically at runtime by the `ng serve` command, which combines all the vendor libraries, our application code, the styles, and inline templates each into individual bundles and injects them into *index.html* to be loaded as soon as the page renders in our browser.

The Entry Point—main.ts

The second important part of our bootstrapping piece is the *main.ts* file. The *index.html* file is responsible for deciding which files are to be loaded. The *main.ts* file, on the other hand, identifies which Angular module (which we will talk a bit more about in the following section) is to be loaded when the application starts. It can also change application-level configuration (like turning off framework-level asserts and verifications using the `enableProdMode()` flag), which we will cover in Chapter 12:

```
import { enableProdMode } from '@angular/core';
import { platformBrowserDynamic } from '@angular/platform-browser-dynamic';

import { AppModule } from './app/app.module';
```

```
import { environment } from './environments/environment';

if (environment.production) {
  enableProdMode();
}

platformBrowserDynamic().bootstrapModule(AppModule)          ❶
  .catch(err => console.log(err));
```

❶ Bootstrap the main `AppModule`

Most of the code in the *main.ts* file is generic, and you will rarely have to touch or change this entry point file. Its main aim is to point the Angular framework at the core module of your application and let it trigger the rest of your application source code from that point.

Main Module—app.module.ts

This is where your application-specific source code starts from. The application module file can be thought of as the core configuration of your application, from loading all the relevant and necessary dependencies, declaring which components will be used within your application, to marking which is the main entry point component of your application:

```
import { BrowserModule } from '@angular/platform-browser';
import { NgModule } from '@angular/core';


import { AppComponent } from './app.component';


@NgModule({                                    ❶
  declarations: [
    AppComponent                               ❷
  ],
  imports: [                                   ❸
    BrowserModule
  ],
  providers: [],
  bootstrap: [AppComponent]                    ❹
})
export class AppModule { }
```

❶ `NgModule` TypeScript annotation to mark this class definition as an Angular module

❷ Declarations marking out which components and directives can be used within the application

❸ Importing other modules that provide functionality needed in the application

❹ The entry point component for starting the application

 This is our first time dealing with a TypeScript-specific feature, which are decorators (you can think of them as annotations). Decorators allow us to decorate classes with annotations and properties as well as meta-functionality.

Angular heavily leverages this TypeScript feature across the board, such as using decorators for modules, components, and more.

You can read more about TypeScript decorators in the official documentation (*http://bit.ly/2IDQd1U*).

We will go over the details of each of these sections in the following chapters, but at its core:

declarations

> The declarations block defines all the components that are allowed to be used in the scope of the HTML within this module. Any component that you create must be declared before it can be used.

imports

> You will not create each and every functionality used in the application, and the imports array allows you to import other Angular application and library modules and thus leverage the components, services, and other capabilities that have already been created in those modules.

bootstrap

> The bootstrap array defines the component that acts as the entry point to your application. If the main component is not added here, your application will not kick-start, as Angular will not know what elements to look for in your *index.html*.

You usually end up needing (if you are not using the CLI for any reason!) to modify this file if and only if you add new components, services, or add/integrate with new libraries and modules.

Root Component—AppComponent

We finally get to the actual Angular code that drives the functionality of the application, and in this case, it is the main (and only) component we have, the AppComponent. The code for it looks something like this:

```
import { Component } from '@angular/core';

@Component({
  selector: 'app-root',                        ❶
  templateUrl: './app.component.html',         ❷
  styleUrls: ['./app.component.css']           ❸
})
export class AppComponent {
  title = 'app';                               ❹
}
```

❶ The DOM selector that gets translated into an instance of this component

❷ The HTML template backing this component—in this case, the URL to it

❸ Any component-specific styling, again pointing to a separate file in this case

❹ The component class with its own members and functions

A *component* in Angular is nothing but a TypeScript class, decorated with some attributes and metadata. The class encapsulates all the data and functionality of the component, while the decorator specifies how it translates into the HTML.

The *app-selector* is a CSS selector that identifies how Angular finds this particular component in any HTML page. While we generally use element selectors (app-root in the preceding example, which translates to looking for <app-root> elements in the HTML), they can be any CSS selector, from a CSS class to an attribute as well.

The templateUrl is the path to the HTML used to render this component. We can also use inline templates instead of specifying a templateUrl like we have done in the example. In this particular case, the template we are referring to is *app.component.html*.

styleUrls is the styling counterpart to the template, encapsulating all the styles for this component. Angular ensures that the styles are encapsulated, so you don't have to worry about your CSS classes from one component affecting another. Unlike templateUrl, styleUrls is an array.

The component class itself finally encapsulates all the functionality backing your component. It makes it easy to think of the responsibilities of the component class as twofold:

- Load and hold all the data necessary for rendering the component
- Handle and process any events that may arise from any element in the component

The data in the class will drive what can be displayed as part of the component. So let's take a look at what the template for this component looks like:

```
<h1>
  {{title}}                    ❶
</h1>
```

❶ Data-bound title from the component

Our HTML is as simple as can be for the component. All it has is one element, which is data-bound to a field in our component class. The double-curly ({{ }}) syntax is an indication to Angular to replace the value between the braces with the value of the variable from the corresponding class.

In this case, once the application loads, and the component is rendered, the {{title}} will be replaced with the text app works!. We will talk in more detail about data binding in "Understanding Data Binding" on page 19.

Creating a Component

So far, we have dealt with the basic skeleton code that the Angular CLI has generated for us. Let's now look at adding new components, and what that entails. We will use the Angular CLI to generate a new component, but look underneath the covers to see what steps it takes. We will then walk through some very basic common tasks we try to accomplish with components.

Steps in Creating New Components

Using the Angular CLI, creating a new component is simply running a simple command. We will first try creating a stock widget, which displays the name of the stock, its stock code, the current price, and whether it has changed for the positive or negative.

We can simply create a new stock-item by running the following command from the main folder of the application:

```
ng generate component stock/stock-item
```

There are a few interesting things to note here:

- The Angular CLI has a command called generate, which can be used to generate components (like we did in the preceding example), and also to generate other Angular elements, such as interfaces, services, modules, and more.
- With the target type, we also specify the name (and the folder) within which the component has to be generated. Here, we are telling the Angular CLI to generate

a component called `stock-item` within a folder called *stock*. If we don't specify stock, it will create a component called `stock-item` in the *app* folder itself.

The command will generate all the relevant files for a new component, including:

- The component definition (named *stock-item.component.ts*)
- The corresponding template definition (named *stock-item.component.html*)
- The styles for the component (in a file named *stock-item.component.css*)
- The skeleton unit tests for the component (named *stock-item.component.spec.ts*)

In addition, it updated the original app module that we saw earlier so that our Angular application recognizes the new module.

This is the recommended convention to follow whenever you are working with components:

- The filename starts with the name of the item you are creating
- This is followed by the type of element it is (in this case, a component)
- Finally, we have the relevant extension

This allows us to both group and easily identify relevant and related files in a simple manner.

When you run the command, you should see something like this:

```
create src/app/stock/stock-item/stock-item.component.css
create src/app/stock/stock-item/stock-item.component.html
create src/app/stock/stock-item/stock-item.component.spec.ts
create src/app/stock/stock-item/stock-item.component.ts
update src/app/app.module.ts
```

The source for the component, HTML, and the CSS remain pretty much barebones, so I won't repeat that here. What is important is how this new component that we create is hooked up and made available to our Angular application. Let's take a look at the modified *app.module.ts* file:

```
import { BrowserModule } from '@angular/platform-browser';
import { NgModule } from '@angular/core';

import { AppComponent } from './app.component';
import { StockItemComponent } from './stock/stock-item/stock-item.component';    ❶

@NgModule({
  declarations: [
    AppComponent,
    StockItemComponent                              ❷
  ],
```

```
  imports: [
    BrowserModule
  ],
  providers: [],
  bootstrap: [AppComponent]
})
export class AppModule { }
```

❶ Importing the newly created `stock-item` component

❷ Adding the new component to the `declarations` section

In the application module, we have to ensure that the new component is imported and added to the `declarations` array, before we can start using it in our Angular application.

Using Our New Component

Now that we have created a new component, let's see how we can use it in our application. We will now try to use this skeleton in the app component. First, take a look at the generated *stock-item.component.ts* file:

```
import { Component, OnInit } from '@angular/core';

@Component({
  selector: 'app-stock-item',                    ❶
  templateUrl: './stock-item.component.html',
  styleUrls: ['./stock-item.component.css']
})
export class StockItemComponent implements OnInit {

  constructor() { }

  ngOnInit() {
  }

}
```

❶ The selector for using this component. Note it is prefixed with `app`, which is added by the Angular CLI by default unless otherwise specified.

The component has no data and does not provide any functionality at this point; it simply renders the template associated with it. The template at this point is also trivial, and just prints out a static message.

To use this component in our application, we can simply create an element that matches the selector defined anywhere inside our main app component. If we had more components and a deeper hierarchy of components, we could choose to use it in any of their templates as well. So let's replace most of the placeholder content in *app.component.html* with the following, so that we can render the `stock-item` component:

```
<div style="text-align:center">
  <h1>
    Welcome to {{ title }}!
  </h1>
  <app-stock-item></app-stock-item>          ❶
</div>
```

❶ Adding our `stock-item` component

All it takes is adding the `<app-stock-item></app-stock-item>` to our *app.component.html* file to use our component. We simply create an element using the selector we defined in our component. Then when the application loads, Angular recognizes that the element refers to a component, and triggers the relevant code path.

When you run this (or if your `ng serve` is still running), you should see both the original "app works" along with a new "stock-item works" in the UI.

Understanding Data Binding

Next, let's focus on getting some data and figuring out how to display it as part of our component. What we are trying to build is a stock widget, which will take some stock information, and render it accordingly.

Let's assume that we have a stock for a company named `Test Stock Company`, with a stock code of `TSC`. Its current price is $85, while the previous price it traded at was $80. In the widget, we want to show both the name and its code, as well as the current price, the percentage change since last time, and highlight the price and percentage change in green if it is an increment, or red if it is a decrement.

Let's walk through this step by step. First, we will make sure we can display the name and code in the widget (we will hardcode the information for now, and we will build up the example to get the data from a different source later).

We would change our component code (the *stock-item.component.ts* file) as follows:

```
import { Component, OnInit } from '@angular/core';

@Component({
  selector: 'app-stock-item',
  templateUrl: './stock-item.component.html',
  styleUrls: ['./stock-item.component.css']
})
export class StockItemComponent implements OnInit {   ❶

  public name: string;                                 ❷
  public code: string;
```

```
    public price: number;
    public previousPrice: number;

    constructor() { }

    ngOnInit() {                              ❸
      this.name = 'Test Stock Company';       ❹
      this.code = 'TSC';
      this.price = 85;
      this.previousPrice = 80;
    }
  }
```

❶ Implement `OnInit` interface from Angular, which gives us a hook to when the component is initialized

❷ Definition of the various fields we will want to access from the HTML

❸ `OnInit` function that is triggered when a component is initialized

❹ Initializing the values for each of the fields

Angular gives us hooks into the lifecycle of a component to let us take certain actions when a component is initialized, when its view is rendered, when it is destroyed, and so on. We've extended our trivial component with a few notable things:

OnInit

Angular's `OnInit` hook is executed after the component is created by the Angular framework, after all the data fields are initialized. It is generally recommended to do any initialization work of a component in the `OnInit` hook, so that it makes it easier to test the functionality of the rest of the component without necessarily triggering the initialization flow every time. We will cover the remaining lifecycle hooks in Chapter 4.

ngOnInit

When you want to hook on the initialization phase of a component, you need to implement the `OnInit` interface (as in the example) and then implement the `ngOnInit` function in the component, which is where you write your initialization logic. We have initialized the basic information we need to render our stock widget in the `ngOnInit` function.

Class member variables

We have declared a few public variables as class instance variables. This information will be used to render our template.

Now, let's change the template (the *stock-item.component.html* file) to start rendering this information:

```
<div class="stock-container">
  <div class="name"><h3>{{name}}</h3> - <h4>({{code}})</h4></div>
  <div class="price">$ {{price}}</div>
</div>
```

and its corresponding CSS (the *stock-item.component.css* file), to make it look nice:

```
.stock-container {
  border: 1px solid black;
  border-radius: 5px;
  display: inline-block;
  padding: 10px;
}

.stock-container .name h3, .stock-container .name h4 {
  display: inline-block;
}
```

Note that the CSS is purely from a visual perspective, and is not needed nor impacts our Angular application. You could skip it completely and still have a functional application.

Once we make these changes and refresh our application, we should see something like Figure 2-2 in our browser.

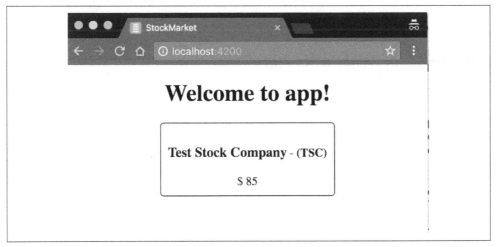

Figure 2-2. Angular app with stock component

We have just used one fundamental building block from Angular to render our data from our component into the HTML. We use the double-curly notation ({{ }}), which is also known as *interpolation*. Interpolation evaluates the expression between the curly braces as per the component backing it, and then renders the result as a string in place in the HTML. In this case, we render the name, code, and the price of the stock using interpolation. This picks up the values of name, code, and price, and then replaces the double-curly expression with its value, thus rendering our UI.

This is Angular's one-way data binding at work. One-way data binding simply refers to Angular's capability to automatically update the UI based on values in the component, and then keeping it updated as the value changes in the component. Without one-way binding, we would have to write code to take the value from our component, find the right element in HTML, and update its value. Then we would have to write listeners/watchers to keep track of when the value in the component changes, and then change the value in the HTML at that time. We can get rid of all of this extra code because of data binding.

In this particular case, we are binding to simple variables, but it is not necessarily restricted to simple variables. The expressions can be slightly more complex. For example, we could render the same UI by changing the binding expression as follows in *stock-item.component.html*:

```
<div class="stock-container">
    <div class="name">{{name + ' (' + code + ')'}}</div>
  <div class="price">$ {{price}}</div>
</div>
```

In this case, we replaced our multiple heading elements with a single div. The interpolation expression is now a combination of both the name and the code, with the code surrounded by parentheses. Angular will evaluate this like normal JavaScript, and return the value of it as a string to our UI.

Understanding Property Binding

So far, we used interpolation to get data from our component code to the HTML. But Angular also provides a way to bind not just text, but also DOM element properties. This allows us to modify the content and the behavior of the HTML that is rendered in the browser.

For example, let's try to modify our stock widget to highlight the price in red if the price is less than the previous price, and in green if it is equal to or more than the previous price. We can first change our component (the *stock-item.component.ts*) to precalculate if the difference is positive or negative like so:

```
import { Component, OnInit } from '@angular/core';

@Component({
  selector: 'app-stock-item',
  templateUrl: './stock-item.component.html',
  styleUrls: ['./stock-item.component.css']
})
export class StockItemComponent implements OnInit {

  public name: string;
  public code: string;
  public price: number;
  public previousPrice: number;
  public positiveChange: boolean;

  constructor() { }

  ngOnInit() {
    this.name = 'Test Stock Company';
    this.code = 'TSC';
    this.price = 85;
    this.previousPrice = 80;
    this.positiveChange = this.price >= this.previousPrice;
  }
}
```

In this code, we added a new public variable called positiveChange, which is of type boolean, and then set the value based on comparing the current price with the previous price. This gives us a singular boolean value that we can use to decide whether to highlight the price in red or green.

Next, let's add some classes in the *stock-item.component.css* file to allow for changing the color of the text:

```
.stock-container {
  border: 1px solid black;
  border-radius: 5px;
  display: inline-block;
  padding: 10px;
}

.positive {
  color: green;
}

.negative {
  color: red;
}
```

We simply added two classes, positive and negative, which change the color of the text to green and red, respectively. Now let's tie this together to see how we can use this information and classes in our *stock-item.component.html* file:

```
<div class="stock-container">
  <div class="name">{{name + ' (' + code + ')'}}</div>
  <div class="price"
       [class]="positiveChange ? 'positive' : 'negative'">$ {{price}}</div>
</div>
```

We have added one new binding on the `price` div element, which reads as:

```
[class]="positiveChange ? 'positive' : 'negative'"
```

This is the Angular syntax for property binding, which binds the value of the expression to the DOM property between the square brackets. The [ ] is the general syntax that can be used with any property on an element to bind one-way from the component to the UI.

In this particular case, we are telling Angular to bind to the class property of the DOM element to the value of the expression. Angular will evaluate it like a normal JavaScript expression, and assign the value (positive in this case) to the class property of the `div` element.

 When you bind to the class property like we did in the example, note that it overrides the existing value of the property. In our example, the `"price"` class is replaced with the class `"positive"`, instead of appending to the existing value of the property. You can notice this for yourself if you inspect the rendered HTML in the browser. Be careful about this if you bind directly to the `class` property.

If the value of the variable `positiveChange` in the component changes, Angular will automatically re-evaluate the expression in the HTML and update it accordingly. Try changing the price so that there is a negative change and then refresh the UI to make sure it works.

Notice that we have been explicitly referring to the data binding working with DOM properties, and not HTML attributes. The following sidebar goes into more detail on the difference between the two, and why it is important to know and understand as you work on Angular. But simplifying it, Angular data binding only works with DOM properties, and not with HTML attributes.

HTML Attribute Versus DOM Property: What's the Difference?

As mentioned, when we work with data binding in Angular, we aren't working with HTML attributes but rather DOM properties. Attributes are defined by HTML, while properties are defined by the Document Object Model. Though some attributes (like ID and class) directly map to DOM properties, others may exist on one side but not the other.

But more importantly, the distinction between the two is that HTML attributes are generally used for initialization of a DOM element, but after that, they have no purpose or effect on the underlying element. Once the element is initialized, its behavior is controlled by the DOM properties from then on.

For example, consider the `input` HTML element. If we bootstrap our HTML with something like:

```
<input type="text" value="foo"/>
```

this initializes an `input` DOM element, with the initial value of the DOM property `value` to be set to `foo`. Now let's assume we type something in the text box, say `bar`. At this point:

- If we do `input.getAttribute('value')`, it would return `foo`, which was the attribute value we used to initialize the HTML.

- If we do `input.value`, we will get the current value of the DOM property, which is `bar`.

That is, the attribute value is used to boostrap and set the initial value of the HTML DOM element, but after that, it is the DOM property that drives the behavior. If you inspect the HTML, you will see that it is still the initial HTML we provided, and does not update either.

In Angular, we thus bind to the DOM property, and not to the HTML attributes. Whenever we think about one-way binding from the component to the UI, we should always keep this in mind!

Just like we did for the `class` property, depending on the use case, we can actually bind to other HTML properties like the `src` property of an `img` tag, or the `disabled` property of `input` and `button`. We will cover this in more depth in the next chapter. We will also cover a simpler and more specific way of binding CSS classes in the next chapter as well.

Understanding Event Binding

So far, we have worked on using the data in our component to both render values and change the look and feel of our component. In this section, we will start understanding how to handle user interactions, and work with events and event binding in Angular.

Say we wanted to have a button that allows users to add the stock to their list of favorite stocks. Generally, with a button like this, when the user clicks it, we would want to make some server call and then process the result. So far, since we are working with very simple examples, let's just say we wanted to handle this click and get a hook to it in our component. Let's see how we might accomplish that.

First, we can change our component code in *stock-item.component.ts* to add a function `toggleFavorite`, which should be triggered each time the click happens from the UI:

```
import { Component, OnInit } from '@angular/core';

@Component({
  selector: 'app-stock-item',
  templateUrl: './stock-item.component.html',
  styleUrls: ['./stock-item.component.css']
})
export class StockItemComponent implements OnInit {

  public name: string;
  public code: string;
  public price: number;
  public previousPrice: number;
  public positiveChange: boolean;
  public favorite: boolean;

  constructor() { }

  ngOnInit() {
    this.name = 'Test Stock Company';
    this.code = 'TSC';
    this.price = 85;
    this.previousPrice = 80;
    this.positiveChange = this.price >= this.previousPrice;
    this.favorite = false;
  }

  toggleFavorite() {
    console.log('We are toggling the favorite state for this stock');
    this.favorite = !this.favorite;
  }

}
```

We have added a new public boolean member variable called `favorite`, which is initialized with a `false` value. We then added a new function called `toggleFavorite()`, which simply flips the boolean value of `favorite`. We are also printing a log in the console to ensure this is getting triggered.

Now, let's update the UI to use this concept of a `favorite` and also allow users to toggle the state:

```
<div class="stock-container">
  <div class="name">{{name + ' (' + code + ')'}}</div>
  <div class="price"
      [class]="positiveChange ? 'positive' : 'negative'">$ {{price}}</div>
  <button (click)="toggleFavorite()"
          [disabled]="favorite">Add to Favorite</button>
</div>
```

We have added a new button in the *stock-item.component.html* file to allow users to click and add the stock to their favorite set. We are using the data-binding concept from the previous section on the `disabled` property. Thus, we are disabling the button based on the boolean value `favorite`. If `favorite` is `true`, the button will be disabled, and if it is `false`, the button will be enabled. Thus, by default, the button is enabled.

The other major thing we have on the element is this fragment:

```
(click)="toggleFavorite()"
```

This syntax is called *event binding* in Angular. The left part of the equals symbol refers to the event we are binding to. In this case, it is the `click` event. Just like how the square-bracket notation refers to data flowing from the component to the UI, the parentheses notation refers to events. And the name between the parentheses is the name of the event we care about.

In this case, we are telling Angular that we are interested in the `click` event on this element. The right part of the equals symbol then refers to the template statement that Angular should execute whenever the event is triggered. In this case, we want it to execute the new function we created, `toggleFavorite`.

When we run this application in our browser, we can see the new button. Clicking it would render something like Figure 2-3.

Notice the other interesting thing, which is Angular data binding at play. When we click the button, our `toggleFavorite` function is executed. This flips the value of `favorite` from `false` to `true`. This in turn triggers the other Angular binding, which is the `disabled` property of the button, thus disabling the button after the first click. We don't have to do anything extra to get these benefits, which is the beauty of data binding.

Figure 2-3. Handling events in an Angular app

There are times when we might also care about the actual event triggered. In those cases, Angular gives you access to the underlying DOM event by giving access to a special variable $event. You can access it or even pass it to your function as follows:

```
<div class="stock-container">
  <div class="name">{{name + ' (' + code + ')'}}</div>
  <div class="price"
      [class]="positiveChange ? 'positive' : 'negative'">$ {{price}}</div>
  <button (click)="toggleFavorite($event)"
          [disabled]="favorite">Add to Favorite</button>
</div>
```

In the HTML, we simply add a reference to the variable $event, and pass it in as an argument to our toggleFavorite function. We can now refer to it in our component as follows:

```
import { Component, OnInit } from '@angular/core';

@Component({
  selector: 'app-stock-item',
  templateUrl: './stock-item.component.html',
  styleUrls: ['./stock-item.component.css']
})
export class StockItemComponent implements OnInit {

  public name: string;
  public code: string;
  public price: number;
  public previousPrice: number;
  public positiveChange: boolean;
  public favorite: boolean;

  constructor() { }

  ngOnInit() {
    this.name = 'Test Stock Company';
    this.code = 'TSC';
    this.price = 85;
    this.previousPrice = 80;
    this.positiveChange = this.price >= this.previousPrice;
    this.favorite = false;
  }

  toggleFavorite(event) {
    console.log('We are toggling the favorite state for this stock', event);
    this.favorite = !this.favorite;
  }

}
```

When you run the application, you will see that when you click the button, your console log now appends the actual MouseEvent that was triggered, in addition to our previous code.

In a similar manner, we can easily hook onto other standard DOM events that are triggered, like focus, blur, submit, and others like them.

Why Angular Shifted to Property and Event Binding

Anyone who has worked on AngularJS would be wondering why the framework developers decided to do such a major breaking change when they created Angular. The binding syntax has changed drastically, as well as the directives and symbols used. In AngularJS, we had `ng-bind`, `ng-src`, and the like for binding from our controllers to the UI, and directives like `ng-click` and `ng-submit` for handling events.

This meant that any time there was a new event or property that we wanted to bind to in AngularJS, we would end up writing a wrapper directive that would do the work of translating from AngularJS to the inner workings and vice versa.

The other problem with the AngularJS syntax was that there was no clear differentiation between data flowing from our controller to the UI or from the UI to the controller. Both follow the same syntax, which made understanding the HTML sometimes difficult, and required developers to understand each directive first.

In Angular, we instead rely on core DOM properties and events for binding. This means that if a property or event exists as per the HTML standards, we can bind to it. This also makes it very easy to work with web components that expose proper properties and events, as Angular works with them simply out of the box, without needing to write any additional code. This has also made obsolete the tons of AngularJS directives from the past, such as `ng-click`, `ng-submit`, and so on, and makes it easier for any web developer to quickly understand and work with Angular. You don't have to spend as much time learning Angular-specific knowledge.

Furthermore, the square bracket and parentheses notation also makes it very obvious about the flow of data. Any time you see the square bracket notation, you can be assured that it is data flowing from the component into the HTML. Any time you see the parentheses notation, you are guaranteed that it refers to an event and flows from a user action to the component.

Using Models for Cleaner Code

The last part of this chapter covers something that is more of a best practice, but it is worth adopting—especially as we aim to build large, maintainable web applications using Angular. We want to use encapsulation to ensure that our components don't work with lower-level abstractions and properties, like we did previously where the stock widget gets an individual name, price, etc. At the same time, we want to leverage TypeScript to make it easier to understand and reason about our application and its behavior. To this extent, we should ideally model our stock itself as a type in TypeScript, and leverage that instead.

The way we would do it in TypeScript is to define an interface or a class with the definition for what belongs in a stock, and use that consistently throughout our application. In this case, since we might want additional logic in addition to just the values (calculating whether the price differential is positive or not, for example), we can use a class.

We can use the Angular CLI to quickly generate a skeleton class for us, by running:

```
ng generate class model/stock
```

This will generate an empty skeleton file called *stock.ts* in a folder called *model*. We can go ahead and change it as follows:

```
export class Stock {
  favorite: boolean = false;

  constructor(public name: string,
              public code: string,
              public price: number,
              public previousPrice: number) {}

  isPositiveChange(): boolean {
    return this.price >= this.previousPrice;
  }
}
```

This gives us a nice encapsulation while we work with stocks across our application. Note that we didn't actually define the variables name, code, and so on as properties of the class. This is because we are using TypeScript's syntactic sugar to automatically create the corresponding properties based on the constructor arguments by using the public keyword. To learn more about TypeScript classes, refer to the official documentation (*https://www.typescriptlang.org/docs/handbook/classes.html*). In short, we have created a class with five properties, four coming through the constructor and one autoinitialized. Let's see how we might use this now in our component:

```
import { Component, OnInit } from '@angular/core';

import { Stock } from '../../model/stock';

@Component({
  selector: 'app-stock-item',
  templateUrl: './stock-item.component.html',
  styleUrls: ['./stock-item.component.css']
})
export class StockItemComponent implements OnInit {

  public stock: Stock;

  constructor() { }

  ngOnInit() {
```

```
    this.stock = new Stock('Test Stock Company', 'TSC', 85, 80);
  }

  toggleFavorite(event) {
    console.log('We are toggling the favorite state for this stock', event);
    this.stock.favorite = !this.stock.favorite;
  }

}
```

In *stock-item.component.ts*, we imported our new model definition at the top, and then replaced all the individual member variables with one variable of type `Stock`. This simplified the code in the component significantly, and encapsulated all the logic and underlying functionality within a proper TypeScript type. Now let's see how *stock-item.component.html* changes to accommodate this change:

```
<div class="stock-container">
  <div class="name">{{stock.name + ' (' + stock.code + ')'}}</div>
  <div class="price"
       [class]="stock.isPositiveChange() ? 'positive' : 'negative'">
    $ {{stock.price}}
  </div>
  <button (click)="toggleFavorite($event)"
          [disabled]="stock.favorite">Add to Favorite</button>
</div>
```

We have made a few changes in the HTML for our stock item. First, most of our references to the variable are now through the `stock` variable, instead of directly accessing the variables in the component. So `name` became `stock.name`, `code` became `stock.code`, and so on.

Also, one more thing of note: our `class` property binding now refers to a function instead of a variable. This is acceptable, as a function is also a valid expression. Angular will just evaluate the function and use its return value to determine the final expression value.

Conclusion

In this chapter, we started building our very first Angular application. We learned how to bootstrap our Angular application, as well as understand the various pieces that the Angular skeleton application generates and their needs and uses. We then created our very first component, and looked at the steps involved in hooking it up to our application.

Following that, we added some very basic data to our component, and then used that to understand how basic Angular data binding works, using both interpolation as well as property binding. We then looked at how event binding works, and handled user interactions through it. Finally, we encapsulated some information in a TypeScript class to make our code cleaner and modular.

In the next chapter, we will go through some basic Angular directives that Angular provides out of the box and how it allows us to work with templates in an effective manner.

Exercise

Each chapter will have an optional exercise at the end to reinforce some of the concepts covered in the chapter, as well as give you some time to experiment and try your hand at Angular code. Over the course of the book, we will build on the same exercise and keep adding more features to it.

The finished source code for the exercise is available in the GitHub repository in each chapter's folder. You can refer to it in case you are stuck or want to compare the final solution. Of course, there are multiple ways to solve every problem, so the solution in the repository is one possible way. You may arrive at a slightly different solution in the course of your attempts.

For the first exercise, try to accomplish the following:

1. Start a new project to build an ecommerce website.
2. Create a component to display a single product.
3. The product component should display a name, price, and image for the product. You can initialize the component with some defaults for the same. Use any placeholder image you want.
4. Highlight the entire element in a different color if the product is on sale. Whether the product is on sale can be an attribute of the product itself.
5. Add buttons to increase and decrease the quantity of the product in the cart. The quantity in the cart should be visible in the UI. Disable the button if the quantity is already zero.

All of this can be accomplished using concepts covered in this chapter. You can check out the finished solution in *chapter2/exercise/ecommerce*.

CHAPTER 3

Useful Built-In Angular Directives

In the previous chapter, we got started with our very first Angular application, and got a feel for using the Angular CLI to begin a new project and create components in it. We got a basic sense of how to use Angular's data and event binding mechanisms as well.

In this chapter, we will first understand what directives are in Angular and how they are different from components. We will then cover some basic directives that Angular provides out of the box and the use cases where they're applicable. By the end of the chapter, you should be comfortable using most of the out-of-the-box directives that Angular provides and understand when and where to use them.

Directives and Components

A directive in Angular allows you to attach some custom functionality to elements in your HTML. A component in Angular, like the one we built in the previous chapter, is a direcive that provides both functionality and UI logic. It is fundamentally an element that encapsulates its behavior and rendering logic.

Noncomponent directives, on the other hand, usually work on and modify existing elements. These can be further classified into two types:

Attribute directives
> Attribute directives change the look and feel, or the behavior, of an existing element or component that it is applied on. `NgClass` and `NgStyle`, which we will see later in this chapter, are examples of attribute directives.

Structural directives

Structural directives change the DOM layout by adding or removing elements from the view. NgIf and NgFor are examples of structural directives that we will see later in this chapter.

Built-In Attribute Directives

We will first explore attribute directives. There are two basic attribute directives that Angular provides out of the box, which are the NgClass and the NgStyle directives. Both of these are alternatives for the class and style bindings, of which we saw the class binding in the previous chapter.

 We generally refer to the directive with the name of its class, which is why we call the directive NgClass or NgIf. But the same directive, when used as an HTML attribute, is usually in camel-case, like ngClass or ngIf. Keep this in mind as we go along.

NgClass

The NgClass directive allows us to apply or remove multiple CSS classes simultaneously from an element in our HTML. Previously, we applied a single class to our element to highlight whether it was a positive or a negative change as follows:

```
<div [class]="stock.isPositiveChange() ? 'positive' : 'negative'">
  $ {{stock.price}}
</div>
```

In this example, we simply look at a boolean value, and then decide whether to apply the class positive or negative based on that. But what if we had to apply multiple CSS classes? And they were all (or a lot of them) conditional? You would end up having to write code that does string generation based on these multiple conditions, so that you could have one string that represents all the classes that need to be applied.

This is cruft code that is not worth writing or maintaining. So for these kinds of situations, Angular provides the NgClass directive, which can take a JavaScript object as input. For each key in the object that has a truthy value, Angular will add that key (the key itself, not the value of the key!) as a class to the element. Similarly, each key in the object that has a falsy value will be removed as a class from that element.

Truthy and Falsy in JavaScript

JavaScript allows us to use non-`boolean` values in conditional statements. Thus, instead of just `true` and `false`, a whole set of values are equivalent to true and false. In JavaScript, the following values are treated as `falsy`:

- `undefined`
- `null`
- `NaN`
- `0`
- `""` (any empty string)
- `false` (the boolean value)

Any other value is treated as `truthy`, including, but not limited to:

- Any nonzero number
- Any nonempty string
- Any nonnull object or array
- `true` (the boolean value)

Another way to easily remember is that any non-falsy value is truthy. We end up using these concepts quite often in conditionals in our applications.

Let's take an example to see this in action. Say we want to extend our example from before, where instead of just a positive and a negative class, we want to add another class that dictates whether it is a large or a small change. We want it to be a small change (denoted by the CSS class `small-change`) if the change percentage is less than 1%; otherwise it would be a large change (denoted by the CSS class `large-change`).

We will build on the example from the previous chapter, so if you don't have it, feel free to grab the final code we were working with from the GitHub repository (*https:// github.com/shyamseshadri/angular-up-and-running*). The codebase is in *chapter2/ stock-market*, which is the base for the code in this chapter.

First, we can add the new classes to the *src/app/stock/stock-item/stock-item.component.css* file:

```
.stock-container {
  border: 1px solid black;
  border-radius: 5px;
  display: inline-block;
  padding: 10px;
}
```

```
.positive {
  color: green;
}

.negative {
  color: red;
}

.large-change {
  font-size: 1.2em;
}

.small-change {
  font-size: 0.8em;
}
```

Next, we can change our component class to calculate and keep the JSON object ready with the classes to apply. We modify the *src/app/stock/stock-item/stock-item.component.ts* file to first calculate the difference between the current and the previous price, and then create an object that holds all the classes we need to apply:

```
import { Component, OnInit } from '@angular/core';

import { Stock } from '../../model/stock';

@Component({
  selector: 'app-stock-item',
  templateUrl: './stock-item.component.html',
  styleUrls: ['./stock-item.component.css']
})
export class StockItemComponent implements OnInit {

  public stock: Stock;
  public stockClasses;

  constructor() { }

  ngOnInit() {
    this.stock = new Stock('Test Stock Company', 'TSC', 85, 80);
    let diff = (this.stock.price / this.stock.previousPrice) - 1;
    let largeChange = Math.abs(diff) > 0.01;
    this.stockClasses = {
      "positive": this.stock.isPositiveChange(),
      "negative": !this.stock.isPositiveChange(),
      "large-change": largeChange,
      "small-change": !largeChange
    };
  }

  toggleFavorite(event) {
    console.log('We are toggling the favorite state for this stock', event);
```

```
      this.stock.favorite = !this.stock.favorite;
    }

  }
```

In the component code, we created a `stockClasses` object with four keys: `positive`, `negative`, `large-change`, and `small-change`. Based on the current price and previous prices, each of these keys will have a value of `true` or `false`.

Now, let's see how we can use the `NgClass` directive to use this instead of the `class` binding we were previously using in the *src/app/stock/stock-item/stock-item.component.html* file:

```
<div class="stock-container">
  <div class="name">{{stock.name + ' (' + stock.code + ')'}}</div>
  <div class="price"
       [ngClass]="stockClasses">$ {{stock.price}}</div>
  <button (click)="toggleFavorite($event)"
          [disabled]="stock.favorite">Add to Favorite</button>
</div>
```

We primarily replaced the

```
[class]="stock.isPositiveChange() ? 'positive' : 'negative'"
```

line with the following:

```
[ngClass]="stockClasses"
```

Now if you run this application in your browser (`ng serve`, in case you have forgotten), you can see the impact of your changes. The price is now shown in green, as well as in slightly larger font, since it has applied both the `positive` and the `large-change` classes. You can play around with the values of price and previous price in the component class to see the different combinations reflected.

Another thing to note is that unlike before, where the `class` binding was overwriting our initial class from the element, the `NgClass` directive retains the classes on the element.

The finished code for the preceding example is available in the *chapter3/ng-class* folder in the GitHub repository.

You should consider using the `NgClass` directive if you have the use case of having to apply various different CSS classes on an element conditionally. It makes it easy to reason and understand how and what classes are applied, and it also makes it easy to unit test the logic of selecting classes separate from the logic of applying classes to the elements.

NgStyle

The `NgStyle` directive is the lower-level equivalent of the `NgClass` directive. It operates in a manner similar to the `NgClass` in that it takes a JSON object and applies it based on the values of the keys. But the `NgStyle` directive works at a CSS style/properties level. The keys and values it expects are CSS properties and attributes rather than class names.

Considering that our example with `NgClass` was using simple CSS classes each affecting only one CSS property, let's see how we can translate the same example using the `NgStyle` directive instead. First, we need to make a change to the *src/app/stock/stock-item/stock-item.component.ts* file to create the style object based on the stock properties:

```
import { Component, OnInit } from '@angular/core';

import { Stock } from '../../model/stock';

@Component({
  selector: 'app-stock-item',
  templateUrl: './stock-item.component.html',
  styleUrls: ['./stock-item.component.css']
})
export class StockItemComponent implements OnInit {

  public stock: Stock;
  public stockStyles;

  constructor() { }

  ngOnInit() {
    this.stock = new Stock('Test Stock Company', 'TSC', 85, 80);
    let diff = (this.stock.price / this.stock.previousPrice) - 1;
    let largeChange = Math.abs(diff) > 0.01;
    this.stockStyles = {
      "color": this.stock.isPositiveChange() ? "green" : "red",
      "font-size": largeChange ? "1.2em" : "0.8em"
    };
  }

  toggleFavorite(event) {
    console.log('We are toggling the favorite state for this stock', event);
    this.stock.favorite = !this.stock.favorite;
  }

}
```

Similar to the previous section, we have created a `stockStyles` object. In the initialization code, we have initialized the `stockStyles` object with the keys `color` and `font-size`. Its values are CSS attributes that are generated based on the stock properties. We can then use this `stockStyles` object as an input to the `NgStyle` directive for binding.

We can now change our HTML to use this information by editing the *src/app/stock/stock-item/stock-item.component.html* file as follows:

```
<div class="stock-container">
  <div class="name">{{stock.name + ' (' + stock.code + ')'}}</div>
  <div class="price"
       [ngStyle]="stockStyles">$ {{stock.price}}</div>
  <button (click)="toggleFavorite($event)"
          [disabled]="stock.favorite">Add to Favorite</button>
</div>
```

We have added a binding for the `NgStyle` directive:

```
[ngStyle]="stockStyles"
```

Angular will look at the keys and values of the `stockStyles` object and add those particular styles to the HTML element. You can again run the application and try changing the values of the price and previous price to see this in action.

The finished code for the preceding example is available in the *chapter3/ng-style* folder in the GitHub repository.

It is generally preferable to use the class or `NgClass` bindings to change the look and feel of your application, but the `NgStyle` does give you another tool in your toolkit, in case you have the use case of changing the CSS style of elements and cannot (for whatever reasons) use classes to perform the same.

Alternative Class and Style Binding Syntax

We covered using the `[class]` binding syntax in the previous chapter, as well as the `NgClass` alternative to dynamically add classes to our elements using Angular. There is a third alternative for both classes and styles, which is to use a singular version of the class and style binding that adds and removes one particular class/style, instead of the all-or-nothing approach of the `[class]` binding.

We can add or remove individual classes based on evaluating a truthy expression in Angular with the following syntax:

```
[class.class-name]="expression"
```

We would replace `class-name` with the particular CSS class we want to apply/remove on our element, and replace `expression` in the syntax with a valid JavaScript expression that would either return a truthy or falsy value.

Let's modify our stock example to apply and remove the `positive` and `negative` CSS classes using this syntax instead. We don't have to make any changes in the component or the CSS, and only make the following changes to the *src/app/stock/stock-item/stock-item.component.html* file:

```
<div class="stock-container">
  <div class="name">{{stock.name + ' (' + stock.code + ')'}}</div>
  <div class="price"
      [class.positive]="stock.isPositiveChange()"
      [class.negative]="!stock.isPositiveChange()">$ {{stock.price}}</div>
  <button (click)="toggleFavorite($event)"
          [disabled]="stock.favorite">Add to Favorite</button>
</div>
```

Notice the two new lines:

```
[class.positive]="stock.isPositiveChange()"
[class.negative]="!stock.isPositiveChange()"
```

We are telling Angular to apply the CSS class `positive` if there is a positive change (based on the call to `stock.isPositiveChange()`), and remove it if this is falsy. Similarly, we are doing the negation of that for `negative`. This is a nice simple way to deal with CSS classes if you only have to add/remove one or two classes. Note that this also works if the class name has dashes and so on. For example, you could do:

```
[class.large-change]="someExpressionHere"
```

and this would apply the class `large-change` if `someExpressionHere` evaluated to true. Also note that this keeps the original class from the element intact (the `price` class), which the basic `[class]` binding does not. That is yet another advantage of this syntax.

It is, though, preferred to use the `NgClass` directive any time you have to deal with more than one or two classes, as it makes it more manageable and easier to test.

The style binding is also something similar, and can be done like follows:

```
[style.background-color]="stock.isPositiveChange() ? 'green' : 'red'"
```

You can read more about the style binding in the official Angular documentation (*https://angular.io/guide/template-syntax#style-binding*).

Built-In Structural Directives

Structural directives, as discussed earlier, are responsible for changing the layout of the HTML by adding, removing, or modifying elements from the DOM. Just like other directives that are not components, structural directives are applied on a preexisting element, and the directive then operates on the content of that element.

Structural directives in Angular follow a very particular syntax, which makes it easy to recognize when a directive is a structural directive versus a normal one. All structural directives in Angular start with an asterisk (*), like:

```
<div *ngIf="stock.favorite"></div>
```

Unlike the data- or event-binding syntaxes, there are no square brackets or parentheses. Just a plain *ngIf followed by the expression. Angular understands the expression and translates it into the final HTML. To understand this process a bit more, refer to the following sidebar.

Syntax and Reasoning

You might be curious about the asterisk syntax, and rightfully so. The star syntax is syntactic sugar that is replaced underneath by Angular to a series of steps, resulting in the final view you get. In fact, unlike the rest of the directives where you can use data/event binding correctly with expressions, with the structural directives, what you instead use is a microsyntax, a mini-language of sorts that Angular uses to accomplish certain things.

You can skip this section if you don't want to dive into the innards of how exactly Angular works with these expressions.

Let's walk through a simple lifecycle of how Angular translates a simple expression into its final state. Say we started with:

```
<div *ngIf="stock.favorite">
  <button>Remove from favorite</button>
</div>
```

Angular will recognize the structural directive and transform it into a template directive, to create something along the lines of the following:

```
<div template="ngIf stock.favorite">
  <button>Remove from favorite</button>
</div>
```

This template directive is using the microsyntax that Angular recognizes and then translates it into an Angular template that surrounds this particular element, to something like:

```
<ng-template [ngIf]="stock.favorite">
  <div>
    <button>Remove from favorite</button>
  </div>
</ng-template>
```

Finally, based on the value of stock.favorite, the inner div would get rendered to the DOM, or removed from it. You can technically use any of these syntaxes to achieve the same effect, but it is recommended for consistency and ease of readability.

NgIf

We will first take a look at the trusty and often used structural directive `NgIf`. The `NgIf` directive allows you to conditionally hide or show elements in your UI. The syntax, as mentioned earlier, starts with an asterisk as it is a structural directive that can conditionally remove or add elements to our rendered HTML.

The `NgIf` uses one of the simplest microsyntaxes of all the structural directives, as it simply expects the expression provided to it to evaluate to a truthy value. This is the JavaScript concept of truthiness (as explained previously), so the boolean true value, a nonzero number, a nonempty string, and a nonnull object would all be treated as true. This also makes it convenient to have templates that show up if certain objects are present and nonnull.

We will build on the examples from the previous chapter, so if you don't have it, feel free to grab the final code we were working with from the GitHub repository (*https://github.com/shyamseshadri/angular-up-and-running*). The codebase is in *chapter2/stock-market*, which is the base for the code in this chapter.

Let's modify the Add to Favorite button such that instead of getting disabled, we hide the button if the stock is already favorited. We don't need to make any changes to the component or CSS code, but instead just to the *src/app/stock/stock-item/stock-item.component.html* file as follows:

```
<div class="stock-container">
  <div class="name">{{stock.name + ' (' + stock.code + ')'}}</div>
  <div class="price"
      [class]="stock.isPositiveChange() ? 'positive' : 'negative'">
      $ {{stock.price}}
  </div>
  <button (click)="toggleFavorite($event)"
          *ngIf="!stock.favorite">Add to Favorite</button>
</div>
```

On the `button`, we added the conditionality with `*ngIf="!stock.favorite"`. This tells Angular to add the element if the stock is not favorited, and remove it from the DOM if it is currently a favorite stock. Now when you load the page, you will see the button by default. Once you click the Add to Favorite button, the boolean will flip and the stock will now be favorited. Angular will automatically at this point hide the button from the UI.

If you inspect the HTML of the page, you will see that the element is actually removed from the rendered DOM.

The `NgIf` directive, along with the `NgFor`, which we will cover in the following sections, are work-horse directives. They do a lot of the heavy lifting and are commonly used in most applications you will develop.

NgFor

While the `NgIf` directive is used for conditionally showing/hiding elements, the `NgFor` directive is used for creating multiple elements, usually one for each instance of some or the other object in an array. It is a common practice to have a template, and then create an instance of that template for each instance of our object.

NgFor or NgForOf

In this book, we use `NgFor` to refer to the `*ngFor` directive. But technically, the `*ngFor` directive uses the class called `NgForOf` under the hood. Thus, you might see people use `NgFor` and `NgForOf` interchangeably when referring to the `*ngFor` directive in Angular.

`NgFor` uses a special microsyntax that comes with a set of mandatory and optional segments. Let's modify our example from Chapter 2 to now show a list of stocks, instead of one individual stock.

First, we will modify the *src/app/stock/stock-item.component.ts* file, just for the sake of demonstration, to have an array of stocks instead of one stock:

```
import { Component, OnInit } from '@angular/core';

import { Stock } from '../../model/stock';

@Component({
  selector: 'app-stock-item',
  templateUrl: './stock-item.component.html',
  styleUrls: ['./stock-item.component.css']
```

```
})
export class StockItemComponent implements OnInit {

  public stocks: Array<Stock>;

  constructor() { }

  ngOnInit() {
    this.stocks = [
      new Stock('Test Stock Company', 'TSC', 85, 80),
      new Stock('Second Stock Company', 'SSC', 10, 20),
      new Stock('Last Stock Company', 'LSC', 876, 765)
    ];
  }

  toggleFavorite(event, index) {
    console.log('We are toggling the favorite state for stock', index, event);
    this.stocks[index].favorite = !this.stocks[index].favorite;
  }
}
```

Generally, we want to keep a `stock-item` for one particular stock only, but we will circumvent that for this particular example. We changed `stock` to be `stocks`, an array of stock objects. We then created some dummy stocks in our initialization. Finally, we changed the `toggleFavorite` to take in an `index` as a parameter, instead of working with the current stock.

Next, let's see how we can now modify our HTML in *src/app/stock/stock-item.component.html* to leverage the power of the `NgFor` directive:

```
<div class="stock-container" *ngFor="let stock of stocks; index as i">
  <div class="name">{{stock.name + ' (' + stock.code + ')'}}</div>
  <div class="price"
      [class]="stock.isPositiveChange() ? 'positive' : 'negative'">
      $ {{stock.price}}
  </div>
  <button (click)="toggleFavorite($event, i)"
          [disabled]="stock.favorite">Add to Favorite</button>
</div>
```

We updated our parent container with the `NgFor` directive. Let's explore how we have used it in a bit more detail:

```
*ngFor="let stock of stocks; index as i"
```

The first part of the microsyntax is basically our `for` loop. We create a template instance variable named `stock`, which will be available within the scope of the element created. This can be equated to a standard `for-each` loop, with the variable `stock` referring to each individual item in the array. The second part after the semicolon is creating another template instance variable `i`, which holds the current index value. We will talk about the other properties in just a bit.

With this statement, Angular will repeat the `stock-container` div element once for each item in the `stocks` array, thus creating three elements in our final rendered HTML. You should see something like Figure 3-1 on your screen.

Figure 3-1. Angular app using *ngFor

Angular encapsulates the `stock` and `i` variables such that each instance of the template has its own copy of them. Thus, when we refer to `stock.name` inside the element, Angular correctly picks up the relevant stock and displays its name. When we click the Add to Favorite button, the correct index is passed and only that particular button is disabled.

Similar to index, there are other local values that are available within the context of an `NgFor` directive that you can assign to a local variable name (like we did with `i`) and bind them to different values:

`index`
> This refers to the current element index

`even`
> This is `true` when the item has an even index

`odd`
> This is `true` when the item has an odd index

`first`
> This is `true` when the item is the first item in the array

`last`
> This is `true` when the item is the last item in the array

You can then use these variables to bind to CSS classes, or display them in the UI, or run any other calculations you might want to. For instance, you might want to add the CSS class `even-item` to each even index item, which you can accomplish with a binding like:

```
[css.even-item]="isEven"
```

where `even` is assigned to the `isEven` variable in the `NgFor` microsyntax like:

```
*ngFor="let stock of stocks; even as isEven; index as i"
```

The last major capability that the `NgFor` directive provides is a hook into how Angular recognizes elements and avoids re-creating element instances unnecessarily. By default, Angular uses object identity to track additions, removals, and modifications to an array. That is, as long as the object reference does not change, Angular will not create new elements for it, and reuse the old element reference. This is mostly for performance reasons, as element creation/removal are two of the more costly operations in the browser.

There are cases when the element reference might change, but you still want to continue using the same element. For example, when you fetch new data from the server, you don't want to blow away your list and re-create it unless the data has fundamentally changed. This is where the `trackBy` capability of the `NgFor` directive comes into play.

The `trackBy` option takes a function that has two arguments: an index and the item. If the `trackBy` function is provided to the `NgFor` directive, then it will use the return value of the function to decide how to identify individual elements. For example, in our particular case, we might want to use the stock's code as an identifier, instead of the object reference.

First, we will add the function used to track individual items in *src/app/stock/stock-item.component.ts*:

```
import { Component, OnInit } from '@angular/core';

import { Stock } from '../../model/stock';

@Component({
  selector: 'app-stock-item',
  templateUrl: './stock-item.component.html',
  styleUrls: ['./stock-item.component.css']
})
export class StockItemComponent implements OnInit {

  public stocks: Array<Stock>;

  constructor() { }

  ngOnInit() {
    this.stocks = [
      new Stock('Test Stock Company', 'TSC', 85, 80),
```

```
      new Stock('Second Stock Company', 'SSC', 10, 20),
      new Stock('Last Stock Company', 'LSC', 876, 765)
    ];
  }

  toggleFavorite(event, index) {
    console.log('We are toggling the favorite state for stock', index, event);
    this.stocks[index].favorite = !this.stocks[index].favorite;
  }

  trackStockByCode(index, stock) {
    return stock.code;
  }
}
```

The last function (`trackStockByCode`) is the one we just added. We are taking both the index and the stock, and returning the `stock.code`. Angular will use this value to identify each element.

Next, we can change the HTML to pass this function to the `NgFor` directive by changing the *src/app/stock/stock-item/stock-item.component.html* file as follows:

```
<div class="stock-container"
    *ngFor="let stock of stocks; index as i; trackBy: trackStockByCode">
  <div class="name">{{stock.name + ' (' + stock.code + ')'}}</div>
  <div class="price"
      [class]="stock.isPositiveChange() ? 'positive' : 'negative'">
      $ {{stock.price}}
  </div>
  <button (click)="toggleFavorite($event, i)"
          [disabled]="stock.favorite">Add to Favorite</button>
</div>
```

We just modified the `*ngFor` to pass in an additional attribute in the microsyntax, which is `trackBy: trackStockByCode`. This will ensure that Angular calls this function to figure out how to identify individual items, instead of using the object reference.

This ensures that even if we reload all the stocks from the server (thus changing all the object references), Angular will still look at the stock code to decide whether or not to reuse the elements present in the DOM.

 Use the `trackBy` option in the `NgFor` directive whenever you know that you are going to reload the list (for example, loading it from an observable that makes a server call). It will definitely help in performance.

NgSwitch

The last built-in directive is actually a set of multiple directives. NgSwitch by itself is not a structural directive, but rather an attribute directive. You would use it with normal data-binding syntax with the square-bracket notation. It is the NgSwitchCase and the NgSwitchDefault directives that are, in fact, structural directives, as they would add or remove elements depending on the case.

Let's take a hypothetical example to see how this might look in action. Let's assume that instead of just stocks, we were dealing with all kinds of securities, like stocks, options, derivatives, and mutual funds. And we had built components to render each one of these. Now, given a security we want to render the right kind of component based on its type. This would be a great example of using an NgSwitch, which might look something like follows:

```
<div [ngSwitch]="security.type">
    <stock-item *ngSwitchCase="'stock'" [item]="security">
    </stock-item>
    <option-item *ngSwitchCase="'option'" [item]="security">
    </option-item>
    <derivative-item *ngSwitchCase="'derivative'" [item]="security">
    </derivative-item>
    <mutual-fund-item *ngSwitchCase="'mutual-fund'" [item]="security">
    </mutual-fund-item>
    <unknown-item *ngSwitchDefault [item]="security">
    </unknown-item>
</div>
```

A few interesting things of note in the example:

- We use normal data binding using square brackets with the ngSwitch directive, as we want it to understand and interpret the value underneath the expression. It is not a structural directive, as we mentioned previously.

- Each *ngSwitchCase is again taking an expression, and in this case, we are passing string constants like 'stock', 'option', and so on. If the value of security.type matches any one of these string constants, then that particular element will get rendered, and all other sibling elements will be removed.

- If none of the sibling *ngSwitchCase statements matches, then the *ngSwitch Default will get triggered and in the example, the unknown-item component will get rendered.

The NgSwitch family of directives is great when you have multiple elements/ templates, of which one has to be rendered based on conditions.

Multiple Sibling Structural Directives

You might run into a case at some point where you want to run an *ngFor on a template, but only if some condition is met. Your instinctive reaction in that case might be to add both *ngFor and *ngIf on the same element. Angular will not let you.

For example, consider the following code:

```
<div *ngFor="let stock of stocks" *ngIf="stock.active">
 <!-- Show stock details here if stock is active -->
</div>
```

Here, we want to run the *ngFor, and then decide if the stock is active before we display it. Now consider the following code.

```
<div *ngFor="let stock of stocks" *ngIf="stocks.length > 2">
  <!-- Show stock details here if more than 2 stocks present -->
</div>
```

Both of these cases look very similar, but the intent and expectation is very different. In the first case, we expect the *ngFor to execute first followed by the *ngIf, and vice versa in the second case.

It is not immediately obvious which one between the two should run first. Rather than creating some innate order that one directive runs before the other, Angular simplifies it by not allowing it on the same element.

When you run into such a case, it is recommended to just use wrapping elements so that you can be explicit about the order in which these structural directives are executed.

Conclusion

In this chapter, we covered what the built-in directives are, and then went over some common directives that you will need and use for your Angular application, such as NgFor, NgIf, and more. We looked at examples of how we could use them for various functionality and saw a little bit of some more complex use cases for NgSwitch as well as advanced usage of NgFor. Of course, Angular does allow you to extend and create your own directives, and you can read up on it in the documentation (*https://angular.io/guide/attribute-directives*).

In the next chapter, we will dive deep into Angular components and understand the various options we have for configuring them as well as the lifecycle of an Angular component.

Exercise

For our second exercise, try to change the exercise code from the previous chapter to perform the following:

1. Move from using simple class binding to using either `ngClass` or the specific class binding from this chapter to highlight on-sale items. Have a combination of some on sale and some not on sale.

2. Instead of disabling the decrease quantity button when the quantity is zero, use `*ngIf` to show the button only if it can be clicked.

3. Add a drop-down with quantity selection from 1 to 20 (generated via `*ngFor`). Don't worry about the action/update of data on selection of a quantity; we will get to that in one of the following chapters.

All of this can be accomplished using concepts covered in this chapter. You can check out the finished solution in *chapter3/exercise/ecommerce*.

CHAPTER 4

Understanding and Using Angular Components

In the previous chapter, we did a deep dive into the built-in directives that Angular offers that allow us to perform common functionality like hiding and showing elements, repeating templates, and so on. We worked with directives like `ngIf` and `ngForOf` and got a feel for how and when to use them.

In this chapter, we will go a bit deeper into components, those elements we have been creating to render the UI and let users interact with the applications we build. We will cover some of the more useful attributes you can specify when creating components, how to think about the lifecycle of the component and the various hooks that Angular gives you, and finally, cover how to pass data into and out of your custom components. By the end of the chapter, you should be able to perform most common tasks related to components while understanding what you are doing and why.

Components—A Recap

In the previous chapter, we saw that Angular only has directives, and that directives are reused for multiple purposes. We dealt with attribute and structural directives, which allow us to change the behavior of an existing element or to change the structure of the template being rendered.

The third kind of directives are components, which we have been using pretty much from the first chapter. To some extent, you can consider an Angular application to be nothing but a tree of components. Each component in turn has some behavior and a template that gets rendered. This template can then continue to use other components, thus forming a tree of components, which is the Angular application that gets rendered in the browser.

At its very simplest, a component is nothing but a class that encapsulates behavior (what data to load, what data to render, and how to respond to user interactions) and a template (how the data is rendered). But there are multiple ways to define that as well, along with other options, which we will cover in the following sections.

Defining a Component

We define a component using the TypeScript decorator `Component`. This allows us to annotate any class with some metadata that teaches Angular how the component works, what to render, and so on. Let's take a look again at the `stock-item` component we created to see what a simple component would look like, and we will build up from there:

```
@Component({
  selector: 'app-stock-item',
  templateUrl: './stock-item.component.html',
  styleUrls: ['./stock-item.component.css']
})
export class StockItemComponent implements OnInit {
    // Code omitted here for clarity
}
```

The very basic component only needs a selector (to tell Angular how to find instances of the component being used) and a template (that Angular has to render when it finds the element). All other attributes in the `Component` decorator are optional. In the preceding example, we have defined that the `StockItemComponent` is to be rendered whenever Angular encounters the `app-stock-item` selector, and to render the *stock-item.component.html* file when it encounters the element. Let's talk about the attributes of the decorator in a bit more detail.

Selector

The selector attribute, as we touched upon briefly in Chapter 2, allows us to define how Angular identifies when the component is used in HTML. The selector takes a string value, which is the CSS selector Angular will use to identify the element. The recommended practice when we create new components is to use element selectors (like we did with `app-stock-item`), but technically you could use any other selector as well. For example, here are a few ways you could specify the selector attribute and how you would use it in the HTML:

- `selector: 'app-stock-item'` would result in the component being used as `<app-stock-item></app-stock-item>` in the HTML.

- `selector: '.app-stock-item'` would result in the component being used as a CSS class like `<div class="app-stock-item"></div>` in the HTML.

- `selector: '[app-stock-item]'` would result in the component being used as an attribute on an existing element like `<div app-stock-item></div>` in the HTML.

You can make the selector as simple or complex as you want, but as a rule of thumb, try to stick to simple element selectors unless you have a very strong reason not to.

Template

We have been using `templateUrl` so far to define what the template to be used along with a component is. The path you pass to the `templateUrl` attribute is relative to the path of the component. In the previous case, we can either specify the `templateUrl` as:

```
templateUrl: './stock.item.component.html'
```

or:

```
templateUrl: 'stock.item.component.html'
```

and it would work. But if you try to specify an absolute URL or anything else, your compilation would break. One interesting thing to note is that unlike AngularJS (1.x), the application Angular builds does not load the template by URL at runtime. Instead, Angular precompiles a build and ensures that the template is inlined as part of the build process.

Instead of `templateUrl`, we could also specify the template inline in the component, using the `template` option. This allows us to have the component contain all the information instead of splitting it across HTML and TypeScript code.

 Only one of `template` and `templateUrl` can be specified in a component. You cannot use both, but at least one is essential.

There is no impact on the final generated application as Angular compiles the code into a single bundle. The only reason you might want to split your template code into a separate file is to get nicer IDE features such as syntax completion and the like, which are specific to file extensions. Generally, you might want to keep your templates separate if they are over three or four lines or have any complexity.

Let's see how our `stock-item` component might look with an inline template:

```
import { Component, OnInit } from '@angular/core';

import { Stock } from '../../model/stock';
```

```
@Component({
  selector: 'app-stock-item',
  template: `
      <div class="stock-container">
        <div class="name">{{stock.name + ' (' + stock.code + ')'}}</div>
        <div class="price"
            [class]="stock.isPositiveChange() ? 'positive' : 'negative'">
            $ {{stock.price}}
  </div>
        <button (click)="toggleFavorite($event)"
              *ngIf="!stock.favorite">Add to Favorite</button>
      </div>
    `,
  styleUrls: ['./stock-item.component.css']
})
export class StockItemComponent implements OnInit {
  // Code omitted here for clarity
}
```

 ECMAScript 2015 (and TypeScript) allows us to define multiline templates using the ` (backtick) symbol, instead of doing string concatenation across multiple lines using the + (plus) operator. We leverage this usually when we define inline templates.

You can find the completed code in the *chapter4/component-template* folder in the GitHub repository.

All we have done is taken the template and moved it into the `template` attribute of the `Component` decorator. In this particular case though, because there are more than a few lines with some amount of work being done, I would recommend not moving it inline. Note that as a result of moving it to `template`, we have removed the previous `templateUrl` attribute.

Styles

A given component can have multiple styles attached to it. This allows you to pull in component-specific CSS, as well as potentially any other common CSS that needs to be applied to it. Similar to templates, you can either inline your CSS using the `styles` attribute, or if there is a significant amount of CSS or you want to leverage your IDE, you can pull it out into a separate file and pull it into your component using the `styleUrls` attribute. Both of these take an array as an input.

One thing that Angular promotes out of the box is complete encapsulation and isolation of styles. That means by default, the styles you define and use in one component will not affect/impact any other parent or child component. This ensures that you can be confident that the CSS classes you define in any component will not unknowingly affect anything else, unless you explicitly pull in the necessary styles.

Again, just like templates, Angular will not pull in these styles at runtime, but rather precompile and create a bundle with the necessary styles. Thus, the choice of using styles or styleUrls is a personal one, without any major impact at runtime.

 Do not use both styles and styleUrls together. Angular will end up picking one or the other and will lead to unexpected behavior.

Let's quickly see how the component might look if we inlined the styles:

```
import { Component, OnInit } from '@angular/core';

import { Stock } from '../../model/stock';

@Component({
  selector: 'app-stock-item',
  templateUrl: 'stock-item.component.html',
  styles: [`
    .stock-container {
      border: 1px solid black;
      border-radius: 5px;
      display: inline-block;
      padding: 10px;
    }

    .positive {
      color: green;
    }

    .negative {
      color: red;
    }
  `]
})
export class StockItemComponent implements OnInit {
    // Code omitted here for clarity
}
```

You can find the completed code in the *chapter4/component-style* folder in the GitHub repository.

You can of course choose to pass in multiple style strings to the attribute. The decision between using styles and styleUrls is one of personal preference and has no impact on the final performance of the application.

Style Encapsulation

In the preceding section, we talked about how Angular encapsulates the styles to ensure that it doesn't contaminate any of your other components. In fact, you can actually tell Angular whether it needs to do this or not, or if the styles can be accessible globally. You can set this by using the `encapsulation` attribute on the `Component` decorator. The `encapsulation` attribute takes one of three values:

`ViewEncapsulation.Emulated`
> This the default, where Angular creates shimmed CSS to emulate the behavior that shadow DOMs and shadow roots provide.

`ViewEncapsulation.Native`
> This is the ideal, where Angular will use shadow roots. This will only work on browsers and platforms that natively support it.

`ViewEncapsulation.None`
> Uses global CSS, without any encapsulation.

> **What Is the Shadow DOM?**
>
> HTML, CSS, and JavaScript have a default tendency to be global in the context of the current page. What this means is that an ID given to an element can easily clash with another element somewhere else on the page. Similarly, a CSS rule given to a button in one corner of the page might end up impacting another totally unrelated button.
>
> We end up having to come up with specific naming conventions, use CSS hacks like `!important`, and use many more techniques to work around this generally in our day-to-day development.
>
> Shadow DOM fixes this by scoping HTML DOM and CSS. It provides the ability to have scoped styling to a component (thus preventing the styles from leaking out and affecting the rest of the application) and also the ability to isolate and make the DOM self-contained.
>
> You can read up on it more in the documentation for self-contained web components (*https://developers.google.com/web/fundamentals/web-components/shadowdom*).

The best way to see how this impacts our application is to make a slight change and see how our application behaves under different circumstances.

First, let's add the following snippet of code to the *app.component.css* file. We are using the same base as the previous chapter, and the completed code is available in the *chapter4/component-style-encapsulation* folder:

```css
.name {
  font-size: 50px;
}
```

If we run the application right now, there is no impact on our application. Now, let's try changing the `encapsulation` property on the main `AppComponent`. We will change the component as follows:

```typescript
import { Component, ViewEncapsulation } from '@angular/core';

@Component({
  selector: 'app-root',
  templateUrl: './app.component.html',
  styleUrls: ['./app.component.css'],
  encapsulation: ViewEncapsulation.None
})
export class AppComponent {
  title = 'app works!';
}
```

We added the `encapsulation: ViewEncapsulation.None` line to our `Component` decorator (of course, after importing the `ViewEncapsulation` enum from Angular). Now if we refresh our application, you will see that the name of the stock has been blown up to 50px. This is because the styles applied on the `AppComponent` are not restricted to just the component but are now taking the global namespace. Thus, any element that adds the `name` class to itself will get this font-size applied to it.

`ViewEncapsulation.None` is a good way of applying common styles to all child components, but definitely adds the risk of polluting the global CSS namespace and having unintentional effects.

Others

There are a lot more attributes than what we covered on the `Component` decorator. We will briefly review a few of those here, and will reserve discussion of others for later chapters when they become more relevant. Here is a quick highlight of some of the other major attributes and their uses:

Stripping white spaces

Angular allows you to strip any unnecessary white spaces from your template (as defined by Angular, including more than one space, space between elements, etc.). This can help reduce the build size by compressing your HTML. You can set this feature (which is set to `false` by default) by using the `preserveWhitespa ces` attribute on the component. You can read more about this feature in the official documentation (*https://angular.io/api/core/Component#preserveWhitespaces*).

Animations

Angular gives you multiple triggers to control and animate each part of the component and its lifecycle. To accomplish this, it provides its own DSL, which allows Angular to animate on state changes within the element.

Interpolation

There are times when the default Angular interpolation markers (the double-curlies {{ and }}) interfere with integrating with other frameworks or technologies. For those scenarios, Angular allows you to override the interpolation identifiers at a component level by specifying the start and end delimiters. You can do so by using the `interpolation` attribute, which takes an array of two strings, the opening and closing markers for the interpolation. By default, they are `['{{', '}}']`, but you override it by, say, providing `interpolation: ['<<', '>>']` to replace the interpolation symbols for just that component to << and >>.

View providers

View providers allow you to define providers that inject classes/services into a component or any of its children. Usually, you won't need it, but if there are certain components where you want to override, or restrict the availability of a class or a service, you can specify an array of providers to a component using the `view Providers` attribute. We will cover this in more detail in Chapter 8.

Exporting the component

We have been working so far by using the component class's functions within the context of the template. But there are use cases (especially when we start dealing with directives and more complex components) for which we might want to allow the user of the component to call functions on the component from outside. A use case might be that we provide a carousel component, but want to provide functionality to allow the user of the component to control the next/previous functionality. In these cases, we can use the `exportAs` attribute of the `Component` decorator.

`changeDetection`

By default, Angular checks every binding in the UI to see if it needs to update any UI element whenever any value changes in our component. This is acceptable for most applications, but as our applications get larger in size and complexity, we might want control over how and when Angular updates the UI. Instead of Angular deciding when it needs to update the UI, we might want to be explicit and tell Angular when it needs to update the UI manually. To do this, we use the `changeDetection` attribute, where we can override the default value of `Change DetectionStrategy.Default` to `ChangeDetectionStrategy.OnPush`. This means that after the initial render, it will be up to us to let Angular know when the value changes. Angular will not check the component's bindings automatically. We will cover this in more detail later in the chapter.

There are a lot more attributes and features with regards to components that we don't cover in this chapter. You should take a look at the official documentation for components (*https://angular.io/api/core/Component*) to get familiar with what else is possible, or dive deeper into the details.

Components and Modules

Before we go into the details of the lifecycle of a component, let's quickly sidetrack into how components are linked to modules and what their relation is. In Chapter 2, we saw how any time we created a new component, we had to include it in a module. If you create a new component, and do not add it to a module, Angular will complain that you have components that are not part of any modules.

For any component to be used within the context of a module, it has to be imported into your module declaration file and declared in the declarations array. This ensures that the component is visible to all other components within the module.

There are three specific attributes on the NgModule that directly impact components and their usage, which are important to know. While only declarations is important initially, once you start working with multiple modules, or if you are either creating or importing other modules, the other two attributes become essential:

declarations

> The declarations attribute ensures that components and directives are available to use within the scope of the module. The Angular CLI will automatically add your component or directive to the module when you create a component through it. When you first start out building Angular applications, you might easily forget to add your newly created components to the declarations attribute, so keep track of that (if you are not using the Angular CLI, that is!) in order to avoid this common mistake.

imports

> The imports attribute allows you to specify modules that you want imported and accessible within your module. This is mostly as a way to pull in third-party modules to make the components and services available within your application. If you want to use a component from other modules, make sure you import the relevant modules into the module you have declared and where the component exists.

exports

> The exports attribute is relevant if you either have multiple modules or you need to create a library that will be used by other developers. Unless you export a component, it cannot be accessed or used outside of the direct module where the

component is declared. As a general rule of thumb, if you will need to use the component in another module, make sure you export it.

 If you are facing issues using a component, where Angular fails to recognize a component or says it does not recognize an element, it most likely is due to misconfigured modules. Check, in order, the following:

- Whether the component is added as a declaration in the module.
- In case it is not a component that you wrote, make sure that you have imported the module that provides/exports the component.
- If you created a new component that needs to be used in other components, make sure that you export the component in its module so that any application including the module will get access to your newly created component.

Input and Output

One common use case when we start creating components is that we want to separate the content that a component uses from the component itself. A component is truly useful when it is reusable. One of the ways we can make a component reusable (rather than having default, hardcoded values inside it) is by passing in different inputs depending on the use case. Similarly, there might be cases where we want hooks from a component when a certain activity happens within its context.

Angular provides hooks to specify each of these through decorators, aptly named Input and Output. These, unlike the Component and NgModule decorators, apply at a class member variable level.

Input

When we add an Input decorator on a member variable, it automatically allows you to pass in values to the component for that particular input via Angular's data binding syntax.

Let's see how we can extend our stock-item component from the previous chapter to allow us to pass in the stock object, rather than hardcoding it within the component itself. The finished example is available in the GitHub repository in the *chapter4/component-input* folder. If you want to code along and don't have the previous code, you can use the *chapter3/ng-if* codebase as the starter to code along from.

We will first modify the `stock-item` component to mark the stock as an input to the component, but instead of initializing the stock object, we will mark it as an `Input` to the component. We do this by importing the decorator and using it for the `stock` variable. The code for the *stock-item.component.ts* file should look like the following:

```
import { Component, OnInit, Input } from '@angular/core';

import { Stock } from '../../model/stock';

@Component({
  selector: 'app-stock-item',
  templateUrl: './stock-item.component.html',
  styleUrls: ['./stock-item.component.css']
})
export class StockItemComponent {

  @Input() public stock: Stock;

  constructor() { }

  toggleFavorite(event) {
    this.stock.favorite = !this.stock.favorite;
  }
}
```

We have removed all instantiation logic from the `app-stock-item` component, and marked the `stock` variable as an input. This means that the initialization logic has been moved out, and the component is only responsible for receiving the value of the stock from the parent component and just rendering the data.

Next, let's take a look at the `AppComponent` and how we can change that to now pass in the data to the `StockItemComponent`:

```
import { Component, OnInit } from '@angular/core';
import { Stock } from 'app/model/stock';

@Component({
  selector: 'app-root',
  templateUrl: './app.component.html',
  styleUrls: ['./app.component.css']
})
export class AppComponent implements OnInit {
  title = 'Stock Market App';

  public stockObj: Stock;

  ngOnInit(): void {
    this.stockObj = new Stock('Test Stock Company', 'TSC', 85, 80);
  }
}
```

We just moved the initialization of the stock object from the `StockItemComponent` to the `AppComponent`. Finally, let's take a look at the template of the `AppComponent` to see how we can pass in the stock to the `StockItemComponent`:

```
<h1>
  {{title}}
</h1>
<app-stock-item [stock]="stockObj"></app-stock-item>
```

We use Angular's data binding to pass in the stock from the `AppComponent` to the `StockItemComponent`. The name of the attribute (`stock`) has to match the name of the variable in the component that has been marked as input. The attribute name is case sensitive, so make sure it matches exactly with the input variable name. The value that we pass to it is the reference of the object in the `AppComponent` class, which is `stockObj`.

HTML and Case-Sensitive Attributes?

You might wonder how this is even possible. Angular has its own HTML parser under the covers that parses the templates for Angular-specific syntax, and does not rely on the DOM API for some of these. This is why Angular attributes are and can be case-sensitive.

These inputs are data bound, so if you end up changing the value of the object in `AppComponent`, it will automatically be reflected in the child `StockItemComponent`.

Output

Just like we can pass data into a component, we can also register and listen for events from a component. We use data binding to pass data in, and we use event binding syntax to register for events. We use the `Output` decorator to accomplish this.

We register an `EventEmitter` as an output from any component. We can then trigger the event using the `EventEmitter` object, which will allow any component bound to the event to get the notification and act accordingly.

We can use the code from the previous example where we registered an `Input` decorator and continue on from there. Let's now extend the `StockComponent` to trigger an event when it is favorited, and move the data manipulation out from the component to its parent. This makes sense as well because the parent component is responsible for the data and should be the single source of truth. Thus, we will let the parent `App Component` register for the `toggleFavorite` event and change the state of the stock when the event is triggered.

The finished code for this is in the *chapter4/component-output* folder.

Take a look at the `StockItemComponent` code in *src/app/stock/stock-item/stock-item.component.ts*:

```
import { Component, OnInit, Input, Output, EventEmitter } from '@angular/core';

import { Stock } from '../../model/stock';

@Component({
  selector: 'app-stock-item',
  templateUrl: './stock-item.component.html',
  styleUrls: ['./stock-item.component.css']
})
export class StockItemComponent {

  @Input() public stock: Stock;
  @Output() private toggleFavorite: EventEmitter<Stock>;

  constructor() {
    this.toggleFavorite = new EventEmitter<Stock>();
  }

  onToggleFavorite(event) {
    this.toggleFavorite.emit(this.stock);
  }
}
```

A few important things to note:

- We imported the `Output` decorator as well as the `EventEmitter` from the Angular library.

- We created a new class member called `toggleFavorite` of type `EventEmitter`, and renamed our method to `onToggleFavorite`. The `EventEmitter` can be typed for additional type safety.

- We need to ensure that the `EventEmitter` instance is initialized, as it is *not* auto-initialized for us. Either do it inline or do it in the constructor as we did earlier.

- The `onToggleFavorite` now just calls a method on the `EventEmitter` to emit the entire stock object. This means that all listeners of the `toggleFavorite` event will get the current stock object as a parameter.

We will also change *stock-item.component.html* to call the `onToggleFavorite` method instead of `toggleFavorite`. The HTML markup remains pretty much the same otherwise:

```
<div class="stock-container">
  <div class="name">{{stock.name + ' (' + stock.code + ')'}}</div>
  <div class="price"
      [class]="stock.isPositiveChange() ? 'positive' : 'negative'">
      $ {{stock.price}}
```

```
    </div>
    <button (click)="onToggleFavorite($event)"
            *ngIf="!stock.favorite">Add to Favorite</button>
</div>
```

Next, we add a method to the AppComponent that should be triggered whenever the onToggleFavorite method is triggered, which we will add event binding on:

```
import { Component, OnInit } from '@angular/core';
import { Stock } from 'app/model/stock';

@Component({
  selector: 'app-root',
  templateUrl: './app.component.html',
  styleUrls: ['./app.component.css']
})
export class AppComponent implements OnInit {
  title = 'app works!';

  public stock: Stock;

  ngOnInit(): void {
    this.stock = new Stock('Test Stock Company', 'TSC', 85, 80);
  }

  onToggleFavorite(stock: Stock) {
    console.log('Favorite for stock ', stock, ' was triggered');
    this.stock.favorite = !this.stock.favorite;
  }
}
```

The only thing new is the onToggleFavorite method we have added, which takes a stock as an argument. In this particular case, we don't use the stock passed to it other than for logging, but you could base any decision/work on that. Note also that the name of the function is not relevant, and you could name it whatever you want.

Finally, let's tie it all together by subscribing to the new output from our StockComponent in the *app-component.html* file:

```
<h1>
  {{title}}
</h1>
<app-stock-item [stock]="stock"
                (toggleFavorite)="onToggleFavorite($event)">
</app-stock-item>
```

We just added an event binding using Angular's event-binding syntax to the output declared in the stock-item component. Notice again that it is case sensitive and it has to exactly match what member variable we decorated with the Output decorator. Also, to get access to the value emitted by the component, we use the keyword $event as a parameter to the function. Without it, the function would still get triggered, but you would not get any arguments with it.

With this, if you run the application (remember, ng serve), you should see the fully functional app, and when you click the Add to Favorite button, it should trigger the method in the AppComponent.

Change Detection

We mentioned changeDetection as an attribute on the Component decorator. Now that we have seen how Input and Output decorators work, let's deep dive a little bit into how Angular performs its change detection at a component level.

By default, Angular applies the ChangeDetectionStrategy.Default mechanism to the changeDetection attribute. This means that every time Angular notices an event (say, a server response or a user interaction), it will go through each component in the component tree, and check each of the bindings individually to see if any of the values have changed and need to be updated in the view.

For a very large application, you will have lots of bindings on a given page. When a user takes any action, you as a developer might know for sure that most of the page will not change. In such cases, you can actually give a hint to the Angular change detector to check or not check certain components as you see fit. For any given component, we can accomplish this by changing the ChangeDetectionStrategy from the default to ChangeDetectionStrategy.OnPush. What this tells Angular is that the bindings for this particular component will need to be checked only based on the Input to this component.

Let's consider a few examples to see how this might play out. Say we have a component tree A → B → C. That is, we have a root component A, which uses a component B in its template, which in turn uses a component C. And let's say component B passes in a composite object compositeObj to component C as input. Maybe something like:

```
<c [inputToC]="compositeObj"></c>
```

That is, inputToC is the input variable marked with the Input decorator in component C, and is passed the object compositeObj from component B. Now say we marked component C's changeDetection attribute as ChangeDetectionStrategy.OnPush. Here are the implications of that change:

- If component C has bindings to any attributes of compositeObj, they will work as usual (no change from default behavior).

- If component C makes any changes to any of the attributes of compositeObj, they will also be updated immediately (no change from default behavior).

- If the parent component B creates a new `compositeObj` or changes the reference of `compositeObj` (think new operator, or assign from a server response), then component C would recognize the change and update its bindings for the new value (no change from default behavior, but internal behavior changes on how Angular recognizes the change).

- If the parent component B changes any attribute on the `compositeObj` directly (as a response to a user action outside component B), then these changes would not be updated in component C (major change from the default behavior).

- If the parent component B changes any attribute on response to an event emitter from component C, and then changes any attribute on the `compositeObj` (without changing the reference), this would still work and the bindings would get updated. This is because the change originates from component C (no change from default behavior).

Angular provides ways for us to signal when to check the bindings from within the component as well, to have absolute control on Angular's data binding. We will cover these in "Change Detection" on page 67. For now, it is good to understand the difference between the two change detection strategies that Angular provides.

Let's now modify the example code to see this in action. First, modify the *stock-item.component.ts* file to change the `ChangeDetectionStrategy` in the child component:

```
import { Component, OnInit, Input, Output } from '@angular/core';
import { EventEmitter, ChangeDetectionStrategy } from '@angular/core';

import { Stock } from '../../model/stock';

@Component({
  selector: 'app-stock-item',
  templateUrl: './stock-item.component.html',
  styleUrls: ['./stock-item.component.css'],
  changeDetection: ChangeDetectionStrategy.OnPush
})
export class StockItemComponent {

  @Input() public stock: Stock;
  @Output() private toggleFavorite: EventEmitter<Stock>;

  constructor() {
    this.toggleFavorite = new EventEmitter<Stock>();
  }

  onToggleFavorite(event) {
    this.toggleFavorite.emit(this.stock);
  }
```

```
  changeStockPrice() {
    this.stock.price += 5;
  }
}
```

In addition to changing the `ChangeDetectionStrategy`, we also added another function to `changeStockPrice()`. We will use these functions to demonstrate the behavior of the change detection in the context of our application.

Next, let's quickly modify *stock-item.component.html* to allow us to trigger the new function. We will simply add a new button to trigger and change the stock price when the button is clicked:

```
<div class="stock-container">
  <div class="name">{{stock.name + ' (' + stock.code + ')'}}</div>
  <div class="price"
      [class]="stock.isPositiveChange() ? 'positive' : 'negative'">
      $ {{stock.price}}
  </div>
  <button (click)="onToggleFavorite($event)"
          *ngIf="!stock.favorite">Add to Favorite</button>
  <button (click)="changeStockPrice()">Change Price</button>
</div>
```

There is no change to the HTML of the template other than adding a new button to change the stock price. Similarly, let's quickly change the main *app.component.html* file to add another button to trigger the change of the price from the parent component (similar to component B in the earlier hypothetical example):

```
<h1>
  {{title}}
</h1>
<app-stock-item [stock]="stock"
                (toggleFavorite)="onToggleFavorite($event)">
</app-stock-item>
<button (click)="changeStockObject()">Change Stock</button>
<button (click)="changeStockPrice()">Change Price</button>
```

We have added two new buttons to this template: one that will change the reference of the stock object directly, and another that will modify the existing reference of the stock object to change the price from the parent AppComponent. Now finally, we can see how all of this is hooked up in the *app.component.ts* file:

```
import { Component, OnInit } from '@angular/core';
import { Stock } from 'app/model/stock';

@Component({
  selector: 'app-root',
  templateUrl: './app.component.html',
  styleUrls: ['./app.component.css']
})
export class AppComponent implements OnInit {
```

```
    title = 'app works!';

    public stock: Stock;
    private counter: number = 1;

    ngOnInit(): void {
      this.stock = new Stock('Test Stock Company - ' + this.counter++,
          'TSC', 85, 80);
    }

    onToggleFavorite(stock: Stock) {
      // This will update the value in the stock item component
      // Because it is triggered as a result of an event
      // binding from the stock item component
      this.stock.favorite = !this.stock.favorite;
    }

    changeStockObject() {
      // This will update the value in the stock item component
      // Because we are creating a new reference for the stock input
      this.stock = new Stock('Test Stock Company - ' + this.counter++,
          'TSC', 85, 80);
    }

    changeStockPrice() {
      // This will not update the value in the stock item component
      // because it is changing the same reference and angular will
      // not check for it in the OnPush change detection strategy.
      this.stock.price += 10;
    }
  }
}
```

The *app.component.ts* file has seen the most changes. The preceding code is also well annotated with comments to explain the expected behavior when each of these functions are triggered. We have added two new methods: changeStockObject(), which creates a new instance of the stock object in the AppComponent, and changeStock Price(), which modifies the prices of the stock object in the AppComponent. We have also added a counter just to keep track of how many times we create a new stock object, but that is not strictly necessary.

Now when you run this application, you should expect to see the following behavior:

- Clicking Add to Favorite within the StockItemComponent still works as expected.

- Clicking Change Price within the StockItemComponent will increase the price of the stock by $5 each time.

- Clicking Change Stock outside the StockItemComponent will change the name of the stock with each click. (This is why we added the counter!)

- Clicking Change Price outside the StockItemComponent will have no impact (even though the actual value of the stock will jump if you click Change Price inside after this). This shows that the model is getting updated, but Angular is not updating the view.

You should also change back the ChangeDetectionStrategy to default to see the difference in action.

Component Lifecycle

Components (and directives) in Angular have their own lifecycle, from creation, rendering, changing, to destruction. This lifecycle executes in preorder tree traversal order, from top to bottom. After Angular renders a component, it starts the lifecycle for each of its children, and so on until the entire application is rendered.

There are times when these lifecycle events are useful to us in developing our application, so Angular provides hooks into this lifecycle so that we can observe and react as necessary. Figure 4-1 shows the lifecycle hooks of a component, in the order in which they are invoked.

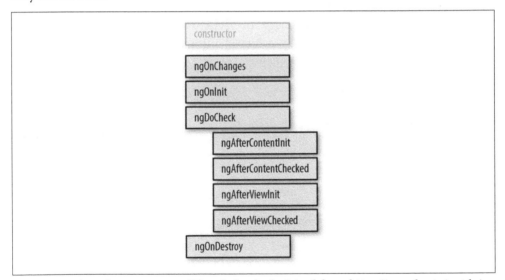

Figure 4-1. Angular component lifecycle hooks (original from https://angular.io/guide/lifecycle-hooks)

Angular will first call the constructor for any component, and then the various steps mentioned earlier in order. Some of them, like the OnInit and AfterContentInit (basically, any lifecycle hook ending with Init) is called only once, when a component is initialized, while the others are called whenever any content changes. The OnDestroy hook is also called only once for a component.

Each of these lifecycle steps comes with an interface that should be implemented when a component cares about that particular lifecycle, and each interface provides a function starting with ng that needs to be implemented. For example, the OnInit lifecycle step needs a function called ngOnInit to be implemented in the component and so on.

We will walk through each of the lifecycle steps here, and then use one example to see this all in action and the ordering of lifecycle steps within a component and across components.

There is also one more concept to learn, which we will briefly touch upon in this chapter, and come back to later in more detail—the concept of ViewChildren and ContentChildren.

ViewChildren is any child component whose tags/selectors (mostly elements, as that is the recommendation for components) appear within the template of the component. So in our case, app-stock-item would be a ViewChild of the AppComponent.

ContentChildren is any child component that gets projected into the view of the component, but is not directly included in the template within the component. Imagine something like a carousel, where the functionality is encapsulated in the component, but the view, which could be images or pages of a book, comes from the user of the component. Those are generally achieved through ContentChildren. We will cover this in more depth later in this chapter.

Interfaces and Functions

Table 4-1 shows the interfaces and functions in the order in which they are called, along with specific details about the step if there is anything to note. Note that we are only covering component-specific lifecycle steps, and they are slightly different from a directive's lifecycle.

Table 4-1. Angular lifecycle hooks and methods

Interface	Method	Applicable to	Purpose
OnChanges	ngOn Changes(changes: SimpleChange)	Components and directives	ngOnChanges is called both right after the constructor to set and then later every time the input properties to a directive change. It is called before the ngOnInit method.
OnInit	ngOnInit()	Components and directives	This is your typical initialization hook, allowing you to do any one-time initialization specific to your component or directive. This is the ideal place to load data from the server and so on, rather than the constructor, both for separation of concerns as well as testability.

Interface	Method	Applicable to	Purpose
DoCheck	ngDoCheck()	Components and directives	DoCheck is Angular's way of giving the component a way to check if there are any bindings or changes that Angular can't or should not detect on its own. This is one of the ways we can use to notify Angular of a change in the component, when we override the default ChangeDetectionStrategy for a component from Default to OnPush.
After Content Init	ngAfterContent Init()	Components only	As mentioned, the AfterContentInit hook is triggered during component projection cases, and only once during initialization of the component. If there is no projection, this is triggered immediately.
After Content Checked	ngAfterContent Checked()	Components only	AfterContentChecked is triggered each time Angular's change detection cycle executes, and in case it is initialization, it is triggered right after the AfterContentInit hook.
AfterView Init	ngAfterViewInit()	Components only	AfterViewInit is the complement to AfterContent Init, and is triggered after all the child components that are directly used in the template of the component are finished initializing and their views updated with bindings. This may not necessarily mean that the views are rendered into the browser, but that Angular has finished updating its internal views to render as soon as possible. AfterViewInit is triggered only once during the load of the component.
AfterView Checked	ngAfterView Checked()	Components only	AfterViewChecked is triggered each time after all the child components have been checked and updated. Again, a good way to think about both this and AfterContent Checked is like a depth-first tree traversal, in that it will execute only after all the children components' AfterView Checked hooks have finished executing.
OnDestroy	ngOnDestroy()	Components and directives	The OnDestroy hook is called when a component is about to be destroyed and removed from the UI. It is a good place to do all cleanup, like unsubscribing any listeners you may have initialized and the like. It is generally good practice to clean up anything that you have registered (timers, observables, etc.) as part of the component.

Let's try to add all these hooks to our existing application to see the order of execution in a real-world scenario. We will add all of these hooks to both our AppComponent and the StockItemComponent, with a simple console.log to just see when and how these functions are executed. We will use the base from the output example to build from, so in case you are not coding along, you can take the example from *chapter4/component-output* to build from there.

The final finished example is also available in *chapter4/component-lifecycle*.

First, we can modify the *src/app/app.component.ts* file and add the hooks as follows:

```
import { Component, SimpleChanges, OnInit, OnChanges, OnDestroy,
        DoCheck, AfterViewChecked, AfterViewInit, AfterContentChecked,
        AfterContentInit } from '@angular/core';
```

```
import { Stock } from 'app/model/stock';

@Component({
  selector: 'app-root',
  templateUrl: './app.component.html',
  styleUrls: ['./app.component.css']
})
export class AppComponent implements OnInit, OnChanges, OnDestroy,
                                    DoCheck, AfterContentChecked,
                                    AfterContentInit, AfterViewChecked,
                                    AfterViewInit {

  title = 'app works!';

  public stock: Stock;

  onToggleFavorite(stock: Stock) {
    console.log('Favorite for stock ', stock, ' was triggered');
    this.stock.favorite = !this.stock.favorite;
  }

  ngOnInit(): void {
    this.stock = new Stock('Test Stock Company', 'TSC', 85, 80);
    console.log('App Component - On Init');
  }

  ngAfterViewInit(): void {
    console.log('App Component - After View Init');
  }
  ngAfterViewChecked(): void {
    console.log('App Component - After View Checked');
  }
  ngAfterContentInit(): void {
    console.log('App Component - After Content Init');
  }
  ngAfterContentChecked(): void {
    console.log('App Component - After Content Checked');
  }
  ngDoCheck(): void {
    console.log('App Component - Do Check');
  }
  ngOnDestroy(): void {
    console.log('App Component - On Destroy');
  }
  ngOnChanges(changes: SimpleChanges): void {
    console.log('App Component - On Changes - ', changes);
  }
}
```

You can see that we have implemented the interfaces for OnInit, OnChanges, OnDestroy, DoCheck, AfterContentChecked, AfterContentInit, AfterView Checked, AfterViewInit on the AppComponent class, and then went ahead and implemented the respective functions. Each of the methods simply prints out a log statement mentioning the component name and the trigger method name.

Similarly, we can do the same for the StockItemComponent:

```
import { Component, SimpleChanges, OnInit,
         OnChanges, OnDestroy, DoCheck, AfterViewChecked,
         AfterViewInit, AfterContentChecked,
         AfterContentInit, Input,
         Output, EventEmitter } from '@angular/core';
import { Stock } from '../../model/stock';

@Component({
  selector: 'app-stock-item',
  templateUrl: './stock-item.component.html',
  styleUrls: ['./stock-item.component.css']
})
export class StockItemComponent implements OnInit, OnChanges,
                                           OnDestroy, DoCheck,
                                           AfterContentChecked,
                                           AfterContentInit,
                                           AfterViewChecked,
                                           AfterViewInit {

  @Input() public stock: Stock;
  @Output() private toggleFavorite: EventEmitter<Stock>;

  constructor() {
    this.toggleFavorite = new EventEmitter<Stock>();
   }

  onToggleFavorite(event) {
    this.toggleFavorite.emit(this.stock);
  }

  ngOnInit(): void {
    console.log('Stock Item Component - On Init');
  }
  ngAfterViewInit(): void {
    console.log('Stock Item Component - After View Init');
  }
  ngAfterViewChecked(): void {
    console.log('Stock Item Component - After View Checked');
  }
  ngAfterContentInit(): void {
    console.log('Stock Item Component - After Content Init');
  }
  ngAfterContentChecked(): void {
    console.log('Stock Item Component - After Content Checked');
  }
  ngDoCheck(): void {
    console.log('Stock Item Component - Do Check');
```

```
  }
  ngOnDestroy(): void {
    console.log('Stock Item Component - On Destroy');
  }
  ngOnChanges(changes: SimpleChanges): void {
    console.log('Stock Item Component - On Changes - ', changes);
  }
}
```

We have done exactly the same thing we did on the AppComponent with the Stock
ItemComponent. Now, we can run this application to see it in action.

When you run it, open the JavaScript console in the browser. You should see, in order
of execution:

1. First, the AppComponent gets created. Then the following hooks are triggered on
   the AppComponent:

   - On Init
   - Do Check
   - After Content Init
   - After Content Checked

   The preceding two immediately execute because we don't have any content projection in our application so far.

2. Next, the StockItemComponent OnChanges executes, with the input to the Stock
   ItemComponent being recognized as the change, followed by the hooks listed here
   within the StockItemComponent:

   - On Init
   - Do Check
   - After Content Init
   - After Content Checked
   - After View Init
   - After View Checked

3. Finally, there are no more subcomponents to traverse down on, so Angular steps
   back out to the parent AppComponent, and executes the following:

   - After View Init
   - After View Checked

This gives us a nice view of how and in which order Angular goes around initializing and the tree traversal it does under the covers. These hooks become very useful for certain trickier initialization logic, and are definitely essential for cleanup once your component is done and dusted, to avoid memory leaks.

View Projection

The last thing we will cover in this chapter is the concept of view projection. Projection is an important idea in Angular as it gives us more flexibility when we develop our components and again gives us another tool to make them truly reusable under different contexts.

Projection is useful when we want to build components but set some parts of the UI of the component to not be an innate part of it. For example, say we were building a component for a carousel. A carousel has a few simple capabilities: it is able to display an item, and allow us to navigate to the next/previous element. Your carousel component might also have other features like lazy loading, etc. But one thing that is not the purview of the carousel component is the content it displays. A user of the component might want to display an image, a page of a book, or any other random thing.

Thus, in these cases, the view would be controlled by the user of the component, and the functionality would be provided by the component itself. This is but one use case where we might want to use projection in our components.

Let's see how we might use content projection in our Angular application. We will use the base from the input example to build from, so in case you are not coding along, you can take the example from *chapter4/component-input* to build from there.

The final finished example is available in *chapter4/component-projection*.

First, we will modify our StockItemComponent to allow for content projection. There is no code change in our component class; we only need to modify the *src/app/stock/stock-item/stock-item.component.html* file as follows:

```
<div class="stock-container">
  <div class="name">{{stock.name + ' (' + stock.code + ')'}}</div>
  <div class="price"
      [class]="stock.isPositiveChange() ? 'positive' : 'negative'">
      $ {{stock.price}}
  </div>
  <ng-content></ng-content>                    ❶
</div>
```

❶ The new ng-content element for projection

We have simply removed the buttons we previously had, and are going to let the user of the component decide what buttons are to be shown. To allow for this, we have replaced the buttons with an `ng-content` element. There is no other change required in the component.

Next, we will make a change to the `AppComponent`, simply to add a method for testing purposes. Modify the *src/app/app.component.ts* file as follows:

```
/** Imports and decorators skipped for brevity **/

export class AppComponent implements OnInit {
  /** Constructor and OnInit skipped for brevity **/

  testMethod() {
    console.log('Test method in AppComponent triggered');
  }
}
```

We have simply added a method that will log to the console when it is triggered. With this in place, now let's see how we can use our updated `StockItemComponent` and use the power of projection. Modify the *app.component.html* file as follows:

```
<h1>
  {{title}}
</h1>
<app-stock-item [stock]="stockObj">
  <button (click)="testMethod()">With Button 1</button>
</app-stock-item>

<app-stock-item [stock]="stockObj">
  No buttons for you!!
</app-stock-item>
```

We have added two instances of the `app-stock-item` component in our HTML. And both of these now have some content inside them, as opposed to previously where these elements had no content. In one, we have a button that triggers the `testMethod` we added in the `AppComponent`, and the other simply has text content.

When we run our Angular application and open it in the browser, we should see something like Figure 4-2.

Notice that the two stock item components on our browser, each with slightly different content, are based on what we provided. If you click the button in the first stock widget, you will see that the method in the `AppComponent` gets called and the `console.log` is triggered.

Thus, users of the component now have the capability to change part of the UI of the component as they see fit. We can even access functionality from the parent component as well, which makes it truly flexible. It is also possible to project multiple different sections and content into our child component. While the official Angular documentation is spare on this topic, there is a great article (*http://bit.ly/2IFX237*) that can give you more insight on content projection.

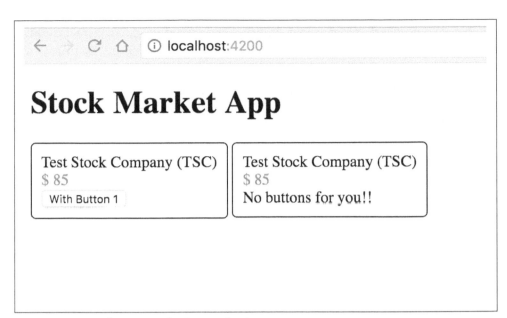

Figure 4-2. Angular app with view projection

Conclusion

In this chapter, we went into a lot more depth on components, and saw some of the more commonly used attributes when creating components. We took a detailed look at the Component decorator, talking about attributes like template versus template Url, styles, and also covered at a high level how Angular's change detection works and how we can override it.

We then covered the lifecycle of a component, as well as the hooks that Angular provides for us to hook on to and react to some of these lifecycle events. Finally, we covered projection in components and how we can make some truly powerful components that allow the user of the component to decide parts of the UI.

In the next chapter, we will do a quick detour to understand unit testing of components, and see how we can test both the logic that drives the component as well as the view that gets rendered.

Exercise

For our third exercise, we can build on top of the previous exercise (*chapter3/exercise*) by including concepts from this chapter:

1. Create a `ProductListComponent`. Initialize an array of products there, instead of initializing a single product in the `ProductComponent`. Change its template to use `NgFor` to create a `ProductItemComponent` for each product.

2. Use inline templates and styles on the `ProductListComponent`. Generate it using the Angular CLI with that setting rather than generating it and changing it manually.

3. Change the `ProductItemComponent` to take the product as an input.

4. Move the increment/decrement logic from the `ProductItem` to the `ProductList` Component. Use an index or product ID to find the product and change its quantity.

5. Move the `ProductItemComponent` to be optimal and move from the default `ChangeDetectionStrategy` to an `OnPush` `ChangeDetectionStrategy`.

All of this can be accomplished using concepts covered in this chapter. You can check out the finished solution in *chapter4/exercise/ecommerce*.

CHAPTER 5

Testing Angular Components

In the chapters so far, we focused on writing our Angular application, and dealt with how to use the Angular CLI, how to create components, some common built-in Angular directives, and the like.

In this chapter, we will take a detour to learn how we can write unit tests for the components we have written so far. To do this, we will first get a sense of the unit testing setup for Angular, the various frameworks and libraries we use to accomplish this, and walk step by step through writing unit tests for a component.

Why Unit Test?

But before we go into all that, let's quickly talk about unit tests and why they are important. Unit tests are called that because they test an individual unit within your application. Given a very large application and its many pieces, it can become very tricky to test each and every flow through the application. This is why we break up the testing to check each individual component, such that we can be assured that when they are hooked up together, they will work correctly under all cases without necessarily testing each and every flow.

This is easily demonstrated with a simple example. Assume we have a very simple application with three different parts. Each part itself might have five different flows through it, giving us a total of 5 * 5 * 5 = 125 flows through the entire application. If we focused only on end-to-end or overall testing, we would have to test 125 flows (or somewhere approaching that number) to get a reasonable assurance on the quality of the application.

Now on the other hand, if we tested each part in isolation, assuming that the other parts were reasonably tested and functional, we would have to write 5 tests for each part, which gives us a total of about 15 tests. Add another 10 to 20 end-to-end tests to make sure the parts are hooked up correctly, and you can have reasonable (not 100% of course) confidence in the overall quality of your application.

That said, unit tests are not just for overall quality. There are a few other good reasons why we write unit tests, some being:

- It is an assertion that what you have written actually does what it is meant to. Without unit tests, there is no way to prove that your code performs correctly.

- It guards your code against future breakages, aka regressions. You write your code today with certain assumptions. You or someone else tomorrow may not remember or know them and may unwittingly change something that breaks your underlying assumption. Unit tests are guards that make sure your code remains future-proof.

- Unit tests are great documentation for your code. Comments have an annoying tendency of becoming obsolete, as people tend to forget to update them. Unit tests, on the other hand, will break if you forget to update your tests as you make changes to your code.

- Unit tests are a great view on how testable and modular your design is. If tests are hard to read or write, it usually is a signal that there might be design flaws or issues in the underlying code.

That said, people have different associations when they hear the term "unit test." The prototypical definition of a unit test is a test of a component, with all dependencies completely mocked out. You are testing only the code you have written and nothing else.

Of course, with frameworks like Angular, sometimes unit tests are useful, and other times you actually want a little bit of integration involved. You want to test how your component behaves rather than the class that defines the component. Angular gives you the capability to write both kinds of tests.

Testing and Angular

Before we go deep into how we write tests for Angular components, let's take a look at the various frameworks and libraries we will use to write and run our Angular tests. Each of these can be used in other non-Angular projects as well, or can be swapped out for something comparable if you have a preference:

Jasmine
Jasmine is a test framework that is oriented toward writing specifications rather than traditional unit tests. It is what is referred to as a behavior-driven development (BDD) framework. It is a standalone framework that can be used to write tests or specifications for any code, not just Angular. The major difference from

traditional unit testing frameworks and something like Jasmine is that Jasmine is more oriented to reading like plain English, so instead of writing a test, you write a specification. A specification is a series of commands, and expectations on what should have happened as a result of these commands.

Karma

If Jasmine is the test-writing framework, then Karma is the test-running framework. Karma's sole task is to take any kind of test, and run it across a suite of real browsers and report the results back. It is highly tuned toward development workflow, as it is heavily oriented toward rapid execution and reporting. It is possible to have Karma run the tests every time you hit save, giving you real-time feedback on whether tests are still passing as you write your code.

Angular testing utilities

Angular provides a suite of various functions and utilities that make testing Angular-specific functionality easier. These are common tasks that you might need to perform in any test, such as initializing modules, components, working with services and routes, and the like. We will touch upon the relevant ones as we work our way through Angular, but in case you want to see all the utility functions upfront, you can check out the documentation (*https://angular.io/guide/testing#atu-apis*).

Protractor

This framework is not relevant with regards to this chapter and unit testing, but for the sake of completeness, we will quickly mention it. Protractor is a framework that is built to write and run end-to-end tests. While the tests we write in this chapter will instantiate various classes and test functionality, it is useful to also test from the perspective of an end user. This would involve opening the browser, clicking, and interacting with the application. Protractor supports this capability of running the real application and simulating actions and verifying behavior, thus completing the circle of testing.

The Test Setup

With that background, let's write our first unit test. Since we generated our applications so far using the Angular CLI, we have the basic infrastructure already set up for us. In fact, every time we generate a component using the Angular CLI, it also generates a skeleton spec for us to write our test code in.

For the purpose of understanding how the testing infrastructure is set up, we'll walk through the major files one by one. The entire finished code for this chapter, including all the tests, is available in the GitHub repository in the *chapter5/component-spec* folder.

Karma Config

The first file of interest is the configuration file for how Karma should find and execute files. The pregenerated *karma.conf.js* is in the main application folder, and looks like the following:

```
// Karma configuration file, see link for more information
// https://karma-runner.github.io/1.0/config/configuration-file.html

module.exports = function (config) {
  config.set({
    basePath: '',
    frameworks: ['jasmine', '@angular/cli'],
    plugins: [
      require('karma-jasmine'),
      require('karma-chrome-launcher'),
      require('karma-jasmine-html-reporter'),
      require('karma-coverage-istanbul-reporter'),
      require('@angular/cli/plugins/karma')
    ],
    client:{
      clearContext: false // leave Jasmine Spec Runner output visible in browser
    },
    coverageIstanbulReporter: {
      reports: [ 'html', 'lcovonly' ],
      fixWebpackSourcePaths: true
    },
    angularCli: {
      environment: 'dev'
    },
    reporters: ['progress', 'kjhtml'],
    port: 9876,
    colors: true,
    logLevel: config.LOG_INFO,
    autoWatch: true,
    browsers: ['Chrome'],
    singleRun: false
  });
};
```

The Karma configuration is responsible for identifying the various plug-ins needed for Karma to run (which includes an Angular CLI–specific plug-in), the files it needs to watch or execute, and then some Karma-specific configuration including coverage reporting (`coverageIstanbulReporter`), which port it needs to run on (`port`), which browsers to run it on (`browsers`), whether it should rerun every time the file changes (`autoWatch`), and which level of logs it needs to capture.

test.ts

The *test.ts* file is the main entry point for our testing, and responsible for loading all our components, the related specifications, and the testing framework and utilities needed to run them:

```
// This file is required by karma.conf.js and loads recursively all the .spec
// and framework files

import 'zone.js/dist/zone-testing';
import { getTestBed } from '@angular/core/testing';
import {
  BrowserDynamicTestingModule,
  platformBrowserDynamicTesting
} from '@angular/platform-browser-dynamic/testing';

declare const require: any;

// First, initialize the Angular testing environment.
getTestBed().initTestEnvironment(
  BrowserDynamicTestingModule,
  platformBrowserDynamicTesting()
);
// Then we find all the tests.
const context = require.context('./', true, /\.spec\.ts$/);
// And load the modules.
context.keys().map(context);
```

The *test.ts* file is basically responsible for loading a series of files for the testing framework, and then initializing the Angular testing environment. Then, it looks for specifications (files ending with *.spec.ts*) recursively in all the folders from the current directory (which is the *src* folder). It then loads all the relevant modules for them and starts executing Karma.

This file is the reason why we don't have to manually list all the specification files in *karma.conf.js*, as it recursively loads them.

Writing Unit Tests

With these two files in place, we can now focus on writing our unit test. To get familiar with Jasmine, we will first start with writing what we call an "isolated unit test."

An Isolated Unit Test

An isolated unit test in Angular terminology is a vanilla JavaScript unit test. This has nothing to do with Angular, but just instantiates classes and methods and executes them. This is sufficient for a large number of classes, as they will mostly be doing simple data manipulation and execution.

We will start with writing a very simple isolated unit test for the `AppComponent` using the example we were working on from Chapter 4. The base codebase to start with can be found in the GitHub repository in the *chapter4/component-output* folder.

The very first thing we will do is create (if it doesn't already exist) a file right beside *app.component.ts* in the *src/app* folder called *app.component.spec.ts*. If it already exists and you haven't deleted it yet, you can go ahead and clear the content, as we will write it from scratch so that we are aware of all the intricacies involved in the test.

The first two tests that we will write will focus on `AppComponent` as a class, and focus on its initialization and how a stock's favorite state is toggled. In these tests, we will not focus on any Angular-specific functionality and see how to test `AppComponent` in isolation:

```
import { AppComponent } from './app.component';        ❶
import { Stock } from 'app/model/stock';

describe('AppComponent', () => {        ❷

  it('should have stock instantiated on ngInit', () => {        ❸
    const appComponent = new AppComponent();        ❹
    expect(appComponent.stock).toBeUndefined();        ❺
    appComponent.ngOnInit();
    expect(appComponent.stock).toEqual(
      new Stock('Test Stock Company', 'TSC', 85, 80));        ❻
  });

  it('should have toggle stock favorite', () => {
    const appComponent = new AppComponent();
    appComponent.ngOnInit();
    expect(appComponent.stock.favorite).toBeFalsy();
    appComponent.onToggleFavorite(new Stock('Test', 'TEST', 54, 55));
    expect(appComponent.stock.favorite).toBeTruthy();
    appComponent.onToggleFavorite(new Stock('Test', 'TEST', 54, 55));
    expect(appComponent.stock.favorite).toBeFalsy();
  });
});
```

❶ Importing all relevant dependencies for our tests

❷ Our main `AppComponent` test suite

❸ The first test, each test being an `it` block

❹ Instantiating the `AppComponent`

❺ An expectation or assertion on what the behavior should be

❻ Our final expectation on what the stock should be

Our isolated unit tests read just like plain old JavaScript, with Jasmine syntax thrown in. We first import our relevant class and interfaces to be able to use them in the specification. Then we define our first describe block, which is Jasmine's way of encapsulating a set of tests as one suite. Describe blocks can be nested any number deep, which we will use in the feature to create separate describe blocks for Angular-aware tests versus isolated unit tests.

We then write our first test block, which uses Jasmine's `it` to define a specification block. Within this, we define and instantiate our `AppComponent` instance, and then write an expectation that, by default, the `stock` instance of the `AppComponent` is `undefined`. We then call the `ngOnInit` method of the `AppComponent` manually, which creates a stock instance for us. We then write another expectation to make sure this value is created as we expect it to be.

Note that this behavior mirrors how the `AppComponent` behaves. When an instance of the `AppComponent` is created, we just have a definition for the `stock` object, but with no initial value. Thus, our initial expectation for the `stock` instance in the test is that it should be `undefined`. Then, we trigger the `ngOnInit` method, which ends up creating a `stock` instance with some values. We then assert in our test that the instance that gets created in the `AppComponent` actually has the values we want.

 Note that in an isolated unit test, Angular lifecycle methods are not called automatically, which is why we manually trigger `ngOnInit` ourselves in the test. This gives us the flexibility that we might want to test some other function and avoid the `ngOnInit`, which might make expensive or complex server calls.

Similarly, we write the second test that evaluates the `onToggleFavorite` method on the `AppComponent` class. We pass a random value to it, as the value is not used in the class except to log it. We use a different expectation, `toBeFalsy` and `toBeTruthy`, instead of the `toEquals` we used in the previous test. These are all in-built matchers that Jasmine provides for us to use in our specifications. You can see the whole list of matchers that Jasmine provides out of the box in the official documentation (*https://jasmine.github.io/api/2.8/matchers.html*).

Running the Tests

Running the actual tests, if you are using the Angular CLI as we are doing in this book, is actually very simple. Simply execute

```
ng test
```

from the command line in the root folder to execute the tests. This will:

1. Pick up the configuration from the *karma.conf.js* Karma configuration file

2. Load all the relevant tests and files as per the *test.ts* file

3. Capture the default browser (which is Chrome in our case)

4. Execute the tests and report the results in the terminal

5. Keep a watch on files to continue executing on change

You should see Karma capturing Chrome, and spawn up a browser that looks like Figure 5-1.

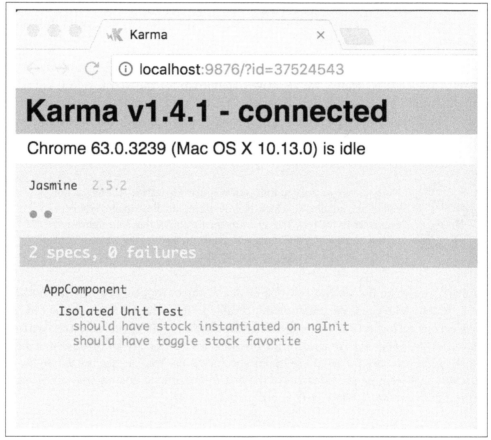

Figure 5-1. Angular tests running via Karma in Chrome

In the terminal, once you run the ng test command, you should see output similar to Figure 5-2.

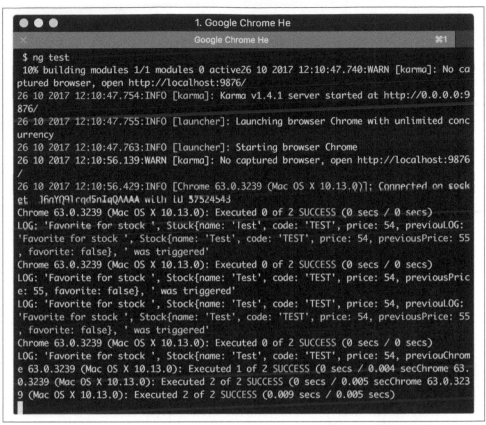

Figure 5-2. Angular test output in the terminal

Once this completes, you should see (in both your Karma captured browser and the terminal) a result of having run two tests with both passing successfully.

Writing an Angular-Aware Unit Test

The next thing we want to learn is how to write a test that is Angular-aware and goes through the Angular lifecycle. In such a test, rather than just instantiating the component class, we want to instantiate a component just the way Angular does, including the HTML for the component.

We will write a test for the StockItemComponent, in which we will make sure that given the right stock input, the template gets rendered with the correct bindings. Furthermore, we want to make sure the input and output bindings are connected and triggered correctly.

Let's create a *stock-item.component.spec.ts* file as a sibling to *stock-item.component.ts*. Again, if this file already exists, replace it with the following contents:

```
import { TestBed, async } from '@angular/core/testing';      ❶

import { StockItemComponent } from './stock-item.component';
import { Stock } from '../../model/stock';
import { By } from '@angular/platform-browser';

describe('Stock Item Component', () => {

  let fixture, component;

  beforeEach(async(() => {                          ❷
    TestBed.configureTestingModule({                ❸
      declarations: [
        StockItemComponent
      ],
    }).compileComponents();                          ❹
  }));

  beforeEach(() => {                                 ❺
    fixture = TestBed.createComponent(StockItemComponent);      ❻
    component = fixture.componentInstance;            ❼
    component.stock = new Stock('Testing Stock', 'TS', 100, 200);
    fixture.detectChanges();                         ❽
  });

  it('should create stock component and render stock data', () => {
    const nameEl = fixture.debugElement.query(By.css('.name'));      ❾
    expect(nameEl.nativeElement.textContent).toEqual('Testing Stock (TS)');      ❿
    const priceEl = fixture.debugElement.query(By.css('.price.negative'));
    expect(priceEl.nativeElement.textContent).toEqual('$ 100');
    const addToFavoriteBtnEl = fixture.debugElement.query(By.css('button'));
    expect(addToFavoriteBtnEl).toBeDefined();
  });

  it('should trigger event emitter on add to favorite', () => {
    let selectedStock: Stock;
    component.toggleFavorite.subscribe((stock: Stock) => selectedStock = stock);
    const addToFavoriteBtnEl = fixture.debugElement.query(By.css('button'));

    expect(selectedStock).toBeUndefined();
    addToFavoriteBtnEl.triggerEventHandler('click', null);
    expect(selectedStock).toEqual(component.stock);
  });
});
```

❶ Importing Angular testing utilities

❷ An async beforeEach, to ensure templates are loaded in the components

❸ Using the Angular testing utilities to configure a module for testing

❹ Compiling all the declared components for later use

❺ A non-async `beforeEach` executed only after the previous one finishes

❻ Creating an instance of the component fixture under test

❼ Getting the underlying component instance from the test fixture

❽ Manually triggering the Angular change detection to update templates

❾ Getting a particular HTML element from the compiled element

❿ Verifying that the element has the expected value

We have added a lot of code, and highlighted most of the important sections in the code as well. But let's walk through it step by step so that we are aware of the intricacies of using the Angular testing utilities to write tests for components:

1. `@angular/core/testing` provides a set of functionality for testing in Angular. We use the `TestBed`, which is used to create modules and components while testing, and `async`, which is to allow the Jasmine framework to understand Angular's async behavior (like loading templates for a component, which in our case is from an external template file). The `async` utility function ensures that we don't start executing the test until these async tasks are finished. Notice how we call the `async` function with a function that does all the tasks which might be asynchronous, and then pass this result to the `beforeEach`.

2. We use the `TestBed` to configure a module for our test. Rather than using an existing module, we create a new module with just our component. This gives us absolute control and can also ensure that we don't inadvertently depend on something else other than what we have defined. In this case, we declare the `StockItemComponent`, and then finally compile the component. This does the task of loading the component, loading all its related templates and styles, and then creating a compiled component for us to use later. This happens asynchronously in some cases, which is why we are wrapping it in an async block.

3. In the non-async `beforeEach`, we create a fixture, which is an instance of the component along with its template and everything related to it. Unlike the previous isolated unit test, where we unit tested just the component class, the fixture is the combination of the template, the component class instance, and Angular's magic to combine the two.

4. From the `fixture` instance, we can get a handle to the underlying component class instance by using the `componentInstance` variable on it. We can then manipulate the inputs and outputs directly from the component instance.

5. In this test, we are not working with a higher-level component, so we cannot directly test the Input and Output bindings. But we can set these values by accessing them directly from the component instance.

6. Finally, in the beforeEach, we trigger fixture.detectChanges(). This is a signal to Angular to trigger its change detection flow, which will look at the values in the component and update the bindings in the corresponding HTML. It is also the trigger to execute the ngOnInit for the component the very first time. Without this, the HTML for the component will not have any values. We trigger this after setting the stock value so that these values will be propagated to the HTML.

7. In the actual tests, we can get access to individual elements from the generated component by using the fixture.debugElement and running CSS queries against it. This allows us to check whether the template has the correct bindings and values. Thus, we can avoid writing an end-to-end test for a lot of these basic checks and simply write Angular tests for them.

8. In the second test, we can actually see that when we trigger a click event on the button element in the template, the corresponding function in the StockItemCom ponent class is triggered, and an event is emitted with the current stock value.

Similarly, we can write a test for most components and test the interaction with the templates and get a good sense for most of the basic functionality and whether it is working as intended.

Testing Component Interactions

The final thing that we'll need to check is whether the AppComponent and the Stock ItemComponent interact with each other correctly, and whether the stock value is passed from the AppComponent to the StockItemComponent as input correctly. We can also test these functionalities and more using the Angular testing utilities. Let's extend our tests for the AppComponent by adding another sub-suite as follows in the *app.com-ponent.spec.ts* file:

```
import { TestBed, async } from '@angular/core/testing';

import { AppComponent } from './app.component';
import { StockItemComponent } from 'app/stock/stock-item/stock-item.component';
import { Stock } from 'app/model/stock';
import { By } from '@angular/platform-browser';

describe('AppComponent', () => {

  describe('Simple, No Angular Unit Test', () => {
    /** Move all the previous test code into a
        child describe block
```

```
    */
  });

  describe('Angular-Aware test', () => {

    let fixture, component;

    beforeEach(async(() => {
      TestBed.configureTestingModule({
        declarations: [
          AppComponent,
          StockItemComponent,
        ],
      }).compileComponents();
    }));

    beforeEach(() => {
      fixture = TestBed.createComponent(AppComponent);
      component = fixture.componentInstance;
      fixture.detectChanges();
    });

    it('should load stock with default values', () => {
      const titleEl = fixture.debugElement.query(By.css('h1'));
      // Trim to avoid HTML whitespaces
      expect(titleEl.nativeElement.textContent.trim())
          .toEqual('Stock Market App');

      // Check for default stock values in template
      const nameEl = fixture.debugElement.query(By.css('.name'));
      expect(nameEl.nativeElement.textContent)
          .toEqual('Test Stock Company (TSC)');
      const priceEl = fixture.debugElement.query(By.css('.price.positive'));
      expect(priceEl.nativeElement.textContent).toEqual('$ 85');
      const addToFavoriteBtnEl = fixture.debugElement.query(By.css('button'));
      expect(addToFavoriteBtnEl).toBeDefined();
    });

  });

});
```

Most of this test will look very similar to the previous test we wrote for the StockItem Component, but here are a few notable differences:

- When we configure our testing module, this time we have to mention both the AppComponent, which is the component under test, as well as the StockItemCompo nent. This is because the AppComponent uses the StockItemComponent internally, and without declaring it, Angular would complain about an unknown element.

- No major changes to either of the beforeEach other than this. One thing to note (and it's worth playing around with and trying it out yourself) is that without the fixture.detectChanges() in the second beforeEach, none of the bindings would happen. You can test this by commenting it out and making sure the test fails.

- Our test follows a similar pattern like before (in fact, it is pretty much a copy/paste of the previous test for StockItemComponent). The one thing to note is we are trimming the actual text contents retrieved from the DOM to account for extra whitespaces in the HTML from how we have done our binding. This can be useful sometimes when the HTML is not an exact replica of your bound value.

Let's quickly add another test that ensures that the end-to-end flow is both ways. We will add a test that makes sure that clicking Add to Favorite updates both the model value as well as hiding the button in the template. The following code is just the test, ignoring the imports and everything else. This is a part of *app.component.spec.ts* like the previous specification:

```
it('should toggle stock favorite correctly', () => {
  expect(component.stock.favorite).toBeFalsy();
  let addToFavoriteBtnEl = fixture.debugElement.query(By.css('button'));
  expect(addToFavoriteBtnEl).toBeDefined();
  addToFavoriteBtnEl.triggerEventHandler('click', null);

  fixture.detectChanges();
  expect(component.stock.favorite).toBeTruthy();
  addToFavoriteBtnEl = fixture.debugElement.query(By.css('button'));
  expect(addToFavoriteBtnEl).toBeNull();
});
```

First, we check the base default value to ensure that the stock is not favorited by default and that the Add to Favorite button is present. Post that, we trigger the click event on the button.

At this point, Angular is supposed to kick in, emit an event from the StockItemCompo nent to the AppComponent, change the model value, trigger the change detection flow, and update the UI. But in our test, we need to tell Angular to trigger the change detection flow, and hence after we trigger the event, we manually call fix ture.detectChanges().

After this, we can write our assertions to ensure that the behavior matches our expectations.

 Forgetting to trigger fixture.detectChanges() is one of the most common mistakes when writing Angular tests. By default, it is manual and thus up to the developer to trigger it when events corresponding to user interactions or server responses happen.

Debugging

Oftentimes, there are cases when your unit test is not working as expected, or is slightly off from what you expect. In these cases, one common approach would be to add tons of `console.log` statements to try and figure out when and where things are going wrong. Figure 5-3 shows how you can see the test results in the Chrome browser captured by Karma.

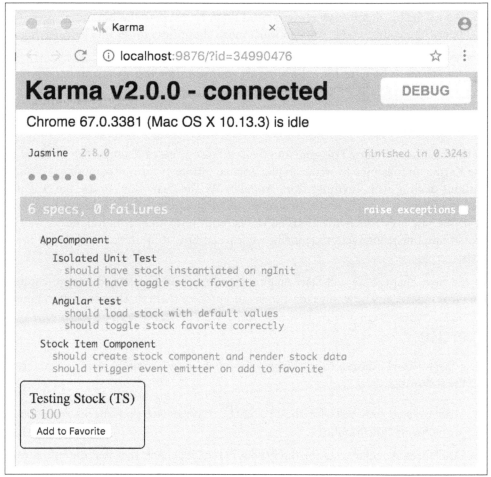

Figure 5-3. Debugging Karma tests using Chrome

Karma allows you to debug your tests and application code the same way you would debug in your normal browser. To debug your tests, simply:

1. Open up the Karma Chrome browser window that Karma spawned on startup. It is the one with the green bar at the top, as shown in Figure 5-3.

2. Click the DEBUG button on the top right of the Karma browser window. This will open up a new tab in debug mode for you to start debugging.

3. Open the Chrome developer tools (Command-Option-I on macOS, Ctrl-Shift-I on Windows) in this tab. Then open up the Sources tab of the developer tools.

4. Select the file you want to debug from the Sources tab. Use Command-P on macOS and Ctrl-P on Windows to start typing the name of the file and select it in case you can't find it.

5. Add your breakpoints where you need them by clicking the line number on the left of the source code. You can learn more about how to do this by referring to the documentation (*http://bit.ly/2s3tdy1*).

6. Run the tests by refreshing the browser; your test should stop at your breakpoint.

Conclusion

In this chapter, we started digging into the testing sections of Angular. We saw how to use Karma and Jasmine to write simple, isolated unit tests for our component classes, without dealing with anything from Angular. We then saw how to use the Angular testing utilities to be able to test the component logic along with the Angular integration. We saw how to use the `TestBed` to test both individual components as well as cross-component interactions. Finally, we learned how to both run and debug these tests.

In the next chapter, we will start digging into forms to understand how to capture data from users, and how to validate them and process them in a convenient manner.

Exercise

Take the finished exercise from the previous chapter (available in *chapter4/exercise*). Do the following:

1. Add isolated unit tests for the `ProductListComponent` that checks the `onQuantityChange` functionality.

2. Add three Angular tests for the `ProductItemComponent` that test the initial rendering, the `incrementInCart`, and the `decrementInCart`.

3. Add an integrated Angular test for the `ProductListComponent` that checks the integration between the `ProductListComponent` and its children `ProductItemComponent`.

All of this can be accomplished using concepts covered in this chapter. You can check out the finished solution in *chapter5/exercise/ecommerce*.

CHAPTER 6

Working with Template-Driven Forms

In the chapters so far, we have worked on a basic Angular application, with the scaffolding in place and working with very simple components and user interactions. We have learned how to create components and do basic data and event binding, and took a look at the capabilities and extensions that this enables.

In this chapter, we will focus purely on how to handle user input, primarily via the use of forms. Forms are the mainstay for many web applications, and are used for everything from logging in and registering to more complex use cases. Creating and using forms is not simply about the template for the form, but also the data binding (both from UI to the code, and vice versa), form state tracking, validation, and error handling. There are two primary mechanisms to work with forms in Angular, and we will explore the *template-driven* approach in this chapter, followed by how we can create *reactive forms* in the following chapter.

Template-Driven Forms

Template-driven forms in Angular are an extension of how we have been creating and working with components so far. This approach is also reminiscent of how forms worked in AngularJS (1.x and below), as it uses a similar syntax and methodology. Anyone well-versed with that would have minimal problems adapting to this. In this section, we will create a simple form that allows us to add new stocks, and build our way up from there.

Template-driven forms, as the name suggests, start with the template, and use data binding to get the data to and from your components. It is template-first, and allows you to drive the logic of your application via your template.

Setting Up Forms

Before we dig into the actual form and the template and how it would work, we need to establish some basic groundwork with Angular. At this point, we still don't know how to create multiple routes, so we will simply, for convenience, add a form on our main page itself.

We can use the same codebase from Chapter 5 as our base to build this in case you are not coding along with the book. You can get that from the *chapter5/component-spec* folder in the GitHub repository.

The very first thing we will do is extend our AppModule to import FormsModule into our main *app.module.ts* file if we have not already done so. The *src/app/app.module.ts* file should look like this:

```
import { BrowserModule } from '@angular/platform-browser';
import { NgModule } from '@angular/core';
import { FormsModule } from '@angular/forms';

import { AppComponent } from './app.component';
import { StockItemComponent } from './stock/stock-item/stock-item.component';

@NgModule({
  declarations: [
    AppComponent,
    StockItemComponent
  ],
  imports: [
    BrowserModule,
    FormsModule                    ❶
  ],
  providers: [],
  bootstrap: [AppComponent]
})
export class AppModule { }
```

❶ The FormsModule in the imports section of your AppModule

What this does is ensure that all the template-driven form features that are built into Angular are made available to your application. The reason form-specific logic and functionality is in a separate module is for performance and size, so that developers can decide whether or not they need form-specific features in their application.

The FormsModule adds the capability of using ngModel, which allows for two-way data binding in Angular. But before we use it, let's explore what other ways we can accomplish this, so that we understand what ngModel does for us.

Alternative to ngModel—Event and Property Binding

At its core, what `ngModel` does for us is two-way data binding. That is, whenever a user enters any text in the UI, it binds that data back to the component. And whenever the value in our component changes (say as a response to a server call, or the initialization logic), then it updates that value in the UI.

If we break it down, the first one (the user entering a value in the UI) can be handled through event binding. We can listen for the `input` event, grab the value from the event property target, and update the value in the component class.

The second one similarly can be simply handled through data binding, in which we can bind the HTML element property value to the variable in our component.

Let's first create a new component, called `CreateStockComponent`. We can use the Angular CLI to create it by running:

```
ng g component stock/create-stock
```

This will create the skeleton component along with its test. Now, let's modify the *app/ stock/create-stock/create-stock.component.ts* file as follows:

```
import { Component, OnInit } from '@angular/core';
import { Stock } from 'app/model/stock';

@Component({
  selector: 'app-create-stock',
  templateUrl: './create-stock.component.html',
  styleUrls: ['./create-stock.component.css']
})
export class CreateStockComponent {

  public stock: Stock;
  constructor() {
    this.stock =  new Stock('test', '', 0, 0);
  }
}
```

We are using the generated template of the Angular CLI, but we have made two small changes. We added a `stock` member variable with visibility `public`, and then initialized it with some dummy values in the constructor. We have also cleaned up and removed the `ngOnInit` because it was unnecessary.

Next, let's take a look at the template for the `CreateStockComponent`, which is where all the magic is. We will edit the file *app/stock/create-stock/create-stock.component .html* as follows:

```
<h2>Create Stock Form</h2>

<div class="form-group">
  <form>
    <div class="stock-name">
      <input type="text"
             placeholder="Stock Name"
             [value]="stock.name"
             (input)="stock.name=$event.target.value">
    </div>
  </form>
  <button (click)="stock.name='test'">Reset stock name</button>
</div>

<h4>Stock Name is {{stock.name}}</h4>
```

We have added a header, followed by a simple form with one `input` element of type `text`. Finally, we have another header that is using interpolation to show the current value of `name` from the `stock` variable in the component class. Now let's take a look at the `input` element in more detail. Other than the `type` and `placeholder`, we have two bindings that we need to talk about:

- The `value` binding is telling Angular to update the value property of the `input` element using the `stock.name` field in the component class. If and when it changes, Angular will be responsible for updating the property as well.

- The `input` event binding is instructing Angular to update the `value` of `stock.name` with the value from the event. The `$event` in this case is the underlying DOM `InputEvent`, through which we access the target and from it, the changed value.

Finally, we have a button that on `click` resets the value of `stock.name` to `'test'`.

When you run this, you should see something like Figure 6-1 on your screen.

To really understand how this works, I would recommend removing one binding and keeping just the other, and then reversing it.

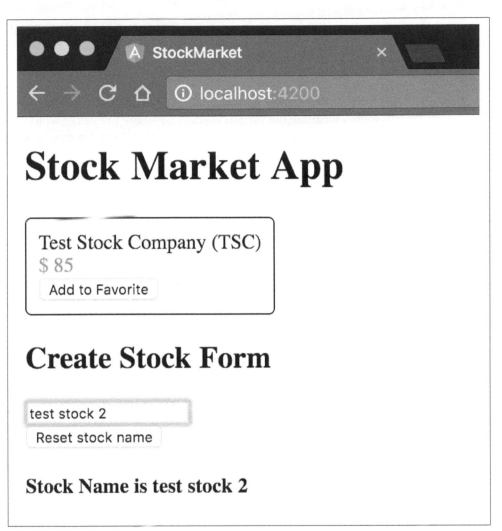

Figure 6-1. Angular template-driven form in action

When you remove just the `value` binding and run the application (`ng serve`, in case you forgot!), you will see that when you type into the text box, the value in the UI gets updated as you type. But when you click the Reset button, then while the header gets updated, the value in the text box does not. Thus, the component gets updated when the event happens, but because we don't have the Component → UI binding, the UI doesn't update if the component gets updated under the covers.

Similarly, we can turn off the `input` event binding. In this case, regardless of what we type in the text box, the underlying model does not get updated.

The combination of the two bindings is what gives us the look and feel of a two-way data binding.

ngModel

Of course, who among us remembers exactly which property is used by each form field? Who can remember what are the various events and where the values would be available? To simplify and abstract this particular information away for ease of use, Angular has the ngModel directive.

The ngModel directive and its special syntax abstracts away the internals of each and every input type from us developers, making it easier for us to quickly develop form-based applications. Let's see how the code gets modified when we use ngModel instead of the input and value binding.

We will only modify the *src/app/stock/create-stock/create-stock.component.html* file as follows; the rest of the code remains the same:

```html
<h2>Create Stock Form</h2>

<div class="form-group">
  <form>
    <div class="stock-name">
      <input type="text"
             placeholder="Stock Name"
             name="stockName"
             [ngModel]="stock.name"
             (ngModelChange)="stock.name=$event">
    </div>
  </form>
  <button (click)="stock.name='test'">Reset stock name</button>
</div>

<h4>Stock Name is {{stock.name}}</h4>
```

Most of the HTML remains the same except for the following changes:

- First, we added a name field to the input form element. This is necessary for the ngModel directive to work. If you remove this, you will see errors in the console.

- We added two bindings. The first one is ngModel data binding. This does the work of the value binding we had previously, but abstracting out which property underneath needs to be bound. It points to the component member variable that it takes the value from.

- The second binding we added is the ngModelChange event binding. In this, we update the underlying component member variable (stock.name) with the value of the $event, which is the changed value of the text field.

There is a simpler version of this, which is what we use in most normal cases, which is the [(ngModel)] banana-in-a-box syntax, as it is called. This encapsulates both of these statements into a single expression, like so:

```
<h2>Create Stock Form</h2>

<div class="form-group">
  <form>
    <div class="stock-name">
      <input type="text"
             placeholder="Stock Name"
             name="stockName"
             [(ngModel)]="stock.name">
    </div>
  </form>
  <button (click)="stock.name='test'">Reset stock name</button>
</div>

<h4>Stock Name is {{stock.name}}</h4>
```

Why Is It Called Banana-in-a-Box?

When used together, a common confusion while using the ngModel directive could be the order of the types of parentheses, whether it is [()] or ([]). This is why the Angular team came up with a nickname to make it easy to remember. The () looks like a banana (yes, it's a stretch, but roll with it!), and it is enclosed in a box []. Hence, the banana-in-a-box, which is [()].

In this, we replaced the two individual ngModel and ngModelChange bindings with the single banana-in-the-box [(ngModel)]. The end result will still be the same, as you should see the text value change as you type, as well as the value in the text box get reset when you press the Reset button.

When to Use the Expanded ngModel Variant

Given that we accomplished the same thing via both the expanded and the collapsed version of the ngModel syntax, is there a need for the expanded version at all?

The combined ngModel syntax only has the capability to set the data-bound property. If you need to do something more complicated (say convert the text into upper-case before setting the model variable), or set it in a different field itself (a calculated value maybe?), or do multiple things, then you might want to consider the expanded syntax. For all other needs, the banana-in-the-box combined syntax works great!

A Complete Form

Now that we have seen a basic form field, let's extend this to a complete form that has different types of controls that are bound to our component along with handling submission of the form. We will continue building on the previous example, the code for which can be found in the *chapter6/simple-ng-model* folder in case you don't have the codebase.

Let's extend our example now to allow users to enter in the other information about a stock, including its code, price, and the exchange it is listed on. In addition, we will have a confirmation checkbox that needs to be checked before the form can be submitted. Finally, we will see how to handle the actual submission event.

First, we'll add an additional field to our stock model (*src/app/model/stock.ts*), which we haven't changed since the initial version, as follows:

```
export class Stock {
  favorite = false;

  constructor(public name: string,
              public code: string,
              public price: number,
              public previousPrice: number,
              public exchange: string) {}

  isPositiveChange(): boolean {
    return this.price >= this.previousPrice;
  }
}
```

Next, let's extend *app/model/create-stock/create-stock.component.ts*:

```
import { Component, OnInit } from '@angular/core';
import { Stock } from 'app/model/stock';

@Component({
  selector: 'app-create-stock',
  templateUrl: './create-stock.component.html',
  styleUrls: ['./create-stock.component.css']
})
export class CreateStockComponent {

  public stock: Stock;
  public confirmed = false;
  constructor() {
    this.stock =  new Stock('test', '', 0, 0, 'NASDAQ');
  }

  setStockPrice(price) {
    this.stock.price = price;
    this.stock.previousPrice = price;
  }
```

```
createStock() {
  console.log('Creating stock ', this.stock);
  }
}
```

We have added a few new pieces here, in particular:

- We added to the stock initialization (an argument `'NASDAQ'` in this case).
- We added `confirmed`, a `boolean` member variable, to the component class, with a default value of `false`.
- We created a new function `setStockPrice`, which takes a price and then sets both the current and previous price for the `stock`.
- Finally, we have a new `createStock` method, which simply logs out the current stock variable to the console.

Now let's see how these are used as we create and hook up the finished template for the form. We will change *src/app/stock/create-stock/create-stock.component.html* as follows :

```
<h2>Create Stock Form</h2>

<div class="form-group">
  <form (ngSubmit)="createStock()">                           ❶
    <div class="stock-name">
      <input type="text" placeholder="Stock Name"
             name="stockName" [(ngModel)]="stock.name">
    </div>
    <div class="stock-code">
      <input type="text" placeholder="Stock Code"
             name="stockCode" [(ngModel)]="stock.code">
    </div>
    <div class="stock-code">
      <input type="number" placeholder="Stock Price"
             name="stockPrice" [ngModel]="stock.price"    ❷
             (ngModelChange)="setStockPrice($event)">
    </div>
    <div class="stock-exchange">
      <div>
        <input type="radio" name="stockExchange"    ❸
               [(ngModel)]="stock.exchange" value="NYSE">NYSE
      </div>
      <div>
        <input type="radio" name="stockExchange"
               [(ngModel)]="stock.exchange" value="NASDAQ">NASDAQ
      </div>
      <div>
        <input type="radio" name="stockExchange"
               [(ngModel)]="stock.exchange" value="OTHER">OTHER
```

```
      </div>
    </div>
    <div class="stock-confirm">
      <input type="checkbox" name="stockConfirm"      ❹
            [(ngModel)]="confirmed">
      I confirm that the information provided above is accurate!
    </div>
    <button [disabled]="!confirmed" type="submit">Create</button> ❺
  </form>
</div>

<h4>Stock Name is {{stock | json}}</h4>
```

❶ Handling the form submission via the ngSubmit event handler

❷ Expanded version of ngModel to handle setting both current and previous price

❸ Handling radio buttons through ngModel

❹ Handling checkboxes through ngModel

❺ Disabling the form while the checkbox is unchecked

In the template, we have added a whole new set of form fields, from input boxes for stock code and price, to radio buttons to select the exchange and a checkbox to confirm if the data is correct. Let's go through this step by step:

1. For the stock code, it remains similar to the stock name which we had. Nothing different other than, of course, the target variable.

2. For the stock price, we are using the expanded version of the ngModel syntax. This is because while we want the value in the text box to come from stock.price, when the user sets it, we want both the price and the previous Price to be set through the method setStockPrice.

3. Next, we have a set of radio buttons that we are using to set the exchange. Each radio button has the same name (which is the standard HTML way of creating a radio group), and are bound to the same model variable (stock.exchange) using ngModel. The value for each radio button is what defines what the value in the stock.exchange variable is, and similarly, the value in the stock.exchange variable defines which of the radio buttons are selected.

4. We then have a checkbox, which is bound to the variable confirmed on the component class. Since it is a checkbox, toggling the checkbox on and off sets the value of the variable confirmed to true and false, respectively.

5. Finally, we have a button of type submit. This is only enabled when the con firmed boolean is set to true. On clicking this, it triggers a form submit, which is

then intercepted by our `ngSubmit` event handler at the form level. This will then trigger the `createStock` method on our component class.

Once you run this, you should see something like Figure 6-2 on your screen.

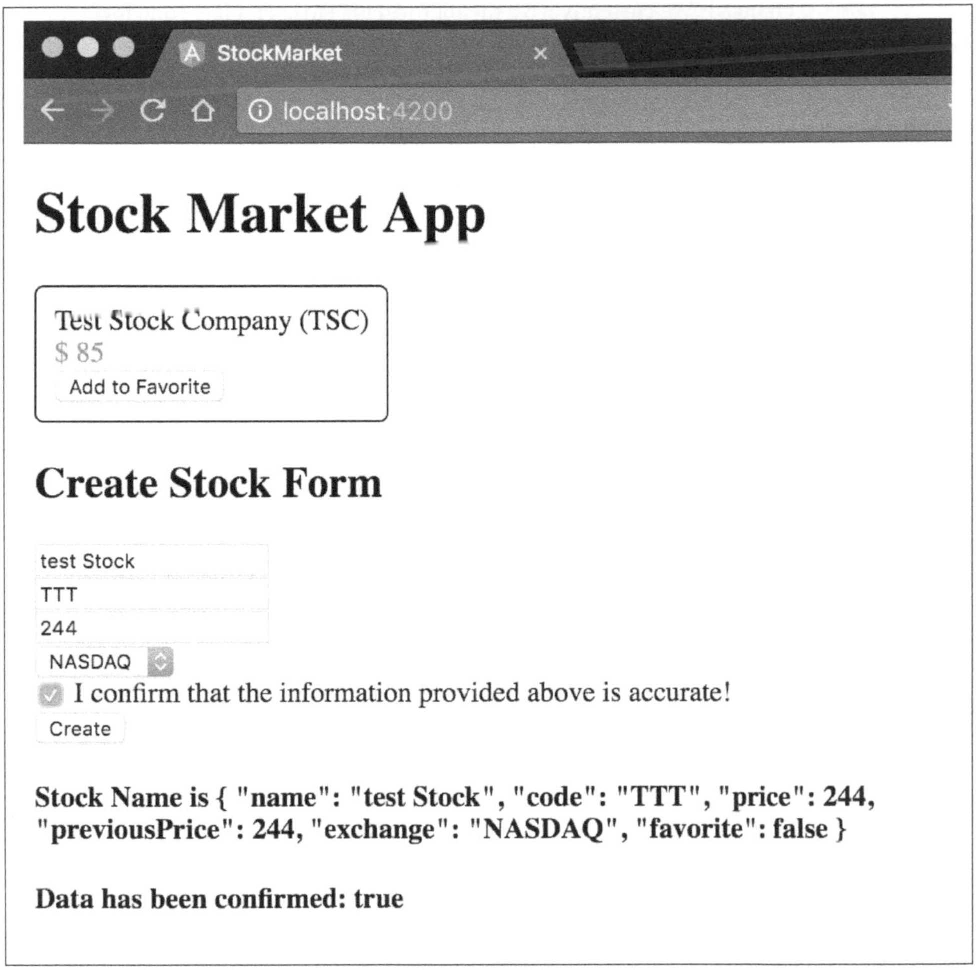

Figure 6-2. Angular form with data binding

We thus have a very simple form that handles different kinds of form elements and binds the value to the component, allowing us to get to the user input once he submits the form. To be fair, we haven't handled any errors or requirements on the form, which we will do shortly in the next section.

What about SELECT Boxes?

One type of input we didn't cover in the preceding example was a select drop-down/combo box. But we could have used it instead of the radio buttons, if we felt like it. How would our example have changed? We currently have the following HTML template code for displaying our radio buttons:

```
<input type="radio" name="stockExchange"
       [(ngModel)]="stock.exchange" value="NYSE">NYSE
<input type="radio" name="stockExchange"
       [(ngModel)]="stock.exchange" value="NASDAQ">NASDAQ
<input type="radio" name="stockExchange"
       [(ngModel)]="stock.exchange" value="OTHER">OTHER
```

We can replace this with a simple select HTML template as follows:

```
<select name="stockExchange" [(ngModel)]="stock.exchange">
  <option value="NYSE">NYSE</option>
  <option value="NASDAQ">NASDAQ</option>
  <option value="OTHER">OTHER</option>
</select>
```

Again, very similar to the other form elements, as long as we have a name and the ngModel directive, Angular internally handles the data binding for us. We could very easily replace the individual option tags with a single option tag and use ngFor to programmatically generate a list of options as well. In those cases, assuming our component has the following code in it:

```
public exchanges = ['NYSE', 'NASDAQ', 'OTHER'];
```

Then we could replace our template code to be as simple as:

```
<select name="stockExchange" [(ngModel)]="stock.exchange">
  <option *ngFor="let exchange of exchanges"
          [ngValue]="exchange">{{exchange}}</option>
</select>
```

Note the *ngFor loop, and the usage of ngValue to ensure that the current value is used instead of a hardcoded value.

Control State

Angular form validation for template-driven forms relies and extends the native form validation from HTML (*https://developer.mozilla.org/en-US/docs/Web/Guide/HTML/ HTML5/Constraint_validation*). Thus, you can simply use most of the constraints that you already know and love out of the box, and they should work directly and cleanly with an Angular form. That said, Angular does the work of integrating these control states and validations with its own internal model (whether it is ngModel or ngForm), and it is up to us to use this internal model to then show the right kind of message to the user.

There are two aspects to this:

- The state, which allows us to peek into the state of the form control, on whether the user has visited it, whether the user has changed it, and finally whether it is in a valid state.
- The validity, which tells us whether a form control is valid or not, and if it is not valid, the underlying reason (or reasons) for which the form element is invalid.

Let's first see how state is made available to us and how we can use it. The ngModel directive changes and adds CSS classes to the element it is on, based on the user's interaction with it. There are three primary modes of interaction that it tracks, and two CSS classes per mode of interation associated with it. They are:

Control state	CSS class if True	CSS class if False
Visited	ng-touched	ng-untouched
Changed	ng-dirty	ng-pristine
Valid	ng-valid	ng-invalid

In particular, these states allow you to present different experiences or views to users under various scenarios. We can use the code from the previous section as a base to work off, in case you are not coding along. The starting code can be found in *chapter6/template-driven/full-form*, which holds the completed code from the previous section.

Now, to use these control state classes, we actually don't need to make any component class code changes. We only need to tweak the CSS a bit and then leverage that in the HTML template for the component.

Let's first add the following CSS class definitions to the *src/app/stock/create-stock/create-stock.component.css* file:

```
.stock-name .ng-valid,
.stock-code .ng-pristine,
.stock-price .ng-untouched {
  background-color: green;
}

.stock-name .ng-invalid,
.stock-code .ng-dirty,
.stock-price .ng-touched {
  background-color: pink;
}
```

Now, we will make minor tweaks (which are more for highlighting different elements rather than any functional changes) to the template HTML in *src/app/stock/create-stock/create-stock.component.html*:

```
<h2>Create Stock Form</h2>

<div class="form-group">
  <form (ngSubmit)="createStock()">
    <div>
      The following element changes from green to red
      when it is invalid
    </div>
    <div class="stock-name">
      <input type="text"
             placeholder="Stock Name"
             required                                      ❶
             name="stockName"
             [(ngModel)]="stock.name">
    </div>
    <div>
      The following element changes from green to red
      when it has been modified
    </div>
    <div class="stock-code">
      <input type="text"
             placeholder="Stock Code"
             name="stockCode"
             [(ngModel)]="stock.code">
    </div>
    <div>
        The following element changes from green to red
        when it is visited by the user, regardless of change
      </div>
    <div class="stock-price">
      <input type="number"
             placeholder="Stock Price"
             name="stockPrice"
             [ngModel]="stock.price"
             (ngModelChange)="setStockPrice($event)">
    </div>
    <div class="stock-exchange">
      <div>
        <select name="stockExchange" [(ngModel)]="stock.exchange">
          <option *ngFor="let exchange of exchanges"
                  [ngValue]="exchange">{{exchange}}</option>
        </select>
      </div>
    </div>
    <div class="stock-confirm">
      <input type="checkbox"
             name="stockConfirm"
             [(ngModel)]="confirmed">
      I confirm that the information provided above is accurate!
    </div>
    <button [disabled]="!confirmed"
            type="submit">Create</button>
```

```
    </form>
  </div>

<h4>Stock Name is {{stock | json}}</h4>
<h4>Data has been confirmed: {{confirmed}}</h4>
```

❶ Adding a required attribute to the stock name

The only change we did to our component HTML is to make the stock name a required field. Angular's Form Module is responsible for reading it and applying the form control state classes accordingly, without any other work on our side.

With these two changes, we now have an application that:

- For the stock name, when it is valid (the class ng-valid), we make the background color of the text box green, and when it is invalid (the class ng-invalid), we change the background color of the text box to be pink.

- For the stock code, when the user has not made any changes to the field (the class ng-pristine), we make the background color of the text box green, and whenever the user makes any change (the class ng-dirty), regardless of whether he reverts the change or not, we change the background color of the text box to pink.

- Finally, for the stock price, the background color remains green as long as the field is not interacted with (the class ng-untouched), and changes to pink as soon as the user interacts and then leaves it (the class ng-touched). Note that the color remains green while the user is interacting/typing on it, and only changes once he moves away from it.

You can test it, of course, by:

1. Removing the default name of the stock (the background color should toggle from green to pink when there is no text in the field)

2. Typing any character in the stock code field (the background color should toggle from green to pink when you do)

3. Focusing and navigating away from the stock price field (the background color should toggle from green to pink when you do)

The end result if you do these actions in order is a screen that looks something like the image in Figure 6-3.

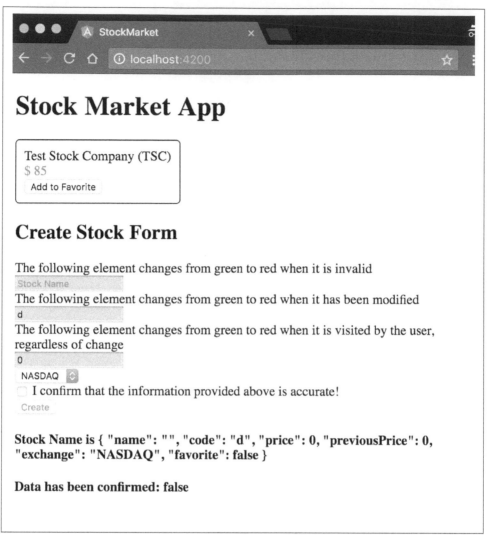

Figure 6-3. Angular form with control state bindings

Control Validity

Next, let's take a look at how we can leverage the HTML form validation to create nice, meaningful errors for our users. We won't get into custom validations just yet in this chapter, but will cover how to use multiple validations on the same elements, and how to display error messages for the same.

Internally, Angular has its own set of validators. These mirror the HTML Form validators that are then used to drive a similar behavior in the context of an Angular application. Once you add any validators to your form elements, Angular will take care of running them every time any of the form control changes. This would then be reflected at each control level, as well as at an aggregate level at the form.

Before we dig into this, you can take a look at the following sidebar to get a brief understanding of template reference variables, which are a major workhorse in how we execute and work with form control validity.

Template Reference Variables

A template reference variable in Angular allows us to get a temporary handle on a DOM element, component, or directive directly in the template. It is denoted by a standard syntax in the HTML, which is a prefix of #. For example, in the following HTML:

```
<input type="text" #myStockField name="stockName">
```

The #myStockField is a template reference variable that gives us a reference to the input form field. We can then use this as a variable in any Angular expression, or directly access its value through myStockField.value and pass it as an argument to a function.

In addition to the DOM elements, it can also be used to reference the class/value underlying a directive, which is how we use it in conjunction with forms and form fields.

By default, when we don't pass it any value, it will always refer to the HTML DOM element.

Once you have looked through the sidebar note, we'll dig into how we can accomplish simple error handling via our template-driven forms. In case you are not coding along, you can use the codebase from the previous section (which is located in *chapter6/template-driven/control-state*) as a base.

We will undo some of the changes from the previous section and now focus purely on form validation. First, let's change our CSS to reflect all invalid form controls with a pink background, by editing the *src/app/stock/create-stock/create-stock.component.css* file as follows:

```
.stock-name .ng-valid,
.stock-code .ng-valid,
.stock-price .ng-valid {
  background-color: green;
}

.stock-name .ng-invalid,
.stock-code .ng-invalid,
.stock-price .ng-invalid {
```

```
    background-color: pink;
  }
```

Next, we will make minor changes to the component class (*src/app/stock/create-stock/create-stock.component.ts*), simply to log out different values under certain conditions as follows:

```
import { Component, OnInit } from '@angular/core';
import { Stock } from 'app/model/stock';

@Component({
  selector: 'app-create-stock',
  templateUrl: './create-stock.component.html',
  styleUrls: ['./create-stock.component.css']
})
export class CreateStockComponent {

  public stock: Stock;
  public confirmed = false;
  public exchanges = ['NYSE', 'NASDAQ', 'OTHER'];
  constructor() {
    this.stock =  new Stock('', '', 0, 0, 'NASDAQ');
  }

  setStockPrice(price) {
    this.stock.price = price;
    this.stock.previousPrice = price;
  }

  createStock(stockForm) {
    console.log('Stock form', stockForm);
    if (stockForm.valid) {
      console.log('Creating stock ', this.stock);
    } else {
      console.error('Stock form is in an invalid state');
    }
  }
}
```

We have made minor changes only to the `createStock` method:

- We have now started taking the `stockForm` as an argument to the function. This is the `ngForm` object representing the form we have in our template, including all its controls and states. We are also logging this out to the web console.

- We are checking if the form is valid using this passed-in object, and then only proceeding to create the stock (for what it's worth, logging it out at this point).

- We have also changed the constructor to initialize the stock with an empty name, unlike before.

Next, let's see the changes made to the template in *src/app/stock/create-stock/create-stock.component.html*:

```
<h2>Create Stock Form</h2>

<div class="form-group">
  <form (ngSubmit)="createStock(stockForm)" #stockForm="ngForm">       ❶
    <div class="stock-name">
      <input type="text"
             placeholder="Stock Name"
             required
             name="stockName"
             #stockName="ngModel"                                       ❷
             [(ngModel)]="stock.name">
    </div>
    <div *ngIf="stockName.errors && stockName.errors.required">        ❸
        Stock Name is Mandatory
    </div>
    <div class="stock-code">
      <input type="text"
             placeholder="Stock Code"
             required
             minlength="2"
             name="stockCode"
             #stockCode="ngModel"                                       ❹
             [(ngModel)]="stock.code">
    </div>
    <div *ngIf="stockCode.dirty && stockCode.invalid">                 ❺
      <div *ngIf="stockCode.errors.required">                          ❻
        Stock Code is Mandatory
      </div>
      <div *ngIf="stockCode.errors.minlength">
        Stock Code must be atleast of length 2
      </div>
    </div>
    <div class="stock-price">
      <input type="number"
             placeholder="Stock Price"
             name="stockPrice"
             required
             #stockPrice="ngModel"                                      ❼
             [ngModel]="stock.price"
             (ngModelChange)="setStockPrice($event)">
    </div>
    <div *ngIf="stockPrice.dirty && stockPrice.invalid">
      <div *ngIf="stockPrice.errors.required">
        Stock Price is Mandatory
      </div>
    </div>
    <div class="stock-exchange">
      <div>
        <select name="stockExchange" [(ngModel)]="stock.exchange">
```

```
              <option *ngFor="let exchange of exchanges"
                      [ngValue]="exchange">{{exchange}}</option>
          </select>
        </div>
      </div>
      <div class="stock-confirm">
        <input type="checkbox"
               name="stockConfirm"
               required
               [(ngModel)]="confirmed">
        I confirm that the information provided above is accurate!
      </div>
      <button type="submit">Create</button>
    </form>
  </div>

  <h4>Stock Name is {{stock | json}}</h4>
  <h4>Data has been confirmed: {{confirmed}}</h4>
```

❶ Template reference variable stockForm to work at the form model level

❷ Template reference variable stockName to expose the name ngModel

❸ Check on the template reference variable for errors and presence

❹ Template reference variable stockCode to expose the code ngModel

❺ Check on the stockCode template reference variable for dirty and invalid form controls

❻ Check on the stockCode for errors

❼ Template reference variable stockPrice to expose the code ngModel

Most of the template remains the same, but there are a few items worth calling out:

- We added a template reference variable at the form level, and at each control level. The form-level template reference variable (stockForm) gets the NgForm model object bound to it, which allows us to check on things like form and control validity and values through it.

- We added template reference variables (stockName, stockPrice, stockCode) on each of the text boxes, and assigned the NgModel model object to it. This allows us to check the form field for all the control states that we were previously using through CSS classes (dirty/pristine, valid/invalid, and touched/untouched), in addition to errors.

- For the first form field (stock name), we added a div to show the error message that it is required, if the error exists.
- For the second and third field messages, we enclosed the error message within another div, which first checks if the form field is dirty and invalid before looking for a particular error message.
- On form submit we pass the `stockForm` template reference variable, which points to the form model, to the `createStock` method. This is another capability of template reference variables: you can pass them in as arguments to your component class.

This completed code is available in the *chapter6/template-driven/control-validity* folder. When you run this application, you should see something like Figure 6-4.

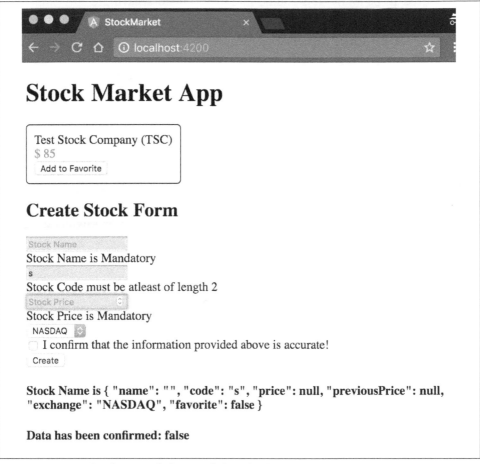

Figure 6-4. Angular form with form validity checks

A few interesting things worth noting:

- Notice that the error message for the stock name is displayed by default, but the error message that the price and code are required is only displayed after we touch the field. This is the advantage of wrapping the error message under the control state (dirty and invalid). Otherwise, the field is invalid by default (because it is empty).

- Most of the default validators (`required`, `minlength`, `maxlength`) will add a corresponding entry on the errors field on the template reference variable, which you can use to display a relevant message.

- Note that for the stock price, the `minlength` and `required` validators are not shown simultaneously. This is handled by the Angular built-in validators, but you need to be aware and handle multiple validators having errors simultaneously, and decide and show messages conditionally.

- Finally, we pass the `stockForm` template reference variable to the `createStock` method in the component class. This actually gives us access to the individual controls, as well as the value of the form model. We can use this (or similar template reference variables) to, for example, start showing error messages only after the first submit, instead of, say, as soon as the user types.

Thus, between the template reference variables and the validators, you get utmost control in how and when you want to show your validation messages. You can choose to do it completely in the template, or choose to have them in the template, but decide when and how to show them from your component class, or go to the extreme of creating your validation messages and drive it completely from your component class. It would be up to you which of the approaches you choose, as Angular gives you the tools and the complete flexibility to choose.

Working with FormGroups

Before we finish with this chapter, we will quickly introduce another method of working with template-driven forms and the `ngModel` directive. So far, we have been declaring a member variable in our component, and then using `ngModel` to bind to it. We can instead let the form model drive the entire form, and copy over or use the values from it once the form has been submitted.

We can use the same codebase from the previous section (*chapter6/template-driven/control-validity*) as the base to work off of.

Let's first modify the `CreateStockComponent` class with minor changes to take the model value from the form instead of relying on it being updated via data binding:

```
import { Component, OnInit } from '@angular/core';
import { Stock } from 'app/model/stock';

@Component({
  selector: 'app-create-stock',
  templateUrl: './create-stock.component.html',
  styleUrls: ['./create-stock.component.css']
})
export class CreateStockComponent {

  public stock: Stock;
  public confirmed = false;
  public exchanges = ['NYSE', 'NASDAQ', 'OTHER'];
  constructor() {
    this.stock =  new Stock('', '', 0, 0, 'NASDAQ');
  }

  createStock(stockForm) {
    console.log('Stock form', stockForm.value);
    if (stockForm.valid) {
      this.stock = stockForm.value.stock;
      console.log('Creating stock ', this.stock);
    } else {
      console.error('Stock form is in an invalid state');
    }
  }
}
```

We have changed the createStock method, to copy over the stock object from the form value field. We have also dropped the setStockPrice method as we won't be using it. Now, let's take a look at the changes needed in the template to be able to support this:

```
<h2>Create Stock Form</h2>

<div class="form-group">
  <form (ngSubmit)="createStock(stockForm)" #stockForm="ngForm" >
    <div ngModelGroup="stock">
      <div class="stock-name">
        <input type="text"
               placeholder="Stock Name"
               required
               name="name"
               ngModel>
      </div>
      <div class="stock-code">
        <input type="text"
               placeholder="Stock Code"
               required
               minlength="2"
               name="code"
               ngModel>
```

```
      </div>
      <div class="stock-price">
        <input type="number"
               placeholder="Stock Price"
               name="price"
               required
               ngModel>
      </div>
      <div class="stock-exchange">
        <div>
          <select name="exchange" ngModel>
            <option *ngFor="let exchange of exchanges"
                    [ngValue]="exchange">{{exchange}}</option>
          </select>
        </div>
      </div>
    </div>
    <button type="submit">Create</button>
  </form>
</div>

<h4>Stock Name is {{stock | json}}</h4>
<h4>Data has been confirmed: {{confirmed}}</h4>
```

We have temporarily removed all validators, so as to not distract us from the core change. The major changes are as follows:

- We have removed the banana-in-a-box syntax from all the ngModel bindings, and just kept it as an attribute. When we use ngModel like this, Angular uses the name field on the form element as the model name and creates a model object corresponding to it on the form.

- We have surrounded the form fields with another div, and used an Angular directive called ngModelGroup on it, providing it a name (stock in this case). What this does is group the form elements, thus creating the name, price, code, and exchange fields as models under the common name stock. This is visible in the component when we access this entire set of values through form.value.stock.

We can similarly create multiple form groups and use ngModel directly, and then finally copy over the entire values to a common field (or not copy it over at all) in our component on form submit. This is another way we can use ngModel and template-driven forms in our applications. The finished code for this is available in the *chapter6/template-driven/form-groups/* folder in the GitHub repository.

Conclusion

In this chapter, we started exploring how to handle user input through the use of forms. In particular, we took a deep dive into how to create and work with template-driven forms, and leverage ngModel for two-way data binding. We further saw what control states Angular provides out of the box and how to leverage that as well as show and deal with validations and error messages.

In the next chapter, we will look at a different way of approaching this: reactive forms. We will discuss how to use reactive forms but will first review the ways they differ from template-driven forms and why you might choose one over the other.

Exercise

Take the finished exercise from the previous chapter (available in *chapter5/exercise/ecommerce*). Do the following:

1. Create a new component that allows us to add new products.

2. Create a form that takes in the product name, price, image URL, and whether or not it is on sale. Try to use the form groups approach rather than two-way binding through ngModel.

3. Make all the fields required, and see if you can add a basic Regex pattern validation for the image URL.

4. Display relevant error messages, but only after the user either edits the field or after the first submit.

5. Copy over the form and print it to the console after successful submission.

All of this can be accomplished using concepts covered in this chapter. You can check out the finished solution in *chapter6/exercise/ecommerce*.

CHAPTER 7

Working with Reactive Forms

In the previous chapter, we started working on our first form-based Angular application. To do this, we explored template-driven forms and how we might build and use them within the context of an Angular application. We saw how to perform data binding, work with different form elements, and also perform validity and show relevant error messages.

In this chapter, we will focus on doing the exact same set of things, though this time, we will use a reactive approach. As mentioned in the previous chapter, Angular allows us to build forms using two approaches: template-driven and reactive. Both these approaches are part of the core `@angular/forms` library, but are part of two different modules, `FormsModule` and `ReactiveFormsModule`, respectively.

Reactive Forms

To understand and get into building forms in a reactive manner, it is important to understand what reactive programming is. Reactive programming, to overly simplify it, is the concept of writing a program in a way that it fundamentally deals with and acts on asynchronous data streams. While most programs (especially web apps) do this, reactive programming does this by providing an amazing toolbox of utilities and functions to combine, filter, and merge these various streams and act on them, which is where it gets real fun real fast.

Unlike template-driven forms in Angular, with reactive forms, you define the entire tree of Angular form control objects in your component code, and then bind them to native form control elements in your template. Because the component has access to the form controls as well as the backing data model, it can push data model changes into the form control and vice versa, thus reacting to changes either way.

Understanding the Differences

Now, with two approaches in front of us (even though we haven't looked at a single line of code of the reactive form approach), the question naturally arises: which one is better? The answer, as you would expect, is that neither is truly "better" than the other. Both have their own advantages and disadvantages.

When we create forms using the template-driven approach, we declare the form controls in the template, and add directives to it (like ngModel). Then Angular is responsible for creating the form controls through the use of directives.

That said, template-driven forms are nice and declarative, and easy to understand. Angular is responsible for the data model sync and pushes data to the model and reads and updates values in the UI via directives like ngModel. This also usually means less code in the component class.

Reactive forms, on the other hand, are synchronous, and you as a developer have absolute control over how and when the data is synced from the UI to the model and vice versa. Because you create the entire form control tree in the component, you have access to it immediately and don't have to deal with Angular's asynchronous lifecycle. While we haven't encountered this ourselves in any of the examples so far, you will run into this if you try to update the form controls from your component class on initialization, as they might not be immediately available. You can read up on this in the official Angular docs (*http://bit.ly/2ki0EcR*). It also fits in better if the rest of your application is following a reactive style of programming.

Using Reactive Forms

Now that we have briefly compared reactive versus template-driven forms and reviewed the pros and cons of each, let's look at building a reactive form. We will do this step by step, starting with the building block of reactive forms, Form Controls, and work our way upwards to the other various components like Form Groups and Form Builders.

Form Controls

The core of any reactive form is the FormControl, which directly represents an individual form element in the template. Thus, any reactive form is nothing but a set of grouped FormControls. It is at the FormControl level that we also assign initial values and validators (both sync and async). Thus, everything that we did in the template with template-driven forms now happens at a FormControl level in the TypeScript code.

We can use the same codebase from Chapter 6 as our base to build this in case you are not coding along with the book. You can get that from the *chapter6/template-driven/simple-ng-model* folder in the GitHub repository.

The very first thing we will do is import ReactiveFormsModule into our main *app.module.ts* file. For this example, we can remove the old FormsModule from it. The *src/app/app.module.ts* file should look like this:

```
import { BrowserModule } from '@angular/platform-browser';
import { NgModule } from '@angular/core';
import { ReactiveFormsModule } from '@angular/forms';          ❶

import { AppComponent } from './app.component';
import { StockItemComponent } from './stock/stock-item/stock-item.component';
import { CreateStockComponent }
    from './stock/create-stock/create-stock.component';

@NgModule({
  declarations: [
    AppComponent,
    StockItemComponent,
    CreateStockComponent
  ],
  imports: [
    BrowserModule,
    ReactiveFormsModule,          ❷
  ],
  providers: [],
  bootstrap: [AppComponent]
})
export class AppModule { }
```

❶   Import the ReactiveFormsModule

❷   Add the ReactiveFormsModule to the NgModule imports section

Now given this base setup, which enables reactive form features in our application, let's see how to create a simple form that allows us to take and work with a name. We will first modify the template for our CreateStockComponent by changing the *src/app/stock/create-stock/create-stock.component.html* file as follows:

```
<h2>Create Stock Form</h2>

<div class="form-group">

    <div class="stock-name">
      <input type="text"
             placeholder="Stock Name"
             name="stockName"
             [formControl]="nameControl">          ❶
    </div>
```

```
    <button (click)="onSubmit()">Submit</button>
</div>

<p>Form Control value: {{ nameControl.value | json }}</p>    ❷
<p>Form Control status: {{ nameControl.status | json }}</p>
```

❶   Using a form control binding instead of ngModel

❷   Accessing the current value in the form field

The way we created this form is very different than the template-driven approach outlined in the previous chapter. Instead of using ngModel, we are binding the form element to nameControl. We can then derive the current value of the form control via this field, whether it is the value (via nameControl.value) or its status (via nameCon trol.status, which is always valid for this simple element). Finally, we have a simple button that triggers the onSubmit() method in the component.

Next, let's take a look at the *src/app/component/stock/create-stock/create-stock.component.ts* file to see what changes we have to make to it to support this form:

```
import { Component, OnInit } from '@angular/core';
import { FormControl } from '@angular/forms';

@Component({
  selector: 'app-create-stock',
  templateUrl: './create-stock.component.html',
  styleUrls: ['./create-stock.component.css']
})
export class CreateStockComponent {

  public nameControl = new FormControl();
  constructor() {}

  onSubmit() {
    console.log('Name Control Value', this.nameControl.value);
  }
}
```

We have removed all references of the Stock model from this. Instead, we import and create an instance of FormControl called nameControl. This is the variable we bound to in the template. Then, on the onSubmit() call, we simply print the current value of the nameControl control. Again, note that unlike traditional non-MVC frameworks, at no point is the control reaching out into the view to get the current value of the element. We rely on the FormControl to provide a representative view of the input element, and keep it up to date.

We have used the default FormControl constructor, but it can also take the initial value along with a list of validators (both sync and async) as arguments. We will see how to add validators in a bit more detail in "Form Groups" on page 128.

When we run this application, we should see something like Figure 7-1, with a simple form field below our stock widgets. If you type into it, you should see the form field below it.

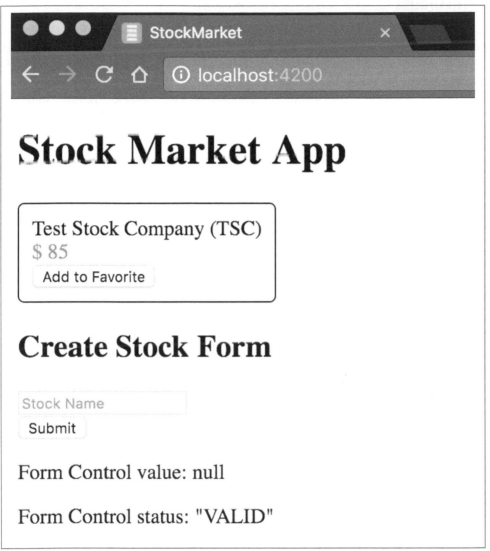

Figure 7-1. Simple Angular reactive form

Summing up, it is helpful to think of FormControl when we need to track the state and value of any individual form element, like an input box or a checkbox. In the next section, we will see how to build a more complete form using FormControl and something called FormGroup.

The finished example is available in the *chapter7/form-control* folder in the GitHub repository.

Form Groups

Usually, when we build any form, it rarely has just one element. We typically have a set of different fields and elements we want to track under one common form or heading. In these cases, the FormGroup is useful as a way to group relevant form fields under one group. This gives us the convenience of whether we want to track the form controls individually, or as a group. For example, we can get the entire form value, or check whether the form as a whole is valid (as a result of individual elements and their state).

Let's see how we can extend the example from the previous section to create a comprehensive form for creating a stock using FormControl and FormGroup instances.

First, we will see how to modify the *src/app/stock/create-stock/create-stock.component .html* template to ask for all the relevant fields of a stock from the user:

```
<h2>Create Stock Form</h2>

<div class="form-group">
  <form [formGroup]="stockForm" (ngSubmit)="onSubmit()">         ❶
    <div class="stock-name">
      <input type="text"
             placeholder="Stock Name"
             name="stockName"
             formControlName="name">                            ❷
    </div>
    <div class="stock-code">
        <input type="text"
               placeholder="Stock Code"
               formControlName="code">
    </div>
    <div class="stock-price">
        <input type="number"
               placeholder="Stock Price"
               formControlName="price">
    </div>
    <button type="submit">Submit</button>
  </form>
</div>

<p>Form Control value: {{ stockForm.value | json }}</p>         ❸
<p>Form Control status: {{ stockForm.status | json }}</p>
```

❶ We now bind to a formGroup instead of a formControl

❷ Once we use a formGroup, we use formControlName inside the group

❸ Change over to printing the form group value instead of the element

The major change from the previous example is that we switched over from binding to formControl to a formGroup. We do this at the form level. Now within it, for each form element, we mention a formControlName. Each of these will bind to an individual element within the formGroup. Finally, we display the current value and status of the form similar to how we did for the FormControl.

Also, for easier readability, we have switched from calling the control nameControl, and instead just call it name, code, and price in the component.

Next, let's take a look at how we change the *src/app/stock/create-stock/create stock.component.ts* component class to get this example to work:

```
import { Component, OnInit } from '@angular/core';
import { FormControl, FormGroup, Validators } from '@angular/forms';

@Component({
  selector: 'app-create-stock',
  templateUrl: './create-stock.component.html',
  styleUrls: ['./create-stock.component.css']
})
export class CreateStockComponent {

  public stockForm: FormGroup = new FormGroup({
    name: new FormControl(null, Validators.required),
    code: new FormControl(null, [Validators.required, Validators.minLength(2)]),
    price: new FormControl(0, [Validators.required, Validators.min(0)])
  });
  constructor() {}

  onSubmit() {
    console.log('Stock Form Value', this.stockForm.value);
  }
}
```

In the component, we now instantiate and expose a FormGroup instance, named stockForm. This is what we had bound to at the form level in the template. FormGroup allows us to instantiate multiple named controls within it, and we have done so to instantiate a form control for the name, code, and price. This time, we are also using the constructor of the FormControl to the maximum extent possible, by adding a default value and validators as required.

The first argument to the FormControl constructor is the default value of the form control. Here, we initialize the default values of the two form controls to be null and 0, respectively.

The second argument to the `FormControl` constructor can either be a single `Valida tor`, or an array of `Validators`. There are a set of built-in validators to ensure that the `FormControl` is `require`, or has a minimum value. These validators can either be synchronous (like the ones we have used), or can also be asynchronous (for example, to check whether a username is available in the server). You can check out the built-in validators in the official Angular docs (*https://angular.io/api/forms/Validators*).

When the form is submitted (using `ngSubmit` event binding), we then print the entire form group value to the console.

When we run this, and type in some values in the form, we should see the form react and print the current value of the form as well as its validity status in the UI. It would look something like Figure 7-2.

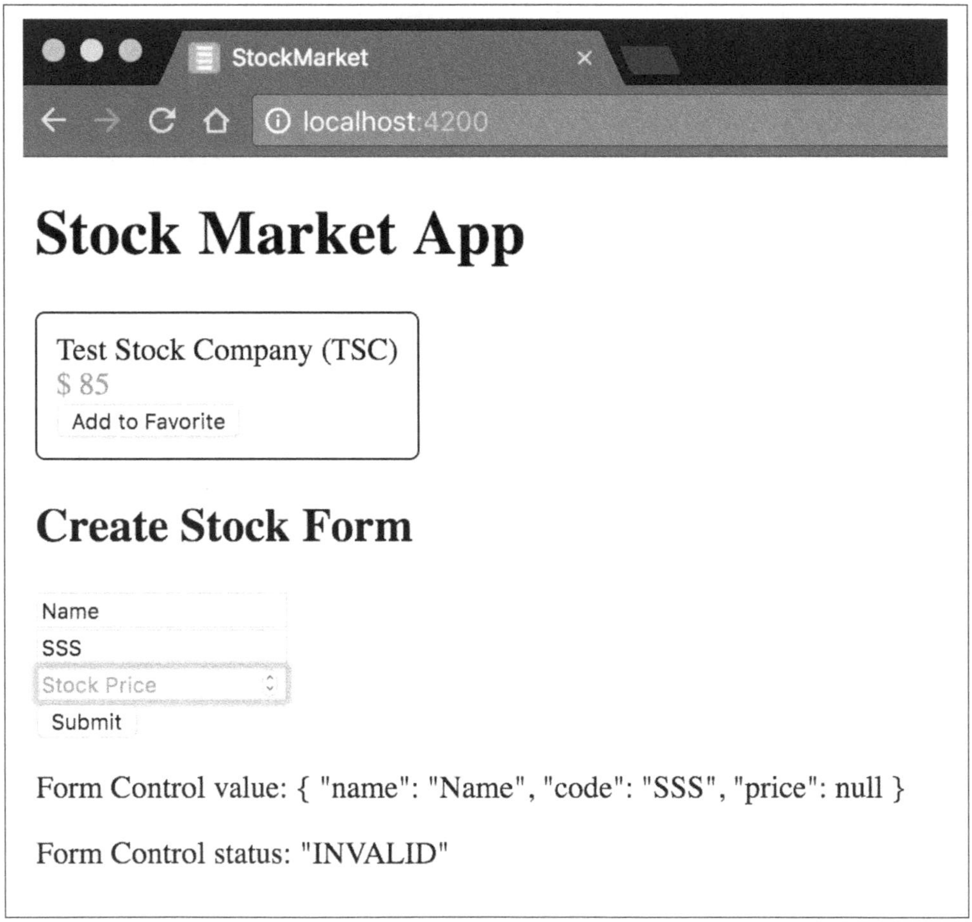

Figure 7-2. Angular reactive form with form control state

The finished example is available in the *chapter7/form-groups* folder in the GitHub repository.

Form Builders

Now, while the FormGroup gives us the flexibility to build complex, nested forms (and by the way, you can absolutely nest further form groups within a form group!), its syntax is slightly verbose. And that's why, to replace it, we have a FormBuilder in Angular, which makes it slightly nicer to build these rich forms in a cleaner manner.

The nice thing about the FormBuilder is that we don't have to change or even touch our template. The FormBuilder fundamentally is syntactic sugar to allow us to quickly create FormGroup and FormControl elements without manually calling new for each one. The reactive form still relies on those elements under the covers for its functioning, and FormBuilder does not do away with them.

Let's see how we can switch our CreateStockComponent to use FormBuilder. We will change the *src/app/stock/create-stock/create-stock.component.ts* file as follows:

```
import { Component, OnInit } from '@angular/core';
import { FormControl, FormGroup } from '@angular/forms';
import { Validators, FormBuilder } from '@angular/forms';          ❶

@Component({
  selector: 'app-create-stock',
  templateUrl: './create-stock.component.html',
  styleUrls: ['./create-stock.component.css']
})
export class CreateStockComponent {

  public stockForm: FormGroup;                    ❷
  constructor(private fb: FormBuilder) {          ❸
    this.createForm();
  }

  createForm() {
    this.stockForm = this.fb.group({              ❹
      name: [null, Validators.required],          ❺
      code: [null, [Validators.required, Validators.minLength(2)]],
      price: [0, [Validators.required, Validators.min(0)]]
    });
  }

  onSubmit() {
    console.log('Stock Form Value', this.stockForm.value);
  }
}
```

❶   Import FormBuilder from @angular/forms

---

❷   We don't initialize the FormGroup while declaring it anymore

❸   Inject an instance of the FormBuilder into the constructor

❹   Create a FormGroup using the injected FormBuilder instance

❺   Initialize the name control with an initial null value and a required validator

The major change from before is how we initialize the stockForm FormGroup instance. Instead of initializing it in line, with the FormBuilder, we first inject an instance of the FormBuilder into our constructor. Then, in the constructor itself, we use the group method on the FormBuilder instance to then create the various form controls.

Even for creating the form controls, we simply use the FormBuilder syntactic sugar. For example, if we just wanted to initialize a text field called name with an empty string as the initial value, we could simply have a key called name, and pass an empty string as the value for it (that is, name: ''). In the preceding code, we actually want to both initialize it with a default value as well as add some validators, so instead of passing it just a value, we pass it an array.

The first value in the array is the default value of the form control (null in the case of name and code, 0 in the case of price). The second value is then either a single validator (like in name), or an array of validators (like in code and price).

Fundamentally, nothing else changes. The result of doing this is we get an application that behaves exactly like the version from the previous section, but we are able to hook it up in a more concise and less verbose manner. For any form with more than a few elements, it almost always makes sense to use the FormBuilder rather than the FormGroup method, as it reduces both the code and makes it a lot more concise and readable.

The finished example is available in the *chapter7/form-builder* folder in the GitHub repository.

Form Data

So far, we have hand-waved over handling the form data. We have simply used the FormControl or FormGroup and accessed the value from it. In this section, we will go into the data and form model and how reactive forms allow us to deal with it as well as control and form state (like valid, invalid, etc.).

Control State, Validity, and Error Messages

Before we go deep into how the form model is structured, and how that corresponds to our data model in the component, we will first cover the simpler aspects, which is dealing with the control's state and validity. Dealing with form control state and validity is quite similar to how we handle it with template-driven forms, in that the base control states and validity are the same. What changes is the method of accessing these properties.

Let's now add error messages to our form that we have been building so far, so that we can show respective error messages along each field. That said, we only want to show these error messages if the user has interacted with a field, and not before. So by default, when the page opens, we don't want to show any error messages.

We will build on the example from the previous section, so in case you are not coding along, you can copy the codebase from *chapter7/form-builder*. Before we start going into the code, here's a quick refresher on the basic Angular control states (repeated from Chapter 6):

Control state	CSS class if True	CSS class if False
Visited	ng-touched	ng-untouched
Changed	ng-dirty	ng-pristine
Valid	ng-valid	ng-invalid

We could use these to highlight and show errors and state of the form, like we did before. But for this section, we will focus on showing only condition error messages, and cleanly handling cases with multiple validators.

Now, let's see how to edit the template to start showing relevant error messages in the form, while using the reactive form approach. We will edit the *src/app/stock/create-stock/create-stock.component.html* file as follows:

```
<h2>Create Stock Form</h2>

<div class="form-group">
  <form [formGroup]="stockForm" (ngSubmit)="onSubmit()">
    <div class="stock-name">
      <input type="text"
             placeholder="Stock Name"
             name="stockName"
             formControlName="name">
      <div *ngIf="stockForm.get('name').invalid &&        ❶
                ( stockForm.get('name').dirty ||
                  stockForm.get('name').touched )">
        Name is required
      </div>
    </div>
  </form>
```

```
<div class="stock-code">
  <input type="text"
         placeholder="Stock Code"
         formControlName="code">
  <div *ngIf="stockForm.get('code').invalid &&
              ( stockForm.get('code').dirty ||
                stockForm.get('code').touched )">
    <div *ngIf="stockForm.get('code').errors.required">     ❷
      Stock Code is required
    </div>
    <div *ngIf="stockForm.get('code').errors.minlength">
      Stock Code must be at least 2 characters
    </div>
  </div>
</div>
<div class="stock-price">
  <input type="number"
         placeholder="Stock Price"
         formControlName="price">
  <div *ngIf="stockForm.get('price').invalid &&
              ( stockForm.get('price').dirty ||
                stockForm.get('price').touched )">
    <div *ngIf="stockForm.get('price').errors.required">
      Stock Price is required
    </div>
    <div *ngIf="stockForm.get('price').errors.min">
      Stock Price must be positive
    </div>
  </div>
</div>
<button type="submit">Submit</button>
  </form>
</div>

<p>Form Control value: {{ stockForm.value | json }}</p>
<p>Form Control status: {{ stockForm.status | json }}</p>
```

❶ Accessing an individual control element's validity through the form group

❷ Checking for individual validator status for a form element

While the base form remains the same from the previous example, we have modified it now to show conditional error messages. There are a few noteworthy things happening in this template, so let's walk through it step by step:

- For each form element, we have added a div element beneath it to show conditional error messages.

- For each element, we first get the individual form element by calling stock Form.get() with the name of the individual form control that we provided while instantiating the FormGroup in the component class.

- With each `FormControl`, we can then check for various properties like whether the form element is touched or not (that is, whether the user has accessed the element), whether the form element has been modified or not (dirty or pristine), and whether it is valid or not.

- For our example, we are relying on these properties to ensure that we display the error message only when the form element is both invalid and the user has interacted with it by either modifying it (`dirty` if modified, `pristine` otherwise) or at least accessing it (`touched` if accessed, `untouched` otherwise).

- For form fields with more than one validator (primarily, the stock code and price), we further look at the `errors` property on the form control. This field allows us to check what kind of error is causing the form field to be invalid, and thus show the respective error message.

Instead of repeating `stockForm.get('price')` every time, you might want to create simple getters in the component class like so:

```
@Component({
  selector: 'app-create-stock',
  templateUrl: './create-stock.component.html',
  styleUrls: ['./create-stock.component.css']
})
export class CreateStockComponent {
/*  Skipping irrelevant code here */

  get name() { return this.stockForm.get('name'); }

  get price() { return this.stockForm.get('price'); }

  get code() { return this.stockForm.get('code'); }
}
```

Now in your HTML, you can simply refer to `name.invalid` instead of `stockForm.get('name').invalid` and so on.

In this way, we can interact with the state of the form controls and provide the correct user experience to the users of our web application.

The finished example is available in the *chapter7/control-state-validity* folder in the GitHub repository.

Form and Data Model

Now we will start digging into accessing and working with the data driving the form, and the interaction between the form and the data model in our component. We simplified this so far in the preceding examples, by simply accessing the `value` from the

FormGroup or the FormControl. This is also what we log in both the template using the json pipe, as well as in the component when we click the Submit button.

Let's use an example to demonstrate how we work with the form and data model, and how the two interact. First, let's change our template slightly from the previous example (in case you want the completed code, you can copy it from the *chapter7/control-state-validity* folder) to provide for a few more actions.

We will edit the template for the CreateStockComponent by changing *src/app/stock/create-stock/create-stock.component.html* as follows:

```html
<h2>Create Stock Form</h2>

<div class="form-group">
  <form [formGroup]="stockForm" (ngSubmit)="onSubmit()">

    <!-- Repeated code from before, omitted for brevity -->

    <button type="submit">Submit</button>
    <button type="button"
            (click)="resetForm()">
      Reset
    </button>
    <button type="button"
            (click)="loadStockFromServer()">
      Simulate Stock Load from Server
    </button>
    <button type="button"
            (click)="patchStockForm()">
      Patch Stock Form
    </button>
  </form>
</div>

<p>Form Control value: {{ stockForm.value | json }}</p>
<p>Form Control status: {{ stockForm.status | json }}</p>
```

Most of the template has not changed, but we have added three new buttons at the end of the form. All three of them call out to a method in the component class, which we will see in just a bit. But the three buttons fundamentally perform the following two actions:

1. Reset the form to its original state

2. Simulate loading a stock from the server

And to perform the latter, we show two methods by which we can accomplish that with our reactive form.

Watch out in case you forget the type on the button element. Depending on the browser, it can take various defaults. For example, Chrome on Mac will assume the type as submit if omitted, causing a form submit even while triggering its event handler.

Now, let's move to the CreateStockComponent class, which is where most of the activity and changes happen. We will edit the *src/app/stock/create-stock/create-stock.component.ts* file as follows:

```
/** NO CHANGE IN IMPORTS **/

let counter = 1;

/** NO CHANGE IN COMPONENT DECORATOR **/
export class CreateStockComponent {

  private stock: Stock;                    ❶
  public stockForm: FormGroup;
  constructor(private fb: FormBuilder) {
    this.createForm();
    this.stock = new Stock('Test ' + counter++, 'TST', 20, 10);  ❷
  }

  createForm() {
    this.stockForm = this.fb.group({
      name: [null, Validators.required],
      code: [null, [Validators.required, Validators.minLength(2)]],
      price: [0, [Validators.required, Validators.min(0)]]
    });
  }

  loadStockFromServer() {
    this.stock = new Stock('Test ' + counter++, 'TST', 20, 10);
    let stockFormModel = Object.assign({}, this.stock);
    delete stockFormModel.previousPrice;
    delete stockFormModel.favorite;
    this.stockForm.setValue(stockFormModel);    ❸
  }

  patchStockForm() {
    this.stock = new Stock(`Test ${counter++}`, 'TST', 20, 10);
    this.stockForm.patchValue(this.stock);      ❹
  }

  resetForm() {
    this.stockForm.reset();        ❺
  }

  onSubmit() {
    this.stock = Object.assign({}, this.stockForm.value);
```

```
        console.log('Saving stock', this.stock);
    }
}
```

❶ We have introduced a `stock` model object, in addition to the form model

❷ Instantiating our stock model with some default value

❸ Setting the entire form model with our `stock` data model values

❹ Patching the form model with whatever fields are available

❺ Resetting the form to its initial state

While it seems like we have added a lot of code, it is actually not that much. Let's walk through the component step by step to understand what has changed and what it does:

1. You can ignore the `counter`; it is there simply to make sure that something (the name) changes every time we click a button. It is not tied into any of the Angular functionality otherwise.

2. We create a `stock` model object, which is a pure data model object. This is not tied to the Angular form models or anything we have been dealing with so far. It parallels the form model, but has a few extra fields that we don't ask for in the form. We instantiate this with a default value in the constructor (but it is not used or tied to the template until this point).

3. We leave the `createForm` method untouched.

4. We create a new method `loadStockFromServer`, to simulate us fetching the stock details from the server. While it is synchronous (unlike a real HTTP server call), it shows us how to take a value and push it to the UI's form model.

5. We use the `setValue` method on the `stockForm` `FormGroup` instance. This method takes a JSON model object that matches the form model exactly. That means for the `setValue` to work in this case, it needs an object with a `name`, `code`, and `price` key. It should not have more or fewer keys than this, as it would throw an error in this case. Based on the object, the form's model object values would get updated and these values would be visible in the form in the UI. This is also the reason why we delete all other keys from the model object before calling `set Value`.

6. Thus, triggering the `loadStockFromServer` method would end up updating the form with the name, code, and price from the newly created `stock` instance.

7. The second method, `patchStockForm`, uses another method on the `stockForm` `FormGroup` instance called `patchValue`. This is a more forgiving method that

takes the fields it has available, and updates the form with them. It will ignore extra fields even if it has fewer fields.

8. Triggering the `patchStockForm` instance would also have the same effect as triggering the previous button. What is more interesting (and left as an exercise to the reader) is to delete the code from the stock object and try patching. In the case of `setValue`, it will fail and throw an exception, while `patchValue` would happily set the other fields (`name`, `price`) and leave the code untouched in the form.

9. The final method is the `resetForm`, which simply resets the form to its initial state.

One final thing to note is that we have changed the `onSubmit` method slightly as well. While in this case our form model mirrors the data model, it is good practice to not directly assign the form model to our data model, but rather make a copy of it. In this case, since it is a simple object, a simple `Object.assign` or the spread operator works, but for slightly more complicated models, it might be necessary to do a deep copy.

The finished example is available in the *chapter7/form-model* folder in the GitHub repository.

Another Advantage of Reactive Forms

Another slightly subtle advantage of using reactive forms over template-driven forms is that it forces developers to have a separation between what the user sees and interacts with (what we call the form model), and the persisted data model that drives our application. This is quite common in most applications, where the presented view is different from what the underlying data model is. Reactive forms make that distinction clear, while also keeping you cognizant of the data flow and giving you control over when and what flows from UI to the component and vice versa.

FormArrays

For the purpose of demonstrating the last thing related to reactive forms, we are going to extend our stock market example in a slightly tangential manner. Let's suppose that for each stock, we wanted to capture and highlight the key people related to the company, as well as their titles. A company may have none, one, or many such people associated with it.

This will allow us to see how we can handle forms where we need to capture multiple values as well as handle nested form elements cleanly. We will take the codebase from the previous section and modify it to support the following:

1. Add a new model to represent one or many notable persons under a stock

2. Add a button in the UI to add a new notable person for a stock

3. Add a button to remove an added notable person from the stock

4. Support basic validation on each notable person added

Let's walk through, step by step, how to accomplish this. In case you are not coding along with the examples, you can copy the codebase from *chapter7/form-model* and work from there.

We will first update the model to understand this new concept of a person. Ideally, we would do this in a model file of its own, but here, we took a shortcut for readability and making it easier to understand. We added our model to the *src/app/model/stock.ts* file as follows:

```
export class Stock {
  favorite = false;
  notablePeople: Person[];

  constructor(public name: string,
              public code: string,
              public price: number,
              public previousPrice: number) {
    this.notablePeople = [];
  }

  isPositiveChange(): boolean {
    return this.price >= this.previousPrice;
  }
}

export class Person {
  name: string;
  title: string;
}
```

We added a new class `Person` with a `name` and a `title`, and then added it as a child to the `Stock` class, with the name `notablePeople`. In the constructor for `Stock` class, we initialized it to an empty array.

Now we move over to our `CreateStockComponent` class. First, let's walk through the changes to the component class, which is located in *src/app/stock/create-stock/create-stock.component.ts*:

```
/**
Omitted for brevity, no change in imports
*/
export class CreateStockComponent {

  private stock: Stock;
```

```
  public stockForm: FormGroup;
  constructor(private fb: FormBuilder) {
    this.createForm();
  }

  createForm() {
    this.stockForm = this.fb.group({
      name: [null, Validators.required],
      code: [null, [Validators.required, Validators.minLength(2)]],
      price: [0, [Validators.required, Validators.min(0)]],
      notablePeople: this.fb.array([])          ❶
    });
  }

  get notablePeople(): FormArray {              ❷
    return this.stockForm.get('notablePeople') as FormArray;
  }

  addNotablePerson() {                          ❸
    this.notablePeople.push(this.fb.group({
      name: ['', Validators.required],
      title: ['', Validators.required]
    }))
  }

  removeNotablePerson(index: number) {          ❹
    this.notablePeople.removeAt(index);
  }

  resetForm() {
    this.stockForm.reset();
  }

  onSubmit() {
    this.stock = Object.assign({}, this.stockForm.value);
    console.log('Saving stock', this.stock);
  }
}
```

❶ Initialize notablePeople as a FormArray instance

❷ Getter to make it easier to access the underlying FormArray from the template

❸ Add a new FormGroup instance to the FormArray

❹ Remove a particular FormGroup instance from the FormArray

There are a few notable things in the code for the component class. Primarily, we have removed all things related to the model, including loading and patching the stock model object from the class. Instead, we have added:

- notablePeople to the main FormGroup. Note that notablePeople is a FormArray instance with an initial value that is empty. In case we have to populate it with existing values, we would pass it to the constructor.

- We have created a simple getter for notablePeople, which goes deep into the stockForm FormGroup instance and returns the notablePeople FormArray instance. This is more for the template to prevent us from writing this.stock Form.get('notablePeople') each time.

- Since we can have zero to many notable people per stock, we need a method to allow us to add as many notable people as we want. This is what the addNotable Person() method does. Note that each instance of notable person in the actual form is represented by a FormGroup. So each time we want to add a new notable person, we add a FormGroup instance with a required name and title.

- Similarly, we want to be able to remove any notable person that we have added, which is what the removeNotablePerson() method does. It takes an index and just removes that particular index from the FormArray instance.

Next, we will add some simple CSS that will allow us to separate out each individual person by adding the following to *src/app/stock/create-stock/create-stock.component .css*:

```css
.notable-people {
  border: 1px solid black;
  padding: 10px;
  margin: 5px;
}
```

Finally, let's now look at how the template changes to hook all of this up. We will modify *src/app/stock/create-stock/create-stock.component.html* as follows:

```html
<h2>Create Stock Form</h2>

<div class="form-group">
  <form [formGroup]="stockForm" (ngSubmit)="onSubmit()">
    <!-- No change until the end of price form element -->
    <!-- Omitted for brevity -->
    <div formArrayName="notablePeople">
      <div *ngFor="let person of notablePeople.controls; let i = index"
           [formGroupName]="i"
           class="notable-people">
        <div>
          Person {{i + 1}}
        </div>
        <div>
          <input type="text"
                 placeholder="Person Name"
                 formControlName="name">
        </div>
```

```
      <div>
        <input type="text"
               placeholder="Person Title"
               formControlName="title">
      </div>
      <button type="button"
              (click)="removeNotablePerson(i)">
        Remove Person
      </button>
    </div>
  </div>
  <button type="button"
          (click)="addNotablePerson()">
    Add Notable Person
  </button>
  <button type="submit">Submit</button>
  <button type="button"
          (click)="resetForm()">
    Reset
  </button>
</form>
</div>

<p>Form Control value: {{ stockForm.value | json }}</p>
<p>Form Control status: {{ stockForm.status | json }}</p>
<p>Stock Value: {{stock | json}}</p>
```

There are a few things to note on how we hooked together the FormArray instance we created in our component to the template for the component:

- Instead of using formControlName, we use formGroupName on the enclosing div element. This is the element that will contain zero to many forms, one for each notable person.

- We then have a div element that is repeated once for each entry in the FormArray instance, which we access through notablePeople.controls. The notable People accesses the getter that we created in the component.

- We also expose the current index of the *ngFor via the variable i.

- We then connect the FormGroup that is each element in the FormArray via the formGroupName binding, binding it to each individual index in the array.

- This allows us to then use formControlName individually for the name and title like we have done so far. This ensures that the name and title are bound to that particular FormGroup instance denoted by the index in the FormArray.

- Finally, we have the Remove Person button within each *ngFor instance, which calls the removeNotablePerson() method, and a global Add Person button, which calls the addNotablePerson() method.

When you run this, you should now see a new button, Add Notable Person. Clicking this should show new form elements to enter a person's details. You can click this multiple times to add more people, and you can click Remove on any individual person to remove them. Your working application should look something like Figure 7-3.

Figure 7-3. Angular form using FormArray

Notice that the form value (printed as JSON) also holds all the person data that you enter. Thus, when the form is submitted, you can capture this data and transform it to the necessary data model before transmitting it.

The finished example is available in the *chapter7/form-arrays* folder in the GitHub repository.

Conclusion

In this chapter, we explored how to create reactive forms as an alternative to using template-driven forms. We reviewed the building blocks of these forms and saw how to use elements like FormControl, FormGroup, and even FormArray to build complex user experiences. We also briefly touched upon the major differences between template-driven forms and reactive forms, and how reactive forms facilitate and highlight the difference between having a form model (or the presentation model), which is different from our underlying data model.

In the next chapter, we will start exploring Angular services, what they are, and when and how to create them. We will also touch upon Angular's dependency injection framework and how to deal with asynchronous behavior using observables.

Exercise

Take the finished exercise from Chapter 5 (available in *chapter5/exercise/ecommerce*). We will repeat the same exercise that we accomplished using template-driven forms, by performing the following:

1. Create a new component that allows us to add new products.

2. Create a form that takes in the product name, price, image URL, and whether it is on sale or not. Create proper FormGroup to encapsulate this form. Use Form Builder ideally.

3. Make all the fields except the On Sale checkbox required. Set the minimum valid price as 1.

4. Add a basic Regex pattern validation for the image URL.

5. Display relevant error messages, but only after the user either modifies a field or after the first submit.

6. Copy over the form and print it to the console after successful submission.

All of this can be accomplished using concepts covered in this chapter. You can check out the finished solution in *chapter7/exercise/ecommerce*.

CHAPTER 8

Angular Services

In the previous two chapters, we worked on creating form-based Angular applications. To this extent, we approached it in two ways: the traditional template-driven approach and then the reactive form-based approach. With both, we looked at the building blocks and then built live working forms with validation and proper messaging.

In this chapter, we will move beyond the UI for a bit, and start exploring Angular services, which are the workhorses of any application. We will take a step back, understand what Angular services are, and how to create one. Then we will dig into the Angular dependency injection system and understand how to use and leverage it, before going off and building our own Angular services.

What Are Angular Services?

We have mostly worked with Angular components so far. Components, to quickly recap, are responsible for deciding what data to display and how to render and display it in the UI. We bind our data from the components to our UI and bind our events from the UI to methods in the components to allow and handle user interactions. That is, components in Angular are our presentation layer, and should be involved in and focus on the presentation aspects of data.

But if components are our presentation layer, it begs the question of what should be responsible for the actual data fetching and common business logic in an Angular application. This is where Angular services come in. Angular services are that layer that is common across your application, that can be reused across various components. Generally, you would create and use Angular services when:

- You need to retrieve data from or send data to your server. This may or may not involve any processing of the data while it is being transferred.

- You need to encapsulate application logic that is not specific to any one component, or logic that can be reused across components.

- You need to share data across components, especially across components that may or may not know about each other. Services by default are singletons across your application, which allows you to store state and access them across various components.

Another simple way to think about Angular services is that it is the layer to abstract the "how" away from the component, so that the component can just focus on the "what," and let the service decide the how.

Creating Our Own Angular Service

Instead of talking in abstract, let's dig into some actual code so that we can more fully understand the concept of services. What we will do is build on the example we have worked on so far, and extend it using Angular services. We will try to accomplish the following things in our stock market application:

- Fetch the list of stocks to show from a service, instead of hardcoding it in the component.

- When we create a stock, we will send it to the service.

- When we create a stock, we want it to show up in our list of stocks.

To do this, if we want to continue using components, we would have to come up with a way for our `CreateStockComponent` to communicate with our `StockItemCompo nent`, and keep the data in sync between the two. This would mean our components would have to know each other, and where in the hierarchy they and all other components fit.

First, we will add a `StockListComponent` that fetches a list of stocks, and displays them using the `StockItemComponent`. This component will use the `StockService` that we will build to act as a layer behind both the components. It will be responsible for figuring out how and where to fetch the list of stocks from, and how to create a stock. In this chapter, we will continue with it being a list on the client, but we will see how to build it in a way that each component does not need to worry about the details. Later, when we learn how to work with an HTTP server, we will see how easy it is to switch once we have a service layer in between.

Digging into the Example

For this example, you can use the code from *chapter6/template-driven/control-validity* as the base to code from. We will modify the example to achieve what we have just outlined.

First, let's tackle the easy stuff. The `StockItemComponent` class does not need any change, but we will change the template for it slightly so that it displays both an Add to Favorite and a Remove from Favorite button depending on the state of the stock. We can modify *src/app/stock/stock-item/stock-item.component.html* as follows:

```html
<div class="stock-container">
  <div class="name">{{stock.name + ' (' + stock.code + ')'}}</div>
  <div class="exchange">{{stock.exchange}}</div>
  <div class="price"
       [class.positive]="stock.isPositiveChange()"
       [class.negative]="!stock.isPositiveChange()">$ {{stock.price}}</div>
  <button (click)="onToggleFavorite($event)"
          *ngIf="!stock.favorite">Add to Favorite</button>
  <button (click)="onToggleFavorite($event)"
          *ngIf="stock.favorite">Remove from Favorite</button>
</div>
```

We have just added a div to show the exchange of the stock, and a button to show Remove from Favorite if the stock is already favorited.

Next, let's create the skeleton for the `StockListComponent` before we try creating and integrating our `StockService`. We can generate the skeleton by executing:

```
ng g component stock/stock-list
```

which we can then modify to our purpose. We will modify the *src/app/stock/stock-list/ stock-list.component.ts* file as follows:

```typescript
import { Component, OnInit } from '@angular/core';
import { Stock } from 'app/model/stock';

@Component({
  selector: 'app-stock-list',
  templateUrl: './stock-list.component.html',
  styleUrls: ['./stock-list.component.css']
})
export class StockListComponent implements OnInit {

  public stocks: Stock[];
  constructor() { }

  ngOnInit() {
    this.stocks = [
      new Stock('Test Stock Company', 'TSC', 85, 80, 'NASDAQ'),
      new Stock('Second Stock Company', 'SSC', 10, 20, 'NSE'),
      new Stock('Last Stock Company', 'LSC', 876, 765, 'NYSE')
    ];
  }

  onToggleFavorite(stock: Stock) {
    console.log('Favorite for stock ', stock, ' was triggered');
    stock.favorite = !stock.favorite;
```

```
    }
  }
```

There are a few things of note here, but nothing fundamentally new or path-breaking so far:

- We have declared an array of stocks at the class level, and initialized it with some default values in the `ngOnInit` block.

- We have a function `onToggleFavorite` that logs the stock and toggles its favorite state.

Let's now look at its corresponding template, in *src/app/stock/stock-list/stock-list.component.html*:

```
<app-stock-item *ngFor="let stock of stocks" [stock]="stock"
                (toggleFavorite)="onToggleFavorite($event)">
</app-stock-item>
```

In the template, we simply loop over all the stocks and display an instance of the `StockItemComponent` for each one. We ask the `StockItemComponent` to trigger the `onToggleFavorite` whenever someone clicks the Add to Favorite or Remove from Favorite button within the stock item.

 Since we generated the component using the Angular CLI, we can avoid the step of having to register the newly created component in the Angular module. Otherwise, there would be one more step here of adding the newly created component in the *app.module.ts* file in the `declarations` section.

The `AppComponent` can now be simplified further. The component class in *src/app/app.component.ts* can be modified to:

```
import { Component, OnInit } from '@angular/core';

@Component({
  selector: 'app-root',
  templateUrl: './app.component.html',
  styleUrls: ['./app.component.css']
})
export class AppComponent implements OnInit {
  title = 'Stock Market App';

  ngOnInit(): void {
  }
}
```

The corresponding template in *src/app/app.component.html* can be modified to:

```
<h1>
  {{title}}
</h1>
<app-stock-list></app-stock-list>
<app-create-stock></app-create-stock>
```

Now finally, let's look at what it takes to build a very simple and trivial `StockService`. We can again generate the base skeleton for the service using the Angular CLI as follows:

```
ng g service services/stock
```

This will generate two files, a skeleton *stock-service.ts* and a dummy test for it in *stock-service.spec.ts*. We will ignore the latter for now but will return to it in Chapter 10, as part of our discussion of unit testing of services. The generated skeleton in *src/app/service/stock.service.ts* should look something like this:

```
import { Injectable } from '@angular/core';

@Injectable()
export class StockService {

  constructor() { }

}
```

The skeleton is literally just an empty shell class, with one decorator of note, which is `Injectable`. The `Injectable` decorator has no current value for us, but is a recommended decorator whenever you are working with services, as it is a hint to the Angular dependency injection system that the service you are working on might have other dependencies. With the `Injectable` decorator, Angular will take care of injecting them into our service.

We will leave the decorator untouched, keeping with the best practices. And pretty soon, as early as the next chapter, we will need it anyway.

Now, let's get to the crux of the work, which is the data that the `StockService` is to provide. This is where services really shine. Components generally will defer and ask a service for data (or a section of the data). It is up to the service to decide how and where to fetch the data from, whether it is from a web service via HTTP calls, a local storage or cache, or even return mock data, as we will in just a bit. Later, if we want to change the source, we can do it in one place without touching any of the components, as long as our API signature remains the same.

Let's define our `StockService` to continue returning mock data. We will edit the *src/app/services/stock.service.ts* file as follows:

```
import { Injectable } from '@angular/core';
import { Stock } from 'app/model/stock';

@Injectable()
export class StockService {

  private stocks: Stock[];
  constructor() {
    this.stocks = [
      new Stock('Test Stock Company', 'TSC', 85, 80, 'NASDAQ'),
      new Stock('Second Stock Company', 'SSC', 10, 20, 'NSE'),
      new Stock('Last Stock Company', 'LSC', 876, 765, 'NYSE')
    ];
  }

  getStocks() : Stock[] {
    return this.stocks;
  }

  createStock(stock: Stock) {
    let foundStock = this.stocks.find(each => each.code === stock.code);
    if (foundStock) {
      return false;
    }
    this.stocks.push(stock);
    return true;
  }

  toggleFavorite(stock: Stock) {
    let foundStock = this.stocks.find(each => each.code === stock.code);
    foundStock.favorite = !foundStock.favorite;
  }
}
```

While it seems like we have added a lot of code, if we dig into it, there is nothing that is Angular specific in the code we added. Most of the added code is business functionality that we have defined and enforced via the StockService. Let's quickly walk through the major functionality we have introduced in the service:

- We have moved our initialization of the mock list of stocks to the constructor of the StockService, initializing it with some dummy values to provide an initial state for our UI when it is rendered.

- We have defined a very simple getStocks() method that simply returns the current list of stocks.

- The createStock method does little more than simply adding the stock to our list of stocks. It first checks if the stock already exists (using the code on the stock to check for uniqueness), exiting early if it does. If not found, it adds the passed-in stock to our list of stocks.

- Finally, we have a `toggleFavorite`, which simply finds the passed-in stock in our array and then toggles the state of the `favorite` key on it.

Now that we have defined our service, let's see what it takes to be able to use it in our components. Before we can start injecting it into our components, we need to define how this service will be provided and at what level. We can define this at the `Stock ListComponent` level, the `AppComponent` level, or the `AppModule` level. We will see what the difference is in a bit, but in the meantime, let's define it at the module level.

Let's edit the *src/app/app.module.ts* file to define the provider as follows:

```
/** Imports same as before, skipped for brevity **/
import { StockService } from 'app/services/stock.service';

@NgModule({
  declarations: [
    AppComponent,
    StockItemComponent,
    CreateStockComponent,
    StockListComponent
  ],
  imports: [
    BrowserModule,
    FormsModule,
    HttpModule
  ],
  providers: [
    StockService                    ❶
  ],
  bootstrap: [AppComponent]
})
export class AppModule { }
```

❶ Registering the provider for `StockService`

We have just made a small addition to the `NgModule` decorator on the `AppModule`. We have registered an array of `providers`, in which the `StockService` is the one and only service right now. The `providers` array in the Angular module tells Angular to create a singleton instance of the service, and make it available for any class or component that asks for it. When we register it at the module level, it means that any component within the module that asks for the service will get the exact same instance injected into it.

We could have skipped the step of manually adding the service to the module by asking the Angular CLI to also perform this. The Angular CLI doesn't know at which level the service is supposed to operate, so it skips the service registration. If we wanted it to register it at the app module level, we could have executed it as:

```
ng g service services/stock --module=app
```

This would have both generated the service and also registered the provider in the AppModule.

At this point, we are ready to start using the service, so first we will use it in the newly created StockListComponent. Let's change the *src/app/stock/stock-list/stock-list.component.ts* file as follows:

```
import { Component, OnInit } from '@angular/core';
import { StockService } from 'app/services/stock.service';
import { Stock } from 'app/model/stock';

@Component({
  selector: 'app-stock-list',
  templateUrl: './stock-list.component.html',
  styleUrls: ['./stock-list.component.css']
})
export class StockListComponent implements OnInit {

  public stocks: Stock[];
  constructor(private stockService: StockService) { }      ❶

  ngOnInit() {
    this.stocks = this.stockService.getStocks();           ❷
  }

  onToggleFavorite(stock: Stock) {
    console.log('Favorite for stock ', stock, ' was triggered');
    this.stockService.toggleFavorite(stock);               ❸
  }
}
```

❶ Inject the StockService into the component

❷ Use the StockService to get the list of stocks

❸ Use the StockService to toggle the favorite status on a stock

This is our first instance of injecting and using a service, so let's walk through it step by step:

1. We can inject any service we want into our component simply by listing it in our constructor. In this case, we have declared a private instance of StockService

with the name `stockService`. The name itself doesn't matter; Angular uses the type definition to figure out what service to inject. For all we care, we could even call the instance of the service `xyz` (not that you should!), and it would still get injected correctly.

2. We simply call the methods we want on our service through our instance (like `stockService.getStocks()` or `stockService.toggleFavorite()`) at the correct time. We initialize our list of stocks, and pass through the toggle call to the service. Note that we need to access the service through an instance variable and cannot access it directly (that is, we need to call `this.stockService`, and cannot directly use `stockService`).

While we don't need to make any changes to the corresponding template, here is what the template for the `StockListComponent` looks like in case you don't remember:

```
<app-stock-item *ngFor="let stock of stocks" [stock]="stock"
                (toggleFavorite)="onToggleFavorite($event)">
</app-stock-item>
```

 We just used one of TypeScript's features in the preceding example to both declare a parameter as well as a property simultaneously. By adding the `private` or `public` keyword in front of a constructor argument, we can make it a member property of the class with the same name.

With this, we need to make no more changes in our template. If we run the application at this point, we should see it running with a list of three stocks displayed at the top.

Let's continue with the minor changes to the `CreateStockComponent` to finish the service integration. First, we'll add a simple `message` to the top of the `CreateStockCompo nent` template, to show a message to the user if the stock was created successfully or if there was any error in creation. We will edit *src/app/stock/create-stock/create-stock.component.html* as follows:

```
<h2>Create Stock Form</h2>

<div *ngIf="message">{{message}}</div>          ❶
<div class="form-group">
  <!-- Rest of the form omitted for brevity -->
  <!-- No change from the base code -->
</div>

<h4>Stock Name is {{stock | json}}</h4>
```

❶ Display a message if it exists

The highlighted line is the only change in this file, which is simply adding a div that shows the `message` class variable if it has a value.

Now, we can change the component in *src/app/stock/create-stock/create-stock.component.ts* to integrate with the `StockService`:

```
import { Component, OnInit } from '@angular/core';
import { Stock } from 'app/model/stock';
import { StockService } from 'app/services/stock.service';

@Component({
  selector: 'app-create-stock',
  templateUrl: './create-stock.component.html',
  styleUrls: ['./create-stock.component.css']
})
export class CreateStockComponent {

  public stock: Stock;
  public confirmed = false;
  public message = null;                                    ❶
  public exchanges = ['NYSE', 'NASDAQ', 'OTHER'];
  constructor(private stockService: StockService) {          ❷
    this.stock =  new Stock('', '', 0, 0, 'NASDAQ');
  }

  setStockPrice(price) {
    this.stock.price = price;
    this.stock.previousPrice = price;
  }

  createStock(stockForm) {
    if (stockForm.valid) {
      let created = this.stockService.createStock(this.stock);    ❸
      if (created) {                        ❹
        this.message = 'Successfully created stock with stock code: '
            + this.stock.code;
        this.stock =  new Stock('', '', 0, 0, 'NASDAQ');
      } else {
        this.message = 'Stock with stock code: ' + this.stock.code
            + ' already exists';
      }
    } else {
      console.error('Stock form is in an invalid state');
    }
  }
}
```

❶ Add a `message` field to display success and error messages

❷ Inject `StockService` into the component

❸ Call `stockService.createStock` when the form is submitted

❹ Deal with success and error scenarios while creating the stock

The `CreateStockComponent` has been changed slightly to integrate with the `StockSer vice` as follows:

- We created a `message` field to show useful messages to the user on successful creation of stock as well as errors while creating it.

- We injected the `StockService` and then called it when the form is submitted by the user.

- We used the return value of the `StockService.createStock()` call to decide what message to show to the user in the UI.

While we are at it, we can remove some of the CSS that makes the form hard to read from *src/app/stock/create-stock/create-stock.component.css*, and just empty the file.

Now when we run this application, it should still look the same as before. The difference is that when you fill the create stock form and click Create, it should clear the form, and you should see the stock you just entered like in Figure 8-1.

Now of course, one of the first things you might ask is "How did adding the stock to the list of stocks in the service make it appear in the `StockListComponent` magically?" It is a very valid question, and the answer to that is JavaScript! We return the reference to the stock array in the `getStocks()` method, which is what the `StockListCom ponent` assigns to its member variable. Thus, any addition in the service automatically makes a change in the component that is holding on to the reference of the array.

This is still hacky in some sense, as we wouldn't want to rely on having the same reference to update the values, but we will fix this shortly. Also, because we are using mock data that is instantiated within the service when it is initialized, you will lose any new stocks you have created when you refresh the page. This is because the service is reloaded and reinitialized when we refresh the page, as we don't have a persistent store.

So just to recap, this is what we accomplished:

- We created a `StockListComponent` to display a list of stocks.

- We created a `StockService` that acts as the layer behind all the components, providing APIs to fetch a list of stocks as well as to create new stocks. Currently, it is working off of mock data.

- We made slight updates to all the components to integrate with this service.

Figure 8-1. Angular service sharing data between components

We have dealt with a very basic and simple Angular service to show what an Angular service is, how it is created, and how it is hooked up and used within the context of an Angular application.

The completed version of this code is available in *chapter8/simple-service* in the GitHub repository.

An Introduction to Dependency Injection

Before we dive deeper into services and other related topics, let's take a step back to understand dependency injection, especially in context to Angular.

Dependency injection started in static languages that are more common in server-side programming. In simple terms, dependency injection is the idea that any class or function should ask for its dependencies, rather than instantiating it themselves. Something else (usually called an injector) would be responsible for figuring out what is needed and how to instantiate it.

Dependency injection has huge benefits when we practice it in our applications, as it allows us to create modular, reusable pieces while allowing us to test components and modules easily. Let's take a simple example to demonstrate how dependency injection can make your code more modular, easier to change, and testable:

```
class MyDummyService {

    getMyData() {
      let httpService = new HttpService();
      return httpService.get('my/api');
    }
}

class MyDIService {

    constructor(private httpService: HttpService) {}

    getMyData() {
      return this.httpService.get('my/api');
    }
}
```

In this example, there is actually not much to differentiate between MyDummyService and MyDIService, except for the fact that one instantiates an HttpService before using it, while the other asks for an instance of it in the constructor. But this small change allows for many things, including:

- It makes it more obvious what is necessary for each service to actually execute, rather than finding out at the time of execution.

- In our example, instantiating the HttpService was trivial, but it might not be in certain cases. In such a case, every user of HttpService will need to know exactly how to create it and configure it, before using it.

- In our test, we might not want to make actual HTTP calls. There, we can replace and instantiate MyDIService with a fake HttpService that does not make real calls, while there is nothing we can do for MyDummyService.

There are many more advantages of dependency injection in general, and the official Angular documentation has a great article (*https://angular.io/guide/dependency-injection-pattern*) that covers this in depth if you want to read further on this.

Angular and Dependency Injection

In the previous section, we covered dependency injection in general. In this section, we will dig deeper into how Angular has set up its dependency injection system, and the major things developers should be aware of. We will not go into each and every detail in this section, but cover the general aspects we expect most developers to encounter in their day-to-day work.

We have seen Angular's dependency injection at work already, with the very first service that we created. For very simple asks, it is enough to think about Angular's dependency injection service as a very simple key-value store, with the ability of any component or class to ask for a key when they are getting initialized. In reality, it is much more complex than a simple key-value store. We will see how to leverage this dependency injection system in our unit tests in Chapter 10.

Every service that we create needs to be registered as a provider with an injector. Then any other class can ask for the service and the injector will be responsible for providing it. However, as briefly mentioned in the previous section, Angular doesn't have just one injector—instead, it has a whole hierarchy of injectors.

At its root, at the application level, Angular has the root module and the root injector. When we created our service, and registered it in the `providers` section of the `NgModule`, the service was in fact registered with the root injector. This would mean that the service is a singleton for the entire application, and that any class or component in the application can ask for the service and would be handed the very same instance of the service.

Let's now understand Angular's hierarchical dependency injection system by taking our example and modifying it to make the dependency injection system apparent. We can use the base code from the previous section in case you are not coding along, which is available in *chapter8/simple-service*. We will continue from there.

Before we get into the code, let's cover what exactly will we be trying to accomplish. We will:

- Add a new service called `MessageService`. This will be used to display messages at various points in the UI, and also as a mechanism to communicate across services.

- Introduce and use the `MessageService` in both the `CreateStockComponent` as well as the `AppComponent`.

First, let's create the `MessageService`. This time, we will use the Angular CLI to create it completely for us, including registering it with its provider in the `AppModule`. Just execute:

```
ng g service services/message --module=app
```

Make sure you don't miss the --module=app argument to the command. In case you do, just open the *app.module.ts* file and manually add the MessageService to the list of providers in the NgModule.

This will create a skeleton MessageService in the *services* folder, and register it with the providers section of the AppModule. Let's now update the *src/app/services/ message.service.ts* file as follows:

```
import { Injectable } from '@angular/core';

@Injectable()
export class MessageService {

  public message: string = null;

  constructor() { }
}
```

MessageService is nothing but a very simple container to hold a message string. It is publicly available, so any class or component can simply reach out and access or change it.

Now, let's modify the AppComponent to use this service and display the current message in the UI. Modify the *src/app/app.component.ts* file as follows:

```
import { Component, OnInit } from '@angular/core';
import { MessageService } from 'app/services/message.service';

@Component({
  selector: 'app-root',
  templateUrl: './app.component.html',
  styleUrls: ['./app.component.css']
})
export class AppComponent implements OnInit {
  title = 'app works!';

  constructor(public messageService: MessageService) {}

  ngOnInit(): void {
    this.messageService.message = 'Hello Message Service!';
  }
}
```

We simply injected our new MessageService into the AppComponent, and while initializing set it to some default value. Notice that we made the default access for the messageService public, so that we can use it from the template. Let's now look at the template in *src/app/app.component.html*:

```
<h1>
  {{title}}
</h1>
<h3>App level: {{messageService.message}}</h3>
<app-stock-list></app-stock-list>
<app-create-stock></app-create-stock>
```

We just added one line, which is an h3 element that shows the current value of the message variable in the MessageService that is injected into our AppComponent.

Next, we'll modify the CreateStockComponent to use the same service. Modify the *src/app/stock/create-stock/create-stock.component.ts* file as follows:

```
import { Component, OnInit } from '@angular/core';
import { Stock } from 'app/model/stock';
import { StockService } from 'app/services/stock.service';
import { MessageService } from 'app/services/message.service';

@Component({
  selector: 'app-create-stock',
  templateUrl: './create-stock.component.html',
  styleUrls: ['./create-stock.component.css'],
  providers: [MessageService]
})
export class CreateStockComponent {

  public stock: Stock;
  public confirmed = false;
  public exchanges = ['NYSE', 'NASDAQ', 'OTHER'];
  constructor(private stockService: StockService,
              public messageService: MessageService) {    ❶
    this.stock =  new Stock('', '', 0, 0, 'NASDAQ');
  }

  setStockPrice(price) {
    this.stock.price = price;
    this.stock.previousPrice = price;
  }

  createStock(stockForm) {
    if (stockForm.valid) {
      let created = this.stockService.createStock(this.stock);
      if (created) {                                  ❷
        this.messageService.message =
            'Successfully created stock with stock code: ' +
            this.stock.code;
        this.stock =  new Stock('', '', 0, 0, 'NASDAQ');
      } else {
        this.messageService.message = 'Stock with stock code: ' +
            this.stock.code + ' already exists';
      }
    } else {
```

```
            console.error('Stock form is in an invalid state');
        }
    }
}
```

❶ Inject `MessageService` into the constructor

❷ Use `MessageService` in both cases of creation

Most of the code remains unchanged from before. We just injected our new service into the class, and then used it instead using `console.log`. We set the `message` variable in the `MessageService` when the stock is created successfully or when there is an error.

Finally, we will use the `MessageService` in the template of the component here as well to display the same message. Let's modify *src/app/stock/create-stock/create-stock.component.html* as follows:

```html
<h2>Create Stock Form</h2>

<div>{{messageService.message}}</div>
<div class="form-group">
  <form (ngSubmit)="createStock(stockForm)" #stockForm="ngForm">
    <div class="stock-name">
      <input type="text"
             placeholder="Stock Name"
             required
             name="stockName"
             #stockName="ngModel"
             [(ngModel)]="stock.name">
    </div>

<!-- Remaining code as before, omitting for brevity -->
```

We have omitted most of the file, as the only change we did was add line 3, where we displayed the current value of `messageService.message` in the UI.

Now when we run this, we should see our application, but with two new lines. One is the second line, which is part of our `AppComponent`, and one within the `CreateStock` Component, both of which are displaying the initial value of the message in the UI. If you now fill up the form and create a stock, you will notice that both the messages change simultaneously. Hence, we are assured that there is only one instance of the `MessageService`, which is being shared across both the components.

Now, let's modify the `CreateStockComponent` slightly as follows:

```typescript
import { Component, OnInit } from '@angular/core';
import { Stock } from 'app/model/stock';
import { StockService } from 'app/services/stock.service';
import { MessageService } from 'app/services/message.service';
```

```
@Component({
  selector: 'app-create-stock',
  templateUrl: './create-stock.component.html',
  styleUrls: ['./create-stock.component.css'],
  providers: [MessageService]          ❶
})
export class CreateStockComponent {

  public stock: Stock;
  public confirmed = false;
  public exchanges = ['NYSE', 'NASDAQ', 'OTHER'];
  constructor(private stockService: StockService,
              public messageService: MessageService) {
    this.stock =  new Stock('', '', 0, 0, 'NASDAQ');
    this.messageService.message = 'Component Level: Hello Message Service';          ❷

  }

  setStockPrice(price) {
    this.stock.price = price;
    this.stock.previousPrice = price;
  }

  createStock(stockForm) {
    /* Code as before, no change */
    /* Omitted for brevity */
  }
}
```

❶ Adding providers declaration for MessageService

❷ Adding an initial value to the MessageService in the component

We've made one addition to the @Component decorator for the CreateStockCompo
nent class. We have added a providers declaration, and provided the MessageSer
vice at the component level. We also added an initial value to the MessageService in
the constructor. We will not make any other changes. We will also leave the Message
Service declared in the providers section of the main module.

Before we talk about what happens as a result of this, it is worth executing the application and seeing it yourself. Execute and note the following:

1. See the message in the AppComponent, which is the default we had set.

2. See the message in the CreateStockComponent, which will be the value we set in
   the component in the constructor "Component Level: Hello Message Ser
   vice".

3. Now fill up the form and create a stock.

---

4. Note that the message is updated only in the `CreateStockComponent`, but the `App Component` message does not change.

When you do all of this, you should see something like Figure 8-2.

Figure 8-2. Angular application with services defined at component level

This is Angular's hierarchical dependency injection at play. As mentioned before, Angular supports multiple dependency injectors within the same application. There is the root injector at the root `AppModule` level, which is where most services you create will be registered and made available. This makes the instance available across your entire application, and this was happening initially.

Then, when we made the change to add the `providers` at the `CreateStockComponent` level, we brought the injector at the component level into play. Angular will create a chain of injectors all the way down, depending on the need and declarations. And all child components will inherit that injector, which will take precedence over the root injector. When we registered our `MessageService` provider at the `CreateStockCompo nent` level, it created a child injector at that level, with its own instance of the `Message Service`. What we injected into the `CreateStockComponent` is in fact this new instance, which has nothing to do with the original root-level `MessageService`. So we, in fact, have two separate instances of `MessageService` with nothing in common.

Just like an Angular application is a tree of components, there is a parallel tree of injectors at play. For most components, these injectors might just be a reference or a proxy to the parent injector. But they may not, as we have just seen.

Whenever a component asks for a dependency, Angular will check the closest injector in the tree to see whether it can satisfy it. If it can (like in `CreateStockComponent`), it will provide it. If not, it will check with the parent injector, all the way to the root injector.

Now when will or can you use this? Usually, it won't even matter and you will just register all your services at the root level. But there might be cases when you want to use this capability of the Angular injector, such as:

- You want to scope services to only certain components and modules, to ensure that a change in the service doesn't impact the entire application.
- You might want different instances of a service in different components. This might be common where you might want to override things, or have different services for different instances, and the like.
- You want to override a particular service with a more specific implementation for a section of your application. Maybe you want a cached version of your service for a certain section as opposed to the general pass-through implementation.

There is more detail in how we can instantiate a service and the various ways we can provide them. You can read up on all the details and ways in the official Angular docs (*https://angular.io/guide/dependency-injection#providers*).

The completed version of this code is available in *chapter8/di-example* in the GitHub repository.

RxJS and Observables: Moving to Asynchronous Operations

The last change we will make before we conclude this particular chapter on services is to work with asynchronous code. The data that we returned from our service in our example was hardcoded, mock data. We returned it as is, and displayed it immediately. But in a real-world application, that would not be the case, as most of the times we would be fetching the data from a server.

Handling responses and data from a server becomes slightly different from what we have done. We might make a call to fetch the list of stocks from the server. And then at some later point in time, after our server finishes processing the request, we would be provided with a list of stocks. Thus, the stocks would not be available immediately on demand, but at a later point in time, asynchronously.

In AngularJS, we used to handle these situations using promises. Promises were a better way to handle asynchronous behavior than callbacks, which was the traditional way, for multiple reasons (*https://developer.mozilla.org/en-US/docs/Web/JavaScript/ Guide/Using_promises*). That said, there are a few drawbacks that Angular tries to do away with, by switching to using *observables*.

Observables are a ReactiveX (*http://reactivex.io/intro.html*) concept that allows us to deal with streams which emit data. Any interested party can then be an observer on this stream, and perform operations and transformations on the events emitted by the stream.

There are a few differences between observables and promises, primarily:

- Promises operate on a single asynchronous event, while observables allow us to deal with a stream of zero or more asynchronous events.

- Unlike promises, observables can be canceled. That is, a promise's success or error handler will eventually be called, while we can cancel a subscription and not process data if we don't care about it.

- Observables allow us to compose and create a chain of transformations easily. The operators it provides out of the box allow for some strong and powerful compositions, and operations like retry and replay make handling some common use cases trivial. All of this while being able to reuse our subscription code.

That said, promises are good for single event cases, and are still an option when you work with Angular. An observable can be converted into a promise and then handled in Angular. But it is recommended to use observables, as Angular provides a lot of out-of-the-box support for RxJS and its extensions within its framework.

Learning RxJS and Observables

We will touch upon the bare minimum of observables and RxJS features in this book, but this book itself is not intended to be a way to learn RxJS and reactive programming in general. There are excellent tutorials and books available, starting with the official documentation for ReactiveX (*http://reactivex.io/intro.html*).

Let's now take our example and move it step by step to using observables and make it ready for our future use cases. You can use the base codebase from *chapter8/simple-service* if you have not been coding along.

First, we will modify our `StockService` to start returning an asynchronous observable to get us ready for the future when we start integrating with servers. Then we will modify our components to subscribe to these observables and deal with success and error cases.

Let's change the *src/app/services/stock.service.ts* file as follows:

```
import { Injectable } from '@angular/core';

import { Observable } from 'rxjs/Observable';                        ❶
import { _throw as ObservableThrow } from 'rxjs/observable/throw';    ❷
import { of as ObservableOf } from 'rxjs/observable/of';
import { Stock } from 'app/model/stock';

@Injectable()
export class StockService {

  private stocks: Stock[];
  constructor() {
    this.stocks = [
      new Stock('Test Stock Company', 'TSC', 85, 80, 'NASDAQ'),
      new Stock('Second Stock Company', 'SSC', 10, 20, 'NSE'),
      new Stock('Last Stock Company', 'LSC', 876, 765, 'NYSE')
    ];
  }

  getStocks() : Observable<Stock[]> {                                 ❸
    return ObservableOf(this.stocks);                                 ❹
  }

  createStock(stock: Stock): Observable<any> {
    let foundStock = this.stocks.find(each => each.code === stock.code);
    if (foundStock) {
      return ObservableThrow({msg: 'Stock with code ' +              ❺
          stock.code + ' already exists'});
    }
    this.stocks.push(stock);
    return ObservableOf({msg: 'Stock with code ' + stock.code +
        ' successfully created'});;
```

```
    }

    toggleFavorite(stock: Stock): Observable<Stock> {
      let foundStock = this.stocks.find(each => each.code === stock.code);
      foundStock.favorite = !foundStock.favorite;
      return ObservableOf(foundStock);
    }
}
```

❶ Importing `Observable`

❷ Import core methods from the Observable API, like `throw` and `of`

❸ Changing the return type of `getStocks` to an observable

❹ Returning an observable for mock data

❺ Throwing an exception to the observer

We completely overhauled the `StockService`, so let's walk through the major changes one by one so we understand what changed and more importantly, why:

- The first thing we do is import `Observable` from the RxJS library. Note that we import operators and classes individually from the respective files, rather than import the entire RxJS library.

- We then make sure to import and add the operators we are planning to use from RxJS to ensure we have them available in our application. In this case, we are simply planning to use the `of` and `throw` operators on the core `Observable` class.

- We then change the return type of each of the methods in the service to return an observable instead of a synchronous value. This is to ensure a consistent API interface to the user of the service. Once we make this change, we can change the implementation underneath (say, changing from mock data to making a server call) without having to change each and every component.

- For the time being, we convert our return value to an observable by using the `Observable.of` operator. The `of` takes a value and returns an observable of that type which is triggered only once.

- In the `createStock` method, we also change the functionality to throw an exception on the observable if the stock already exists.

Instead of importing each class and operator from RxJS manually, we also have the option to import the entire RxJS library and access the classes and operators through it, like so:

```
import { Rx } from 'rxjs/Rx';
```

We would then be able to access `Rx.Observable` and so on. But this comes with a downside, which is that Angular won't be able to optimize your build, as it would not be able to understand which parts of RxJS are being used at the time of compilation. RxJS as a library is large, and most applications would only end up using bits and pieces of it.

Thus I would always recommend using individual imports as a general practice.

Now let's change the components to integrate with the new asynchronous APIs in the service. First, we will change the `StockListComponent`, to read the list of stocks from the observable instead of reading the array directly. We will change the *src/app/stock/ stock-list/stock-list.component.ts* file as follows:

```
/** Imports skipped for brevity **/
export class StockListComponent implements OnInit {

  public stocks: Stock[];
  constructor(private stockService: StockService) { }

  ngOnInit() {
    this.stockService.getStocks()
        .subscribe(stocks => {
          this.stocks = stocks;
    });
  }

  onToggleFavorite(stock: Stock) {
    this.stockService.toggleFavorite(stock);
  }
}
```

We have made one small change, which is to the `ngOnInit` block of the component. Instead of directly assigning the return value of the `stockService.getStocks()` call to the `stocks` array, we now instead subscribe to the observable that it returns. The observable gets triggered with the array of stocks once, at which point we assign the value to our local array. There is no change as such to the `onToggleFavorite`, though we should also subscribe to the observable it returns for proper handling.

Let's also change the `CreateStockComponent` and see how the *src/app/stock/create-stock/create-stock.component.ts* file changes:

```
/** Imports skipped for brevity **/
export class CreateStockComponent {

  /** No changes, skipping for brevity **/

  createStock(stockForm) {
    if (stockForm.valid) {
      this.stockService.createStock(this.stock)
          .subscribe((result: any) => {        ❶
            this.message = result.msg;
            this.stock =  new Stock('', '', 0, 0, 'NASDAQ');
          }, (err) => {
            this.message = err.msg;
          });
    } else {
      console.error('Stock form is in an invalid state');
    }
  }
}
```

❶ Subscribing to the observable

Again, most of our changes are focused on one method, the createStock. Instead of handling all the work immediately after triggering the stockService.create Stock(), we now subscribe to the observable. In the previous case, we just handled the success case, but the subscribe method allows us to take two functions as arguments. The first argument is called in the case of a successful call, while the second is the error handler callback.

Both of our flows return an object with a msg key, so we handle it accordingly and update the message with the value returned.

At this point, we can now run our application to see it working. When you run it, you shouldn't see any difference in the functionality, but all our stocks should be visible and you should be able to add stocks.

Let's alter our code one final time to make it simpler and easier to read. In a lot of cases, we simply want to make a call to our server, and display the return value in our UI. We don't need to process the data, make any transformations, or anything else. In those cases, Angular gives us a slight shortcut that we can use.

We'll change the *src/app/stock/stock-list/stock-list.component.ts* file first:

```
/** Imports skipped for brevity **/
export class StockListComponent implements OnInit {

  public stocks$: Observable<Stock[]>;        ❶
  constructor(private stockService: StockService) { }

  ngOnInit() {
```

```
    this.stocks$ = this.stockService.getStocks();      ❷
  }

  onToggleFavorite(stock: Stock) {
    this.stockService.toggleFavorite(stock);
  }
}
```

❶ Storing the observable as a member variable

❷ Calling and directly storing the observable

We have made two changes to our `StockListComponent` class:

- Instead of having an array of `stocks` as a member variable, we now have an `Observable<Stock[]>` as the member. That is, we are saving the observable that the API returns directly, instead of its underlying return value.

- In `ngOnInit`, we simply save the observable returned by our `stockService.get Stocks()` call.

Given this, how do we display our array of stocks in the template? How do we handle this asynchronous behavior? Let's look at what we can do in the template to take care of this:

```
<app-stock-item *ngFor="let stock of stocks$ | async"
                [stock]="stock"
                (toggleFavorite)="onToggleFavorite($event)">
</app-stock-item>
```

We have made one tweak here, which is to use a `Pipe` in the `ngFor` expression. Angular provides a pipe called `async`, which allows us to bind to `Observable`. Angular would then be responsible for waiting for events to be emitted on the observable and displaying the resultant value directly. It saves us that one step of having to manually subscribe to the observable.

Again, this is useful in only a few situations where the data returned by an API call is something we can directly display. But it does save a few lines of code, leaving it to the framework to handle most of the boilerplate. Run your application to make sure that this still works, and you should see the same application running without any issues.

The completed version of this code is available in *chapter8/observables* in the GitHub repository.

Conclusion

In this chapter, we started understanding Angular services in more detail. We covered what Angular services are and some common uses for them, primarily:

- Abstraction of the data fetching aspects
- Encapsulation of shared application logic
- Sharing of data across components

We also discussed Angular's dependency injection system and how its hierarchical dependency injection works with an example. Finally, we looked at how `Observable` works and how to integrate very simple observables into our application.

In the next chapter, we will dig into how to work with and make HTTP calls and deal with their responses. We will also cover some common use cases that we have when working with servers and how to build solutions for them.

Exercise

Take the finished exercise from Chapter 6 (available in *chapter6/exercise/ecommerce*). Try to accomplish the following:

1. Create a common service backing the `ProductListComponent` and the `CreatePro ductComponent` called `ProductService`.

2. Make the components simple and move any logic into the service. Register the service correctly at the module level (either using the CLI or manually).

3. Start from the beginning with observables and make all the components deal with asynchronous APIs.

4. Use the `async` pipe where possible instead of manually subscribing to the results.

All of this can be accomplished using concepts covered in this chapter. You can check out the finished solution in *chapter8/exercise/ecommerce*.

CHAPTER 9

Making HTTP Calls in Angular

In the previous chapter, we started our groundwork on Angular services. In particular, we took a look at what Angular services are and when to use them. We then dealt with creating Angular services and using them in our application, followed by a very cursory glance at dealing with asynchronous behavior in Angular using observables.

In this chapter, we will build on that base and start using the built-in Angular modules and services to make and parse HTTP calls to a server. We will use that to explore common paradigms, the API options, and how to chain and really use the power of observables in our application.

Introducing HttpClient

In this section, we will start using Angular's HttpClient to make GET and POST calls to a server. Through this, we will see how to set up our application so that we can make the calls, walk through the process of actually making the calls and dealing with the response, and then go into the API signature and all the various options that we have to tweak it to our needs.

As for the server, we won't be spending any time building it out, but rather using a prebuilt server for this application. It is a Node.js server, and available in the repository in case you are interested in digging deeper into it, but it is not required to understand this part of the book.

HttpClient Versus Http

If you happened upon some older tutorials and examples, you might encounter a slightly different way of making HTTP calls, by directly importing from *@angular/http* and then making calls. This was the old way of working with HTTP in Angular, before `HttpClient` was introduced in Angular version 4.3. In version 5 of Angular, the old `http` service was deprecated in favor of `HttpClient`, so just use the method described in this chapter in your applications.

We will continue building on our application, and try to move it over to communicate with a real server instead of our mock data that it was working with so far. In particular, in this section, we will switch over all three service calls (getting a list of stocks, creating a stock, and toggling the favorite on a stock level) to server calls using HTTP GET/POST. By the end of this section, we should not be operating with any mock data on our client side.

Server Setup

As mentioned, the server we will be working with is already developed and available in the repository in the *chapter9/server* folder. Before we start any web development, let's get our server up and running.

Checkout and browse to the *chapter9/server* folder in the GitHub repository (*https://github.com/shyamseshadri/angular-up-and-running*). From within the folder, execute the following commands in your terminal :

```
npm i
node index.js
```

This installs all the necessary dependencies for our Node.js server, and then starts the server on port 3000. Keep this server running in the background; don't kill it. This will be what our application hits to fetch and save stocks.

Note that this is a very simplistic server with an in-memory data store. Anything you create or save will be reset if you restart the server.

Using HttpClientModule

In case you are not coding along, you can get the base code from the *chapter8/observables* folder in the GitHub repository.

Now let's get to our web application, and see step by step how to convert our local web application to talk to a server and fetch its data. While doing this, we will also see how easy this switch is, since we are already using observables in our code.

The very first thing we will do is add a dependency on `HttpClientModule` in our App Module. Let's modify the *src/app/app.module.ts* file as follows:

```
import { BrowserModule } from '@angular/platform-browser';
import { NgModule } from '@angular/core';
import { FormsModule } from '@angular/forms';
import { HttpClientModule } from '@angular/common/http';        ❶

import { AppComponent } from './app.component';
import { StockItemComponent } from './stock/stock-item/stock-item.component';
import { CreateStockComponent } from './stock/create-stock/create-stock.component';
import { StockListComponent }
    from './stock/stock-list/stock-list.component';
import { StockService } from 'app/services/stock.service';

@NgModule({
  declarations: [
    AppComponent,
    StockItemComponent,
    CreateStockComponent,
    StockListComponent
  ],
  imports: [
    BrowserModule,
    FormsModule,
    HttpClientModule                                            ❷
  ],
  providers: [
    StockService,
  ],
  bootstrap: [AppComponent]
})
export class AppModule { }
```

❶ Import the `HttpClientModule` instead of `HttpModule`

❷ Add `HttpClientModule` to the `imports` array

Making HTTP GET/POST Calls

Next, we will change the implementation of our `StockService` to actually make an HTTP service call instead of just returning an observable of mock data. To do this, we get the `HttpClient` service injected into the constructor (thanks, Angular dependency injection!), and then use it to make our calls. Let's see how we can modify the *src/app/services/stock.service.ts* file:

```
import { Injectable } from '@angular/core';
import { HttpClient } from '@angular/common/http';

import { Observable } from 'rxjs/Observable';

import { Stock } from 'app/model/stock';

@Injectable()
export class StockService {

  constructor(private http: HttpClient) {}

  getStocks() : Observable<Stock[]> {
    return this.http.get<Stock[]>('/api/stock');
  }

  createStock(stock: Stock): Observable<any> {
    return this.http.post('/api/stock', stock);
  }

  toggleFavorite(stock: Stock): Observable<Stock> {
    return this.http.patch<Stock>('/api/stock/' + stock.code,
      {
        favorite: !stock.favorite
      });
  }
}
```

Our server exposes three APIs:

- GET on */api/stock* to get a list of stocks
- POST on */api/stock* with the new stock as a body to create a stock on the server
- PATCH on */api/stock/:code* with the stock code in the URL and the new favorite status in the body of the request, to change the state of favorite for the particular stock.

Our `StockService` mirrors this API, with each of the three methods making the respective call. The `HttpClient` APIs directly mirror the HTTP methods, as we can call `httpClient.get`, `httpClient.post`, and `httpClient.patch` directly. Each of them take the URL as the first argument, and a request body as the second (if the method supports it).

One important thing to note is that the `HttpClient` can give you type-assurance across your code. We leverage this feature in the `getStocks()` and the `toggleFavorite()` methods.

One effect of this is that we need to change our *stock.ts* from a TypeScript class to a TypeScript interface. Why is this? While we don't need to, Angular does a simple typecast of the response body into the type we have defined. But TypeScript (and ECMAScript underneath it) has no nice and easy way to convert a simple plain-old JavaScript object into a prototypical JavaScript/TypeScript class object. This means that while our response from `StockService` will have all the properties of the class `Stock`, it would not have the functions (in particular, `isPositiveChange()`) available.

We could write a converter, but it is only worth it in very specific cases. It is easier to simply leverage TypeScript for type safety and work with other ways of encapsulation (either at a component level, or maybe as an Angular service).

For these reasons, let's switch our `Stock` class to an interface, by editing *src/app/model/stock.ts* as follows:

```typescript
export interface Stock {
  name: string;
  code: string;
  price: number;
  previousPrice: number;
  exchange: string;
  favorite: boolean;
}
```

We have simply converted it to an interface, and defined all the properties on it. No more constructor, no more built-in functions. With that groundwork done, let's now move to changing the components over to using the service correctly. We will first start with `StockListComponent`, which has minimal changes. All we will do is remove the toggling of favorites functionality away from this component, and let each individual stock component handle it. Let's see the changes to *src/app/stock/stock-list/stock-list.component.ts*:

```typescript
import { Component, OnInit } from '@angular/core';
import { StockService } from 'app/services/stock.service';
import { Stock } from 'app/model/stock';
import { Observable } from 'rxjs/Observable';

@Component({
  selector: 'app-stock-list',
  templateUrl: './stock-list.component.html',
  styleUrls: ['./stock-list.component.css']
})
export class StockListComponent implements OnInit {

  public stocks$: Observable<Stock[]>;
  constructor(private stockService: StockService) { }

  ngOnInit() {
    this.stocks$ = this.stockService.getStocks();
  }
}
```

Our StockListComponent becomes simplified with this change. We also have to make a slight tweak to its template, to remove the toggleFavorite event binding. Change *src/app/stock/stock-list/stock-list.component.html* as follows:

```
<app-stock-item *ngFor="let stock of stocks$ | async"
                [stock]="stock">
</app-stock-item>
```

Next, let's move on to the StockItemComponent. We will move the toggleFavorite logic into the component here, and ask each individual stock to make the respective server call through StockService.toggleFavorite directly, and handle the response. We will remove the EventEmitter while we are at it. The finished *src/app/stock/stock-item/stock-item.component.ts* file should look like this:

```
import { Component, OnInit, Input } from '@angular/core';

import { Stock } from '../../model/stock';
import { StockService } from 'app/services/stock.service';

@Component({
  selector: 'app-stock-item',
  templateUrl: './stock-item.component.html',
  styleUrls: ['./stock-item.component.css']
})
export class StockItemComponent {

  @Input() public stock: Stock;                    ❶

  constructor(private stockService: StockService) {}    ❷

  onToggleFavorite(event) {                         ❸
    this.stockService.toggleFavorite(this.stock)
      .subscribe((stock) => this.stock.favorite = !this.stock.favorite);
  }
}
```

❶ Only have input, remove the output binding

❷ Inject StockService into the constructor

❸ Change onToggleFavorite to call the service instead

Note that we are taking responsibility for toggling the local state of favorite on the stock on successful toggle favorite call. Without it, it would change the state on the server, but the local browser state would not be changed. We could also have chosen to refresh the entire list of stocks on every toggle favorite, by keeping the EventEmitter and asking the parent StockListComponent to refetch the list of stocks every time. That is a call we can make as we develop our applications, depending on our needs. There will be times when we want the latest and greatest information from the server, and times when handling changes locally is acceptable.

There is also a change in our template for the StockItemComponent, as we no longer have access to the isPositiveChange() function on the stock. We instead directly calculate whether it is positive or not using the underlying properties in our template. Our changed *src/app/stock/stock-item/stock-item.component.html* should look as follows:

```
<div class="stock-container">
  <div class="name">{{stock.name + ' (' + stock.code + ')'}}</div>
  <div class="exchange">{{stock.exchange}}</div>
  <div class="price"
      [class.positive]="stock.price > stock.previousPrice"        ❶
      [class.negative]="stock.price <= stock.previousPrice">      ❷
      $ {{stock.price}}
  </div>
  <button (click)="onToggleFavorite($event)"
          *ngIf="!stock.favorite">Add to Favorite</button>
  <button (click)="onToggleFavorite($event)"
          *ngIf="stock.favorite">Remove from Favorite</button>
</div>
```

❶ Add positive class binding based on stock price

❷ Add negative class binding based on stock price

Now, we will move to the last component, the CreateStockComponent. We only have to accommodate the change over from the class to the interface, which means we don't have a nice constructor for a Stock object. While we are it, we will refactor the class for reuse. But there is no change required with respect to HttpClient, since we abstracted out the logic and used observables from the beginning. The finished *src/app/stock/create-stock/create-stock.component.ts* file should look like this:

```
import { Component, OnInit } from '@angular/core';
import { Stock } from 'app/model/stock';
import { StockService } from 'app/services/stock.service';

@Component({
  selector: 'app-create-stock',
  templateUrl: './create-stock.component.html',
  styleUrls: ['./create-stock.component.css']
})
export class CreateStockComponent {

  public stock: Stock;
  public confirmed = false;
  public message = null;
  public exchanges = ['NYSE', 'NASDAQ', 'OTHER'];
  constructor(private stockService: StockService) {
```

```
      this.initializeStock();                   ❶
    }

    initializeStock() {                          ❷
      this.stock = {
        name: '',
        code: '',
        price: 0,
        previousPrice: 0,
        exchange: 'NASDAQ',
        favorite: false
      };
    }

    setStockPrice(price) {
      this.stock.price = price;
      this.stock.previousPrice = price;
    }

    createStock(stockForm) {
      if (stockForm.valid) {
        this.stockService.createStock(this.stock)
            .subscribe((result: any) => {
              this.message = result.msg;
              this.initializeStock();             ❸
            }, (err) => {
              this.message = err.error.msg;
            });
      } else {
        console.error('Stock form is in an invalid state');
      }
    }
  }
```

❶ Call `initializeStock` to create a stock instance

❷ Define `initializeStock` method for reuse

❸ Use `initializeStock` after stock is successfully created

We just pulled out an `initializeStock` function, which we call both from the constructor as well as after the stock is successfully created. The only other change we did in this class is how we handled the error. With `HttpResponse` for errors, the response body is actually available in the `error` key inside the response, so we grab the `msg` key from there instead. There are no other changes we need to do in this class. The template also remains as is.

We are now almost ready to run our application, but we have one final change we need to make. The browser, for security reasons, does not allow you to make calls across domains and origins. Thus, even while both our server and the Angular application are running on localhost, they are running on different ports, and thus the browser treats them as different origins. To get around this, the Angular CLI allows us to set up a proxy, so that our requests would be sent to the server, which would then proxy it to our final endpoint.

To do this, we will create a file *proxy.conf.json* in the main folder of our Angular application, with the following contents:

```
{
  "/api": {
    "target": "http://localhost:3000",
    "secure": false
  }
}
```

What we have done is simply asked Angular to proxy all requests made to the server with the path starting with */api* to our Node.js server running on port 3000 locally. Technically, this filename can be anything, but we are just following a certain pattern. This file supports a lot more configuration, but we will not get into it in this book. You can read up on it in the official Angular CLI docs (*https://github.com/angular/angular-cli/blob/master/docs/documentation/stories/proxy.md*).

Now we are finally ready to run our application. So far, we have been running the application using `ng serve`. Now, we need to run it with the following command:

```
ng serve --proxy-config proxy.conf.json
```

This will let Angular run our application, but taking our proxy configuration into account. Now, when you browse to our application (*http://localhost:4200*), you should see the list of stocks coming from the server. Note that if you create a new stock, you will see a message saying it has been added successfully, but you will have to manually refresh the page to see it updated in the UI. Toggling the stock should also work, and this should be persisted even after you refresh the page. The application should look exactly the same as it has been looking so far, as we have not made any UI-specific changes.

The finished code sample for this section is available in the GitHub repository in the *chapter9/simple-http* folder.

Advanced HTTP

In the previous section, we started with the basics of Angular's `HttpClient` and learned how to make simple HTTP GET and POST calls to our server, and deal with its response. In this section, we will dig a little bit deeper into our HTTP API, and other features that are supported by Angular's HTTP module.

Options—Headers/Params

First, let's take a closer look at the HTTP API we invoke. So far, we passed it a URL, along with a body for the request if necessary. The HTTP API also allows us to pass an `options` object as the second (or third in case the API allows for a body like POST and PATCH) argument to the function. Again, let's modify our existing application to see these options, and add in some common requirements as well. We will use the codebase from the previous section, which can be obtained from the *chapter9/simple-http* folder in case you are not coding along, as a base.

First, one of the common tasks that any developer has with an HTTP API is to send additional query parameters, or certain HTTP headers along with the request. Let's see how we can accomplish this using the `HttpClient`. We will change the *src/app/services/stock.service.ts* file as follows:

```
import { Injectable } from '@angular/core';
import { HttpClient, HttpHeaders } from '@angular/common/http';

import { Observable } from 'rxjs/Observable';

import { Stock } from 'app/model/stock';

@Injectable()
export class StockService {

  constructor(private http: HttpClient) {}

  getStocks() : Observable<Stock[]> {
    return this.http.get<Stock[]>('/api/stock', {
      headers: new HttpHeaders()                              ❶
          .set('Authorization', 'MyAuthorizationHeaderValue')
          .set('X-EXAMPLE-HEADER', 'TestValue'),
      params: {                                               ❷
        q: 'test',
        test: 'value'
      }
    });
  }

  /** Unchanged after this, omitted for brevity */
}
```

❶ Add HTTP headers to the outgoing call

❷ Add query params `q` and `test` to the outgoing call

In the preceding code, we have made two changes. We have added a second argument to the `http.get` call, which is an options object. There are certain keys we can pass to it, to configure the outgoing HTTP request. In the code, we have added two options:

headers

We can set the outgoing/request HTTP headers. There are two ways we can set both the headers as well as the parameters. One option, as we have done in the code, is to pass an `HttpHeaders` object, which is a typed class instance, on which we can call `set` to set the correct headers. It follows a builder pattern, so you can chain multiple headers as we have done. The second option is to just pass it a plain-old JavaScript object. Of course, for the values, we have hardcoded it here, but you can just as well access it from some variable, or even some other service (in case you need to get authorization headers from, say, an `AuthService`).

params

Just like the headers, HTTP query parameters can also be configured in two ways: using the typed, built-in `HttpParams` class, or using a plain-old JavaScript object.

Now, when we run this code (making sure that the Node.js server is also running in parallel), open your network inspector to see the outgoing requests. You should see something like Figure 9-1.

Figure 9-1. Sending query params and headers with an Angular HTTP request

The finished code is available in the *chapter9/http-api* folder.

Options—Observe/Response Type

We will next move on to two other options on the HTTP request, which give you flexibility in a variety of use cases. The first one we will focus on is the observe property on the options parameter.

The observe parameter takes one of three values:

body

> This is the default value, which ensures that the observable's subscribe gets called with the body of the response. This body is auto-casted to the return type specified when calling the API. This is what we have been using so far.

response

> This changes the response type of the HTTP APIs from returning the entire HttpResponse instead of just the body. The response still holds a typed response, so you can still access it underneath, but you also get access to the headers of the response and the status code. Note that instead of a raw HttpResponse, what you really get is an HttpResponse<T>, where T is the type of the body. So in the case of getStocks, what you would end up returning is actually an observable of HttpResponse<Stock[]>.

events

> This is similar to response, but gets triggered on all HttpEvents. This would include the initialization event, as well as the request finished event. These correspond to the XMLHttpRequest states. This is more useful when we have an API that sends progress events, as we can catch and listen to progress events as well with the observe parameter set to events.

The second parameter that we will explore is the responseType property on the options parameter. This can take one of four values:

json

> This is the default, which basically ensures that the response body is parsed and treated as a JSON object. In most cases, you wouldn't need to change this from the default.

text

> This allows you to treat the response body as a string, without parsing it at all. In this case, the response from your HTTP request would be an Observable<string> instead of a typed response.

blob

> Both this and the next option are more useful when dealing with binary responses that you need to handle in your application. blob gives you a file-like object containing the raw immutable data, which you can then process as you see fit.

arraybuffer

> The last option gives us the underlying raw binary data directly.

Let's take a look at some of these in action. We will change the StockService temporarily to try the same API with a few of these values set as options. Change the *src/app/services/stock.service.ts* file as follows:

```
/** No Change in Imports */

@Injectable()
export class StockService {

  constructor(private http: HttpClient) {}

  getStocks() : Observable<Stock[]> {
    return this.http.get<Stock[]>('/api/stock', {
      headers: new HttpHeaders()
          .set('Authorization', 'MyAuthorizationHeaderValue')
          .set('X-EXAMPLE-HEADER', 'TestValue'),
      params: {
        q: 'test',
        test: 'value'
      },
      observe: 'body'                    ❶
    });
  }

  getStocksAsResponse(): Observable<HttpResponse<Stock[]>> {
    return this.http.get<Stock[]>('/api/stock', {
      observe: 'response'                ❷
    });
  }

  getStocksAsEvents(): Observable<HttpEvent<any>> {
    return this.http.get('/api/stock', {
      observe: 'events'                  ❸
    });
  }

  getStocksAsString(): Observable<string> {
    return this.http.get('/api/stock', {
      responseType: 'text'               ❹
    });
  }

  getStocksAsBlob(): Observable<Blob> {
```

```
        return this.http.get('/api/stock', {
          responseType: 'blob'                ❺
        });
    }

    /** Remaining code unchanged, omitted for brevity */
}
```

❶ Observe response body only

❷ Observe entire response

❸ Observe all events

❹ Response to be treated as text

❺ Response to be treated as blob

We have added four new methods to the `StockService` as follows:

- `getStocksAsResponse` makes the same HTTP call, but sets the `observe` value to `response`. This also changes the response of the function to return an `Observable<HttpResponse<Stock[]>>`.

- `getStocksAsEvents` makes the same HTTP call, but sets the `observe` value to `events`. This also changes the response of the function to return an `Observable<HttpEvent<any>>`. This is because we will get multiple instances of `Http Event` that are not just the response, but also progress, initialization, etc. Thus the format of the response is not defined.

- `getStocksAsString` makes the same HTTP call, but sets the `responseType` value to `text`. We also change the response type of the function to return an `Observable<string>`, and the string is the entire body as a string.

- `getStocksAsBlob` makes the same HTTP call, but sets the `responseType` value to `blob`. We also change the response type of the function to return an `Observable<Blob>` to allow the subscriber to work with the blob once we get a response from the server.

Now, let's hook this up in the component so that we see the effect of calling each of these slightly different APIs. We will modify the `StockListComponent` to make calls to each of these APIs so that we can see and compare them side by side. Modify the *src/app/stock/stock-list/stock-list.component.ts* file as follows:

```
import { Component, OnInit } from '@angular/core';
import { StockService } from 'app/services/stock.service';
import { Stock } from 'app/model/stock';
import { Observable } from 'rxjs/Observable';
```

```
@Component({
  selector: 'app-stock-list',
  templateUrl: './stock-list.component.html',
  styleUrls: ['./stock-list.component.css']
})
export class StockListComponent implements OnInit {

  public stocks$: Observable<Stock[]>;
  constructor(private stockService: StockService) { }

  ngOnInit() {
    this.stocks$ = this.stockService.getStocks();
    this.stockService.getStocksAsResponse()
        .subscribe((response) => {
          console.log('OBSERVE "response" RESPONSE is ', response);
        });

    this.stockService.getStocksAsEvents()
        .subscribe((response) => {
          console.log('OBSERVE "events" RESPONSE is ', response);
        });

    this.stockService.getStocksAsString()
        .subscribe((response) => {
          console.log('Response Type "text" RESPONSE is ', response);
        });

    this.stockService.getStocksAsBlob()
        .subscribe((response) => {
          console.log('Response Type "blob" RESPONSE is ', response);
        });
  }
}
```

In the `StockListComponent`, we leave the original call untouched, and simply add calls to each of the other functions we added in the service below it. For each, we simply subscribe to the response, and then print it (with a respective log so that we can identify them separately). Now, when you run it, make sure you have your browser developer tools open so that you can see the logs it prints. You should see something like Figure 9-2.

Figure 9-2. Different kind of response types in Angular

There are a few interesting things to note in the example we ran:

- For the `getStocksAsEvents()` call, our subscription is actually called twice, once for the initialization/request being sent and once when the actual information has been loaded with the response. The second event is the one that has the actual data. If our API supported progress, then the subscription would get called for progress events as well.

- The `getStocksAsResponse()` call is similar to our initial `getStocks()` call, except it gives the body along with other HTTP request fields like status, headers, etc.

- The `getStocksAsString()` call is similar to our original call, but instead of getting a typed JSON response, we get our entire JSON response as a string. As mentioned before, this is more useful for working with non-JSON APIs.

- The final `getStocksAsBlob()` call returns a blob containing our data that we can then work with. This is more useful for working with binary data and the like, rather than JSON APIs.

For the most part, you wlll only need the default setting of observing the body and using the json response type. These other options exist for that 5% of use cases where the default is not enough, and you need access to something more. The new HttpClient gives you that flexibility to work with your APIs the way you want to, while making it easy for the most common use cases.

The finished code sample for this section is available in the GitHub repository in the *chapter9/http-api* folder.

Interceptors

One other common use case is to be able to hook into all incoming and outgoing requests to be able to either modify them in flight, or listen in on all responses to accomplish things like logging, handling authentication failures in a common manner, etc.

With the HttpClient API, Angular allows easily defining interceptors, which can conceptually sit between the HttpClient and the server, allowing it to transform all outgoing requests, and listen in and transform if necessary all incoming responses before passing them on. Let's see how we might create a very simple interceptor in Angular that allows us to:

- Modify all outgoing requests by adding a header if we have an authorization token.
- Log all incoming responses before passing them along.
- In case the request ends up in a failure (a non-200 or non-300 response), we will log it differently.

We will fetch the authorization token from another service, which we will create just for the purpose of storing and returning our authorization information. To complete this example, we will build on our codebase from the first section. So if you want, you can obtain the base code from the *chapter9/simple-http* folder. Note that we are not using the additions we did while we were exploring the HTTP API.

We will first add a very simple service that acts as a holder of authorization-related information. We can add it simply by running this from the terminal:

```
ng generate service services/auth --module=app
```

This will create an AuthService for you, and also hook up the provider in the AppMod ule. We will just make a small change to the generated service to hold a property that we can use in our interceptor. The changed service in *src/app/services/auth.service.ts* should look like the following:

```
import { Injectable } from '@angular/core';

@Injectable()
export class AuthService {

  public authToken: string;

  constructor() { }
}
```

We have added a public property on the class called `authToken` in the `AuthService`. Because we generated the service using the Angular CLI, it automatically added the provider in the `AppModule`. Otherwise, we would have had to do it ourselves. We will add one more HTTP API call in the `StockService` to an API that always returns a 403. Make the change so that the *src/app/services/stock.service.ts* file looks like this:

```
import { Injectable } from '@angular/core';
import { HttpClient } from '@angular/common/http';

import { Observable } from 'rxjs/Observable';

import { Stock } from 'app/model/stock';

@Injectable()
export class StockService {

  constructor(private http: HttpClient) {}

  /** No changes to other calls, omitting for brevity */

  makeFailingCall() {
    return this.http.get('/api/fail');
  }
}
```

We only added the last method, `makeFailingCall()`, to the `StockService`. The remaining code remains untouched. We will then change the `StockListComponent` to display a few extra buttons, which we will hook up to the `StockService` and the `Auth Service` that we have just created. First, change the *src/app/stock/stock-list/stock-list.component.ts* file as follows:

```
import { Component, OnInit } from '@angular/core';
import { StockService } from 'app/services/stock.service';
import { Stock } from 'app/model/stock';
import { Observable } from 'rxjs/Observable';
import { AuthService } from 'app/services/auth.service';

@Component({
  selector: 'app-stock-list',
  templateUrl: './stock-list.component.html',
  styleUrls: ['./stock-list.component.css']
```

```
})
export class StockListComponent implements OnInit {

  public stocks$: Observable<Stock[]>;
  constructor(private stockService: StockService,
              private authService: AuthService) { }

  ngOnInit() {
    this.fetchStocks();
  }

  fetchStocks() {
    this.stocks$ = this.stockService.getStocks();
  }

  setAuthToken() {
    this.authService.authToken = 'TESTING';
  }

  resetAuthToken() {
    this.authService.authToken = null;
  }

  makeFailingCall() {
    this.stockService.makeFailingCall().subscribe(
      (res) => console.log('Successfully made failing call', res),
      (err) => console.error('Error making failing call', err));
  }
}
```

We made a slight change to the initialization logic, and added a few new methods to the StockListComponent. First, we pulled out the stock$ Observable subscription to a new method called fetchStocks(), and just called it in the ngOnInit. Next, we have added a few more methods, namely setAuthToken(), resetAuthToken(), and make FailingCall(), all of which are trivial and basically call out to AuthService and StockService, respectively.

Next, we will hook these four new methods to buttons in the template for the Stock ListComponent. Let's change *src/app/stock/stock-list/stock-list.component.html* as follows:

```
<app-stock-item *ngFor="let stock of stocks$ | async"
                [stock]="stock">
</app-stock-item>

<div>
  <button type="button"
          (click)="fetchStocks()">
    Refetch Stocks
  </button>
  <button type="button"
```

```
            (click)="makeFailingCall()">
      Make Failing Call
    </button>
    <button type="button"
            (click)="setAuthToken()">
      Set Auth Token
    </button>
    <button type="button"
            (click)="resetAuthToken()">
      Reset Auth Token
    </button>
  </div>
```

We have added four new buttons to the template, with each one calling out to one of the new methods we just added.

So far, we have not added anything related to interceptors, but rather just set up our application to demonstrate various things related to the interceptors and how we might be able to use them in our application. Let's create our interceptor now. Sadly, the Angular CLI does not yet support generating the skeleton of the interceptor, so we will do it manually. Create a file at *src/app/services/stock-app.interceptor.ts* with the following content:

```
import {Injectable} from '@angular/core';
import {HttpEvent, HttpInterceptor, HttpResponse} from '@angular/common/http';
import {HttpHandler, HttpRequest, HttpErrorResponse} from '@angular/common/http'

import {Observable} from 'rxjs/Observable';

@Injectable()
export class StockAppInterceptor implements HttpInterceptor {     ❶

  constructor() {}

  intercept(req: HttpRequest<any>, next: HttpHandler):
      Observable<HttpEvent<any>> {     ❷
    console.log('Making a request to ', req.url);
    return next.handle(req);     ❸
  }
}
```

❶ Implement the HttpInterceptor interface

❷ Implement the intercept API

❸ Continue the chain by calling handle with the request

We have a mostly straightforward StockAppInterceptor class that implements the Angular HttpInterceptor interface. This interface provides one method, intercept, which we implement in the class. The `intercept` method is called with two arguments, the `HttpRequest` and an `HttpHandler`.

A good way to think of `HttpInterceptor` is that it is a chain. Each interceptor is called with the request, and it is up to the interceptor to decide whether it continues in the chain or not. Within this context, each interceptor can decide to modify the request as well. It can continue the chain by calling the handler provided to the `intercept` method with a request object. If there is only one interceptor, then the handler would simply call our backend with the request object. If there are more, it would proceed to the next interceptor in the chain.

Let's hook up this simple interceptor, which at this point simply logs all outgoing requests to the console, to the application. We do so in the `AppModule` (available in *src/app/app.module.ts*) as follows:

```
/** Skipping other standard imports for brevity **/
import { HttpClientModule, HTTP_INTERCEPTORS } from '@angular/common/http';
import { AuthService } from './services/auth.service';
import { StockAppInterceptor } from './services/stock-app.interceptor';

@NgModule({
  declarations: [
    /** Skipping for brevity **/
  ],
  imports: [
    /** Skipping for brevity **/
  ],
  providers: [
    StockService,
    AuthService,
    {
      provide: HTTP_INTERCEPTORS,
      useClass: StockAppInterceptor,
      multi: true,
    }
  ],
  bootstrap: [AppComponent]
})
export class AppModule { }
```

The major focus is on the last element in the `providers` section, which is how we provide the `HttpInterceptor`. Here, we are using the basic form of a provider, where we mention what we are providing (using the `provide` key), how to provide it (using the `useClass`, which points at our newly created `StockAppInterceptor`), and the fact that it is an array of interceptors (`multi: true` takes care of this). We can similarly add another entry for each interceptor we want.

Now we can run this application (using ng serve --proxy-config proxy.conf.json, after making sure our Node.js server is running). When you run this, open the console in your developer tools and you should see a log entry each time a server call is made. You can trigger more server calls by clicking the Refetch Stocks button.

Now, let's extend to make the interceptor nontrivial. Modify the *src/app/services/stock-app.interceptor.ts* file as follows:

```
import {Injectable} from '@angular/core';
import {HttpEvent, HttpInterceptor, HttpResponse} from '@angular/common/http';
import {HttpHandler, HttpRequest, HttpErrorResponse} from '@angular/common/http'

import {Observable} from 'rxjs/Observable';
import 'rxjs/add/operator/do';

import { AuthService } from './auth.service';

@Injectable()
export class StockAppInterceptor implements HttpInterceptor {

  constructor(private authService: AuthService) {}

  intercept(req: HttpRequest<any>, next: HttpHandler):
      Observable<HttpEvent<any>> {            ❶
    if (this.authService.authToken) {          ❷
      const authReq = req.clone({
        headers: req.headers.set(
          'Authorization',
          this.authService.authToken
        )
      });
      console.log('Making an authorized request');
      req = authReq;                           ❸
    }
    return next.handle(req)                     ❹
        .do(event => this.handleResponse(req, event),
            error => this.handleError(req, error));
  }


  handleResponse(req: HttpRequest<any>, event) {   ❺
    console.log('Handling response for ', req.url, event);
    if (event instanceof HttpResponse) {
      console.log('Request for ', req.url,
          ' Response Status ', event.status,
          ' With body ', event.body);
    }
  }

  handleError(req: HttpRequest<any>, event) {      ❻
```

```
        console.error('Request for ', req.url,
              ' Response Status ', event.status,
              ' With error ', event.error);
      }
    }
  }
```

❶ Implement the `intercept` API

❷ Check for presence of auth token in the service

❸ Change the request to an authorized request with extra headers

❹ Call the `handle` API on the request to proceed in the chain

❺ Handle any successful response

❻ Handle any error

We have changed a few things of note in the interceptor now:

- First, we check for the presence of the `authToken` in the `AuthService`. If it is available, we then modify the request to add an `Authorization` header with the current value from the `AuthService`.

- We have added an operator to `Observable` using the `import 'rxjs/add/opera tor/do';` statement. We then use this on the `next.handle`.

- The do operator on an observable allows us to hook onto the results of an observable in a pass-through manner, but still make changes or have side effects. It is useful for cases like these where we want to see the response and possibly even make changes to it or log it.

- We subscribe to both the success and error events on the observable, and add the appropriate logging in both.

Why Clone the Request?

One very important thing to note is how we handle adding headers (or making any other changes) to the outgoing request.

`HttpRequest` (and `HttpResponse`) instances are *immutable*. This means that once created, its values cannot be changed. We want the `HttpRequest` and `HttpResponse` to be immutable because there are various `Observable` operators, some of which might want to retry the request.

For example, assume a simple flow where before we make the request, we add a counter that counts the number of requests from our client. If the request was retried, then the count might get updated again, even though it is still the original request that was being retried.

If request instances were mutable, then on retrying the request through an interceptor chain, the request might be completely different. For this reason, both `HttpRequest` and `HttpResponse` instances are immutable. Thus, any changes we make on them result in a new immutable instance. This allows us to ensure that retrying a request through an interceptor chain would result in exactly the same request being made, and not result in unexpected behavior because of mutability.

We therefore call `clone()` on the request to get a new instance with modified/updated properties that we pass to the instance. This gives us back a new instance with updated values. We pass this instance to the handler instead of the original request.

Now when you run your application, take the following actions:

1. See the initial request to get the list of stocks in the network inspector. Ensure that there is no `Authorization` header in the request.

2. Click the Set Auth Token button. Now click the Refetch Stocks button. Notice that the `Authorization` header is now set and sent in the request. Corresponding logs will also be printed.

3. Click Reset Auth Token to ensure that header is removed and try Refetch Stocks once again.

4. Click the Make Failing Call button and ensure that the error handler in the interceptor gets called and the logs are correctly printed.

Service Dependencies and Interceptors

Note that we pulled in an `AuthService` dependency in the interceptor via dependency injection. But there is one exception that you would need to watch out for, which is if the dependency you are pulling in within the interceptor in turn depends on `HttpClient`. This would compile, but when you run the application in your browser, you will see an error about *circular dependency*. This is because the `HttpClient` underneath requires all the interceptors, and when we add a service as a dependency that requires `HttpClient`, we end up with a circular ask that breaks our application.

How do we fix this? There are a few approaches we can take:

- Split apart your service if possible into a data service that does not depend on `HttpClient` and one that makes server calls using `HttpClient`. Then you can pull in the first service as a dependency only, which won't cause this circular dependency. This is usually the easier and preferred approach.

- Do not inject your `HttpClient` dependency in the constructor, but rather lazily inject it later as and when you need it. To do this, you would need the `Injector` injected in the constructor. You can then do `this.injector.get(MyService)` to get a handle on your service and use it. Refer to this GitHub issue (*https://github.com/angular/angular/issues/18224*) for more details.

The finished code is available in *chapter9/interceptors*.

Advanced Observables

In this final section, we will go a little bit more in depth into how we can accomplish some usually complex things using observables. We will also see some common pitfalls that you should be aware of when using observables. From an application perspective, we will try to add the capability to search stocks as you type from the application. This will allow us to see many things in actions. Search is the prototypical example for demonstrating the power of ReactiveX as it really demonstrates how observables can make certain tasks simpler, especially when you treat everything as a stream of events.

Search-as-you-type is generally difficult, for the following reasons:

- If you trigger an HTTP call every time someone performs a keypress, then you would end up with a lot of calls, most of which will need to be ignored.

- Users rarely type correctly in one shot, often having to erase and retype. This will also result in unnecessary duplicate calls.
- You need to worry about how to deal with out-of-order responses. If the result for the previous query returns after the current one, you need to handle it in your application logic.

Thankfully, observables give us powerful operators to handle each of these. Before we get into how to fix these using observables, let's start by first adding a line to show how many search results we are seeing. This will also demonstrate one thing to watch out for when using observables.

We will again use the code from the first finished example, which is available in *chapter9/simple-http*. We will build on this for the rest of the section.

First, let's edit *src/app/stock/stock-list.component.html* to show the number of stocks we have in addition to the stocks themselves. We might end up with something like:

```
<h2>
  We have found {{(stocks$ | async)?.length}} stocks!
</h2>

<app-stock-item *ngFor="let stock of stocks$ | async"
                [stock]="stock">
</app-stock-item>
```

We have added a div, which shows the length (if present, which is what the ? syntax does—it marks the element as optional, thus preventing failure in case of nulls, etc.). Now if you run the application, you will see the list of stocks as well as "We have found 3 stocks!"

But open up the network inspector and you will notice an interesting thing. There will actually be two different calls going for fetching the list of stocks. Why? Because Angular observables are cold by default. And so every time someone subscribes to it, the observable is triggered. In this case, we have two subscribers, which are the two Async pipes, one for the ngFor and one for the length. Thus, instead of using the same observable, we end up with two different calls being made.

Cold Versus Hot Observables

We just mentioned that Angular observables are cold observables by default. What does this mean for us? Fundamentally, an observable is nothing but a function that connects a producer to a consumer.

A cold observable is responsible for creating the producer as well, while a hot observable ends up sharing the producer.

For us, this just means that if whenever someone subscribes to an observable in Angular, the producer is created for that instance. This is why for each subscribe, we end up with a new producer.

You can read up more on hot and cold observables in this article (*http://bit.ly/2s2HETa*).

Now how can we solve it? We have a few options:

- We can tell Angular to share the same observable, thus preventing two calls.
- We can manually subscribe to the observable in the component, and capture the event response and save it to a class variable. Then the template can access the class variable instead of relying on the `Async` pipe.
- We can choose not to use observables and instead use the promise to get at the underlying value. Promises do work in Angular, and you can convert any observable into a promise by calling `toPromise` on the observable (after adding the operator `toPromise` first of course by importing it).

All of these are acceptable options, depending on the use case. While Angular pushes us toward using observables, there is no hard-and-fast rule that you can't convert it into a promise. And there are cases where it makes sense to deal with a promise instead of an observable.

We won't go into code snippets for the latter two, though. Let's see how we can share the same observable, by changing the *src/app/stock/stock-list/stock-list.component.ts* file as follows:

```
import { Component, OnInit } from '@angular/core';
import { StockService } from 'app/services/stock.service';
import { Stock } from 'app/model/stock';
import { Observable } from 'rxjs/Observable';

import { share } from 'rxjs/operators';

@Component({
  selector: 'app-stock-list',
  templateUrl: './stock-list.component.html',
  styleUrls: ['./stock-list.component.css']
})
```

```
export class StockListComponent implements OnInit {

  public stocks$: Observable<Stock[]>;

  constructor(private stockService: StockService) { }

  ngOnInit() {
    this.stocks$ = this.stockService.getStocks()
      .pipe(share());
  }
}
```

We have simply imported and used the share operator from RxJS. Then, in the ngOn
Init, instead of saving the getStocks() observable directly, we pipe our base observable and add the share() operator to our pipe. We save this observable as a member
variable. This ensures that regardless of how many subscriptions are present on the
observable, there would be only one underlying trigger to the server. Now when you
run the application, you should see only one request being made to fetch the list of
stocks, and still see both the number of stocks as well as the individual stocks.

Be careful when you use AsyncPipe in your application, as using
multiple async pipes on the same observable without sharing the
underlying observable underneath would result in multiple server
calls.

Another option is to use the as operator along with the async pipe.
This assigns the variable to a template variable for easy access and
use. We can do something like:

```
<li *ngFor="let stock of stocks$ | async as stocks;
        index as i">
  {{ stock.name }} ({{ i }} of {{ stocks.length }})
</li>
```

The problem is that the template variable is scoped to the element,
and cannot be accessed outside like in our example.

Next, let's add a simple search field, and see how we might fetch a list of stocks based
on the search term from the server. We will take this step by step, by first updating
our service to make the modified server call, and then adding a search field in the UI.

First, let's change our StockService to support searching for stocks with a query
string. We will update the *src/app/services/stock.service.ts* file as follows:

```
import { Injectable } from '@angular/core';
import { HttpClient } from '@angular/common/http';

import { Observable } from 'rxjs/Observable';

import { Stock } from 'app/model/stock';
```

```
@Injectable()
export class StockService {

  constructor(private http: HttpClient) {}

  getStocks(query: string) : Observable<Stock[]> {
    return this.http.get<Stock[]>(`/api/stock?q=${query}`);
  }

  /** Remaining same, omitted for brevity */
}
```

We have changed the definition of the getStocks method to take a query parameter, which is then passed to the */api/stock* server call as a query parameter. Note that we could have passed it as an options object as the second argument as well instead of appending it to the URL.

Now we need to change our StockListComponent to make the updated call. While we are doing that, we will also add an input field bound to a model in the component, which will drive our search-as-you-type capability. Let's modify the template first to add the new form field, by changing *src/app/stock/stock-list/stock-list.component.html* as follows:

```
<div>
  <input name="searchBox"
         [(ngModel)]="searchString"
         placeholder="Search Here"
         (keyup)="search()">
</div>

<h2>
  We have found {{(stocks$ | async)?.length}} stocks!
</h2>

<app-stock-item *ngFor="let stock of stocks$ | async"
                [stock]="stock">
</app-stock-item>
```

We have added an input field named searchBox to the template, and bound it using ngModel to a member variable called searchString. In addition, on every keyup event, we are triggering a method called search(). Let's see how the component in *src/app/stock/stock-list/stock-list.component.ts* has to evolve:

```
import { Component, OnInit } from '@angular/core';
import { StockService } from 'app/services/stock.service';
import { Stock } from 'app/model/stock';
import { Observable } from 'rxjs/Observable';

import { share } from 'rxjs/operators';
```

```
@Component({
  selector: 'app-stock-list',
  templateUrl: './stock-list.component.html',
  styleUrls: ['./stock-list.component.css']
})
export class StockListComponent implements OnInit {

  public stocks$: Observable<Stock[]>;
  public searchString: string = '';

  constructor(private stockService: StockService) { }

  ngOnInit() {
    this.stocks$ = this.stockService.getStocks(this.searchString)
      .pipe(share());
  }

  search() {
    this.stocks$ = this.stockService.getStocks(this.searchString)
      .pipe(share());
  }
}
```

We've not done much at this point; we've simply replicated our logic of fetching the stocks in another method called search(). We have also ensured that we are passing along the query term to our StockService. If you run the application at this point, you will see the new search box. And if you type into the box, it does actually make a request to the server and search. But opening the network inspector in the developer tools tells the underlying story, which is that:

- For every keystroke, we make a request to the server. This is horrifyingly inefficient.

- We make requests for duplicate values even if we had already made a request for the previous one.

Thankfully, because we only hold the reference to the latest observable, we don't have to worry about out-of-order responses, but if we were subscribing to the observable in our component, then we would have to ensure that the response we are working with is the latest and not an older, out-of-date response.

Now let's see how we can leverage observable operators to solve these problems in a clean, simple manner. We will change the component's implementation to the following now:

```
import { Component, OnInit } from '@angular/core';
import { StockService } from 'app/services/stock.service';
import { Stock } from 'app/model/stock';
import { Observable } from 'rxjs/Observable';
import { Subject } from 'rxjs/Subject';
```

```
import { debounceTime, switchMap,
         distinctUntilChanged, startWith,
         share } from 'rxjs/operators';

@Component({
  selector: 'app-stock-list',
  templateUrl: './stock-list.component.html',
  styleUrls: ['./stock-list.component.css']
})
export class StockListComponent implements OnInit {

  public stocks$: Observable<Stock[]>;
  public searchString: string = '';

  private searchTerms: Subject<string> = new Subject();
  constructor(private stockService: StockService) { }

  ngOnInit() {
    this.stocks$ = this.searchTerms.pipe(
      startWith(this.searchString),
      debounceTime(500),
      distinctUntilChanged(),
      switchMap((query) => this.stockService.getStocks(query)),
      share()
    );
  }

  search() {
    this.searchTerms.next(this.searchString);
  }
}
```

We have given the component a major overhaul, so let's talk through the various changes and why we have done them:

- The first major thing we have done is that we have introduced a member variable called searchTerms, which is a Subject. A Subject is a special type in RxJS that acts as both an observer as well as an observable. That is, it is capable of both emitting events as well as subscribing to one. We will use this searchTerms subject to trigger an event whenever the user types in our search box.

- At this point, our ngOnInit now starts with the Subject we created, rather than the StockService. This means our chain of observable operators will be triggered each time the Subject gets a new term. The Subject is hooked in the search() to emit an event each time the user enters a letter.

- Of course, we don't want to trigger the server call each time the user enters a key, so we introduce the debounceTime() operator in the chain. To chain, we use the pipe operator on the observable, and then can add any number of operators separated as arguments to the pipe function. Here, we instruct the stream to hold until there are no more new events for a period of 500 milliseconds. This ensures that we only send a call once the user stops typing for half a second.

- The next thing we want to do is to avoid unnecessary calls, like if the user enters a search term (say, "test"), then types a few more characters and then erases them to land back at the same word he started with. Instead of adding checks and local variables, we use another observable operator called distinctUntilChanged(). This ensures that the event is only emitted if the new value is different from the previous value, thus saving a few more network calls.

- So far, we are using a Subject that emits string values. But our observable that we bind to is one of Stock[]. Converting an observable chain from one type to another is usually the work of the map operator. But we will use a particular type of map operator called the switchMap. The switchMap has a nice behavior that in addition to converting from one type of observable to another, it also has the capability to cancel old, in-flight subscriptions. This helps to solve our out-of-order response problem in a nice, clean manner. Note that it does not necessarily cancel the underlying HTTP request, but simply drops the subscription.

- If we leave it at just this, our chain will only start the first moment the user starts typing into the search box, and will result in an empty list of stocks when the page loads. We can solve this by using an operator called startWith, which sets the initial value with which the observable chain is to be triggered. We start it with an empty string, which ensures that when the page is loaded, we see our original list of stocks.

At this point, with a chain of four RxJS operators, we can now run our application. When you type in the search box, it will wait for you to stop typing for a period before making the request. If you type and erase to land back at the starting value, it will not make the request at all.

There are many more operators available in RxJS than what I can reasonably cover in this book, so I won't even try. This section is more to give you an idea of what RxJS is really capable of. Whenever you are trying to do any complex work, see if you can tackle it using operators rather than doing it manually. The official RxJS documentation (*http://reactivex.io/rxjs/manual/overview.html#operators*) is a great place to start on learning them.

Conclusion

In this chapter, we learned how to make HTTP calls using the HttpClient in Angular. We started with GET and POST calls using the HttpClient, before diving deeper into the API provided in the HttpClient. This included working with headers and query parameters, as well as working with different levels of detail in the response and different response types. We then moved on to handling common use cases of hooking onto every HTTP request and response using interceptors, and saw how to create and hook our own interceptor to the Angular HTTP chain. Finally, we saw how to leverage observables to accomplish some complex tasks in a simple, efficient manner with an example of search-as-you-type.

In the next chapter, we will take a step back and learn how to write unit tests for services, as well as how to unit-test flows where HTTP calls are being made through the HttpClient.

Exercise

Take the finished exercise from Chapter 8 (available in *chapter8/exercise/ecommerce*). Install and run the server in the *chapter9/exercise/server* folder by running:

```
npm i
node index.js
```

from within the folder. This will start a local Node.js server, which can work with products (similar to one we had for stocks). It exposes the following APIs:

- GET on */api/product* to get a list of products. It can also take an optional query param q, which is the product name to search for.
- POST on */api/product* with product information in the body to create a product on the server (in-memory of course; restarting the server would lose all created products).
- PATCH on */api/product/:id* with the product ID in the URL and a field changeIn Quantity in the body would change the quantity in cart of the product by that amount.

Given this, now try to accomplish the following:

1. Change over the ProductService to make HTTP calls instead of responding with mock data. Support searching for a list of products as well.
2. Implement both product listing and search-as-you-type using the power of observables.
3. Handle product creation, as well as change in quantity of an individual product and hook it up end-to-end.
4. See if you can continue using the same observable chain to now reload the entire list of products each time a product is created or the quantity is changed.

Most of this can be accomplished using concepts covered in this chapter. The only tricky thing is how to reload the list of products when it happens in a different component, for which you can leverage template reference variables to access the component and make a call. The other thing you might need to use is the merge operator in the observable so that you can leverage the same observable for loading the list, searching products, and reloading the list. You can check out the finished solution in *chapter9/exercise/ecommerce*.

CHAPTER 10

Unit Testing Services

In the previous two chapters, we started understanding what Angular services are, when to create them, and how to use them. We also started learning how to make HTTP calls and handle the various use cases that crop up when working with servers.

In this chapter, we will take a step back and try to see how we can unit test these services. We will first see how to unit test a service, followed by understanding how to leverage the Angular dependency injection system to mock out service dependencies in unit tests. Finally, we will dig into writing unit tests when we are working with `HttpClient`.

If you want to quickly recap what unit tests are and how to write them for components, you can refer to Chapter 5.

How to Unit Test Services

The first thing we will start with is learning how to unit test very simple services. These might be services without any dependencies that act as encapsulators of business logic or functionality that needs to be reused across our application.

We will start with testing the very simple service we built in Chapter 8. You can use the codebase in *chapter8/simple-service* as the base for this section. The finished code is available in *chapter10/simple-service*.

Any time we are unit testing our service, we must do a few things over and above what we did for testing components. Namely:

- Configure the Angular `TestBed` with a provider for the service we want to test.

- Inject an instance of the service we want to test either into our test or as a common instance in the beforeEach.

When you generate a service using the Angular CLI, this initial skeleton is generated for you out of the box. Regardless, let's first take a look at the skeleton spec that was generated in *src/app/services/stock.service.spec.ts*:

```
import { TestBed, inject } from '@angular/core/testing';

import { StockService } from './stock.service';

describe('StockService', () => {
  beforeEach(() => {
    TestBed.configureTestingModule({
      providers: [StockService]
    });
  });

  it('should be created', inject([StockService],
      (service: StockService) => {
    expect(service).toBeTruthy();
  }));
});
```

The basic skeleton itself allows us to walk through some of the initial setup that we mentioned. Let's cover the most important bits:

- In the beforeEach, like we used to register the components, we now register the provider for the StockService. This ensures that the test is now running in the context of our testing module.

- In the it, which is the actual test, instead of just passing the test function to it, we call inject, which is a function provided by the Angular testing utilities. We pass an array to it as the first argument, which are the Angular services that need to be injected into our test. The second argument is a function that gets the arguments in the same order that we passed to the array. We write our actual test within this function.

In the skeleton code, we instantiate the StockService provider with the testing module, and then just make sure that when we inject it in the test, we get an instantiated version of the service for use in the test.

Before we get on to the actual test, let's quickly review the service that we will be testing. The StockService currently looks like the following:

```
import { Injectable } from '@angular/core';
import { Stock } from 'app/model/stock';

@Injectable()
```

```
export class StockService {

  private stocks: Stock[];
  constructor() {
    this.stocks = [
      new Stock('Test Stock Company', 'TSC', 85, 80, 'NASDAQ'),
      new Stock('Second Stock Company', 'SSC', 10, 20, 'NSE'),
      new Stock('Last Stock Company', 'LSC', 876, 765, 'NYSE')
    ];
  }

  getStocks() : Stock[] {
    return this.stocks;
  }

  createStock(stock: Stock) {
    let foundStock = this.stocks.find(each => each.code === stock.code);
    if (foundStock) {
      return false;
    }
    this.stocks.push(stock);
    return true;
  }

  toggleFavorite(stock: Stock) {
    let foundStock = this.stocks.find(each => each.code === stock.code);
    foundStock.favorite = !foundStock.favorite;
  }
}
```

The StockService has three stocks that are instantiated by default. When we call get
Stocks(), this list of three stocks is returned. We can also add stocks by calling
createStock, which checks for the presence of the stock and then adds it.

Now let's improve it to actually test the service, which had the capability of getting a
list of stocks and adding stocks. We will add two tests for these two methods:

```
/** Other imports skipped for brevity **/
import { Stock } from 'app/model/stock';

describe('StockService', () => {
  var stockService: StockService;
  beforeEach(() => {
    /** No change in first beforeEach, skipping for brevity **/
  });

  beforeEach(inject([StockService],              ❶
    (service: StockService) => {
      stockService = service;
  }));

  it('should allow adding stocks', () => {
```

```
    expect(stockService.getStocks().length).toEqual(3);        ❷
    let stock = new Stock('Testing A New Company', 'TTT',
        850, 800, 'NASDAQ');
    expect(stockService.createStock(stock)).toBeTruthy();      ❸
    expect(stockService.getStocks().length).toEqual(4);        ❹
    expect(stockService.getStocks()[3].code).toEqual('TTT')
  });

  it('should fetch a list of stocks', () => {
    expect(stockService.getStocks().length).toEqual(3);        ❺
    expect(stockService.getStocks()[0].code).toEqual('TSC');   ❻
    expect(stockService.getStocks()[1].code).toEqual('SSC');
    expect(stockService.getStocks()[2].code).toEqual('LSC');
  });
});
```

❶   Inject StockService into another beforeEach and save it for access across tests

❷   Ensure that we start with the original three stocks from our service

❸   Add the stock and ensure that it returns true

❹   Check for the presence of the stock we added in the service

❺   Ensure that we start with the original three stocks from our service

❻   Check each stock to ensure it is the data we expect

We have made a slight change to the initialization logic, and added two pretty mundane, run-of-the-mill tests:

- Instead of writing an inject block in each test (each it block), we have moved that logic to another beforeEach block, which is solely responsible for setting up local variables that will be repeatedly used across all the tests. Note that this does not mean the same instance is used in all the tests, but that we don't have to inject the service into each test individually.

- We have added two tests, one to test adding of stocks and another to check the default getStocks() call. Again, note that the two tests are independent. Our adding a stock in the first stock does not result in there being four stocks in the second test. Before each test, we are creating a new testing module with a new instance of the service.

Other than this, the test itself is pretty straightforward and self-explanatory. To run this test, simply execute:

```
ng test
```

That should automatically start Karma, capture Chrome, run the tests, and report the results right in your terminal window.

Handling Service Dependencies?

What if our service itself had a dependency on another service? Well, we would handle it exactly the same way. We have a few options:

- Register the dependency as a service with the Angular `TestBed` module, and let Angular be responsible for injecting it into the service we are testing.

- Override/mock the dependent service by registering a fake/ stub provider with the `TestBed`, and rely on that instead of the original service.

For both of these, we would simply add another `provider` in the `TestBed.configureTestingModule` call for the other service. We will see this principle in action in the next section.

Testing Components with a Service Dependency

Next, let's see how to deal with two slightly different situations:

- If we had to test a component, and actually use the real service underneath in the test.

- If we had to test a component, and we wanted to mock out the service it depends on in the test.

Testing Components with a Real Service

First, let's take a look at the test for `StockListComponent` if we were using the real service underneath. Our *src/app/stock/stock-list/stock-list.component.spec.ts* file would look like the following:

```
import { async, ComponentFixture, TestBed } from '@angular/core/testing';

import { StockListComponent } from './stock-list.component';
import { StockService } from 'app/services/stock.service';
import { StockItemComponent } from 'app/stock/stock-item/stock-item.component';
import { Stock } from 'app/model/stock';

describe('StockListComponent With Real Service', () => {
  let component: StockListComponent;
  let fixture: ComponentFixture<StockListComponent>;
```

```
beforeEach(async(() => {
  TestBed.configureTestingModule({
    declarations: [ StockListComponent, StockItemComponent ],   ❶
    providers: [ StockService ]                                 ❷
  })
  .compileComponents();
}));

beforeEach(() => {
  fixture = TestBed.createComponent(StockListComponent);
  component = fixture.componentInstance;
  fixture.detectChanges();
});

it('should load stocks from real service on init', () => {
  expect(component).toBeTruthy();
  expect(component.stocks.length).toEqual(3);                   ❸
});
});
```

❶ Add `StockItemComponent` to the `TestBed` declarations array

❷ Add `StockService` to the `providers` array

❸ Ensure that the stocks in the component are loaded from the service

Most of the test is the autogenerated skeleton from the Angular CLI. The changes we have made in particular are:

- We have added a declaration of `StockItemComponent` in addition to the `Stock ListComponent`. This is because the template for our `StockListComponent` uses the `StockItemComponent` and hence it is needed for our test to succeed.

- We have added `StockService` in the array passed to the `providers` section of the testing module created. This ensures that in our test, we use the actual underlying `StockService` whenever it is asked for by any component.

- Finally, we have added an assertion to ensure that we load the three stocks that are returned by our `StockService` when the component is initialized.

If you notice, this should be similar to how we tested the service itself in the previous section. We simply add a provider for our service and then we have the real live service in our tests accessible.

Testing Components with a Mock Service

Next, let's see how we could write a similar test, but instead of using the real service in the test, how to mock out certain calls instead of creating a brand-new fake service just for our test. This approach is useful when we do actually want to use most of the service, but just override/mock out certain calls. This is also less cumbersome than creating and maintaining a full parallel fake implementation.

Let's see how we could use the real service with just some calls mocked out in our test. Our revamped test in *src/app/stock/stock-list/stock-list.component.spec.ts* would look like this:

```
/** Standard imports, skipping for brevity **/

describe('StockListComponent With Mock Service', () => {
  let component: StockListComponent;
  let fixture: ComponentFixture<StockListComponent>;
  let stockService: StockService;

  beforeEach(async(() => {
    /** No change in TestBed configuration, skipping for brevity **/
  }));

  beforeEach(() => {
    fixture = TestBed.createComponent(StockListComponent);
    component = fixture.componentInstance;
    // Always get the Service from the Injector!
    stockService = fixture.debugElement.injector.get(StockService);    ❶
    let spy = spyOn(stockService, 'getStocks')                         ❷
        .and.returnValue([
          new Stock('Mock Stock', 'MS', 800, 900, 'NYSE')
        ]);
    fixture.detectChanges();
  });

  it('should load stocks from mocked service on init', () => {
    expect(component).toBeTruthy();
    expect(component.stocks.length).toEqual(1);                        ❸
    expect(component.stocks[0].code).toEqual('MS');
  });
});
```

❶ Get the `StockService` instance through the component's injector

❷ Mock out the `getStocks()` call and return a hardcoded value instead

❸ Ensure that the stocks are provided from our mocked-out call now

Our test looks mostly similar to the test in the previous section, especially in how we hook up the service as a provider to the `TestBed`. The major difference is in the second `beforeEach`, where we use the injector in the test fixture to get a handle on the `StockService`.

There are two ways for us to get the service instance in our tests. We can either rely on the `inject` function from the Angular testing utilities to inject the service instance, like we did in our test for `StockService`, or we can use the `injector` reference on the element, like we just did here.

Once we have a handle on the service instance, we can use *Jasmine spies* to spy on different methods on the service. A spy (whether it is from Jasmine or any other framework) allows us to stub any function or method, and track any calls to it along with its arguments and also define our own return values.

In this case, we use `spyOn` to spy on a particular method in the service (the `get Stocks()` call), and use it to change the return value to what we want, rather than the original underlying call. This way, the actual service call never gets invoked.

Our test then just has assertions to make sure the return value is from our mocked service call rather than the original service.

Testing Components with a Fake Service

The last option we have when we are writing tests for components or services that depend on other services is to replace the actual service with a fake that we have created just for the purpose of testing. This allows us to create a service tuned just for the test that gives us maybe more access, or just tracks what APIs are called with what values. Most of this could also be accomplished with Jasmine spies, but if you have a repeated use case, then it might make more sense to create a fake that can be reused.

For us, a fake would simply be an object that we create, which has the same API as the service we are mocking, but our own (hardcoded) implementation of the methods underneath. For example, our fake could simply return a different hardcoded list of stocks instead of making a server call in a test.

Let's see how we could use a fake service in our test. Our revamped test in *src/app/ stock/stock-list/stock-list.component.spec.ts* would look like this:

```
/** Skipping imports for brevity **/

describe('StockListComponent With Fake Service', () => {
  let component: StockListComponent;
  let fixture: ComponentFixture<StockListComponent>;

  beforeEach(async(() => {
    let stockServiceFake = {                              ❶
      getStocks: () => {
        return [new Stock('Fake Stock', 'FS', 800, 900, 'NYSE')];
      }
    };
    TestBed.configureTestingModule({
      declarations: [ StockListComponent, StockItemComponent ],
      providers: [ {
        provide: StockService,
        useValue: stockServiceFake                        ❷
```

```
    } ]
  })
  .compileComponents();
}));

beforeEach(() => {
  fixture = TestBed.createComponent(StockListComponent);
  component = fixture.componentInstance;
  fixture.detectChanges();
});

it('should load stocks from fake service on init', () => {
  expect(component).toBeTruthy();
  expect(component.stocks.length).toEqual(1);
  expect(component.stocks[0].code).toEqual('FS');          ❸
});
});
```

❶ Define a stockServiceFake JavaScript object that implements a getStocks() method

❷ Specify the instance to use when providing the StockService

❸ Ensure that the values are coming from our fake service

There are a lot of differences in the test from the previous sections, so let's walk through some of the major changes:

- We first create a fake service instance, called stockServiceFake. Note that we initialize it with only one of the methods (getStocks()), and not necessarily all the APIs in the service.

- When we configure the testing module using the TestBed, instead of registering the StockService, we register a provider. We tell Angular that whenever someone asks for StockService (using the provide key), provide the value stockSer viceFake (using the useValue) key. This overrides the default behavior of providing the class instance.

Providing an Instance of a Service

Generally, when we identify a class as a `provider` to Angular, Angular would be responsible for instantiating an instance of the class and providing it when a component or a service depends on it.

In certain cases, we don't want Angular to instantiate it, but rather we want to define what value to use. That is when we use the mechanism we used in the preceding code, where we can define what class is being provided (using the `provide` key) and specify the instance to use, rather than letting Angular create the instance (using the `useValue` key).

You can read up more on the different ways you can configure Providers in the official Angular docs (*http://bit.ly/2IVt8Hl*).

Other than this, our test looks similar. We again assert that the data returned to the component is from our fake service, and not from the original service.

Always Get Services from the Injector

Note that the recommended way to get the handle on an instance of a service, even when using fakes, is through the injector. This is because the `fakeStockService` instance we create in our test will not be the same as the instance provided by the Angular dependency injector. Thus, even with a fake, if you want to assert, for example, that a stock was added successfully to the service, you would want to do it against the service returned by the injector, and not the original instance we used.

You can either let Angular's dependency injection provide it for you using the `inject` method from the Angular testing utilities or use the `injector` instance on the element created.

Angular's dependency injector creates a clone of the stub/fake you provide to it and injects that instead of the original instance.

You can check this out by tring to write the test against the service instance in the test versus the way we have written it here, and see the behavior of the test. You will see that the test fails, because the original instance does not change.

All three of these tests are available in *chapter10/simple-service/src/app/stock/stock-list/ stock-list.component.spec.ts*, one after the other as three `describe` blocks.

Unit Testing Async

So far, we have seen how we might test simple and straightforward services, with or without further dependencies, as well as test components. But the services we have worked with so far have been synchronous. In this section, we will dig a little bit into how to handle and write tests when the underlying service or code deals with asynchronous flows.

With any code that touches an asynchronous flow, we have to be careful in our tests and recognize at which point the hand-off happens from synchronous flow to asynchronous, and deal with it accordingly. Thankfully, Angular provides enough helpers to abstract out some of the complexities of this in our test.

Fundamentally, we have to make sure our test itself is identified and running as an asynchronous test. Secondly, we must ensure that we identify when we have to wait for the asynchronous part to finish, and validate the changes after that.

Let's see how a test for the `CreateStockComponent` might look, when we had just switched to using observables (but not HTTP yet). We will use the codebase from *chapter8/observables* as the base on which to write our tests.

We will add (or modify if the skeleton already exists) the *src/app/stock/create-stock/create-stock.component.spec.ts* file, and change it as follows:

```
import { async, ComponentFixture, TestBed } from '@angular/core/testing';

import { CreateStockComponent } from './create-stock.component';
import { StockService } from 'app/services/stock.service';
import { Stock } from 'app/model/stock';
import { FormsModule } from '@angular/forms';
import { By } from '@angular/platform-browser';


describe('CreateStockComponent', () => {
  let component: CreateStockComponent;
  let fixture: ComponentFixture<CreateStockComponent>;

  beforeEach(async(() => {
    TestBed.configureTestingModule({
      declarations: [ CreateStockComponent ],
      providers: [ StockService ],
      imports: [ FormsModule ]          ❶
    })
    .compileComponents();
  }));

  beforeEach(() => {
    fixture = TestBed.createComponent(CreateStockComponent);
    component = fixture.componentInstance;
    fixture.detectChanges();
```

```
    });

    it('should create stock through service', async(() => {        ❷
      expect(component).toBeTruthy();
      component.stock = new Stock(
        'My New Test Stock', 'MNTS', 100, 120, 'NYSE');

      component.createStock({valid: true});

      fixture.whenStable().then(() => {                              ❸
        fixture.detectChanges();                                     ❹
        expect(component.message)
            .toEqual('Stock with code MNTS successfully created');
        const messageEl = fixture.debugElement.query(
            By.css('.message')).nativeElement;
        expect(messageEl.textContent)
            .toBe('Stock with code MNTS successfully created');
      });
    }));
  });
```

❶ The CreateStockComponent needs FormsModule to work

❷ Pass the return value of calling async as the second param to the it function

❸ Wait for the test fixture to finish executing asynchronous flows

❹ Update the view after the changes

The early part of the unit test remains pretty much the same, from initializing the TestBed with the module to the beforeEach. We also have to import the FormsModule for the CreateStockComponent to work.

The first difference comes in the it declaration itself of our asynchronous test. Instead of simply passing the function containing our test code to the it block, we now pass an async function, which in turn is passed the function containing our test code. Do not forget this part when writing an asynchronous unit test.

The second major difference is after calling the function under test, createStock(), which actually triggers the asynchronous flow. Normally, we would write our assertions right after this. In the case of an asynchronous flow, we need to ask Angular's test fixture to stabilize (that is, wait for the asynchronous parts to finish). The when Stabilize returns a promise that on completion allows us to run the remaining part of the test. In this case, we tell Angular to detect any changes and update the UI, and then make our assertions.

In this particular case, even if we had skipped the whenStabilize bit and directly written our assertions, our test might still have passed. But that is only because our actual underlying service is also synchronous, even though it does return an observable. If it was truly asynchronous, then the whenStable becomes critical for us. Thus, it is generally a good practice to aways use it when it comes to async tests.

The finished code for this example is available in the *chapter10/observables* folder in the GitHub repository.

async Versus fakeAsync

In the preceding test, we passed an async function to the it block, which is our test. This allowed us to deal with any asynchronous behavior in the test and still be able to assert everything we needed to.

Angular also provides a fakeAsync function, which can be used instead of the async function. Both are very similar and used for the same purpose, which is to abstract away some of Angular's internals and handling of asynchronous behavior in our code. The async function still exposes some of the underlying asynchronous behavior, since we have to deal with promises in our test with the whenStable() function.

The fakeAsync does away with all of that. It allows us to write our unit test (for async and sync code) in a completely synchronous manner (almost that is, unless we are actually making XHR requests in our tests). Here is how the same test might look if rewritten using fakeAsync:

```
import { async, fakeAsync, tick,
         ComponentFixture, TestBed } from '@angular/core/testing';

import { CreateStockComponent } from './create-stock.component';
import { StockService } from 'app/services/stock.service';
import { Stock } from 'app/model/stock';
import { FormsModule } from '@angular/forms';
import { By } from '@angular/platform-browser';


describe('CreateStockComponent', () => {
  /** Skipped for brevity, same as before */

  it('should create stock through service', fakeAsync(() => {    ❶
    expect(component).toBeTruthy();
    component.stock = new Stock(
      'My New Test Stock', 'MNTS', 100, 120, 'NYSE');

    component.createStock({valid: true});
```

```
        tick();                      ❷
        fixture.detectChanges();
        expect(component.message)
            .toEqual('Stock with code MNTS successfully created');
        const messageEl = fixture.debugElement.query(
            By.css('.message')).nativeElement;
        expect(messageEl.textContent)
            .toBe('Stock with code MNTS successfully created');
    }));
});
```

❶ Using the fakeAsync instead of async

❷ Using tick() to simulate and finish all async behavior

We pass a fakeAsync function, and instead of the whenStable call, we now have a
simple tick() function call that does similar work. It allows the code to look linear
and makes it more readable.

There are in fact two methods to simulate a passage of time in a fakeAsync test,
namely tick() and flush(). tick simulates the passage of time (and can take the
number of milliseconds as an argument). flush, on the other hand, takes the number
of turns as an argument, which is basically how many times the queue of tasks is to be
drained.

So why use one over the other? If you would like to keep your code linear and
abstract away the async behavior, then the fakeAsync is great. But if you would like to
ensure that you are thinking about how your code flows, and want to keep it similar
to your actual code, then you can use the async method. It is completely a matter of
preference. Feel free to pick whichever works better for your style of coding!

Unit Testing HTTP

The last thing we will take a look at in this chapter is to see how to test HTTP communication. In particular, we will dig into how to mock out server calls. We will see
how to leverage Angular's built-in testing utilities that it provides to test HTTP
communication.

For this section, we will use the code from *chapter9/simple-http* as the base, and see
how we can test both GET calls like fetching a list of stocks as well as POST calls that
we make to create stocks.

First, let's test the StockListComponent to see how we can test the initialization logic
of fetching the list of stocks from our server. We want to ensure the entire flow of
making a server call, getting the list of stocks, and then displaying it.

We will modify *src/app/stock/stock-list/stock-list.component.spec.ts* as follows:

```
/** Standard imports, skipping for brevity **/

import { HttpClientModule } from '@angular/common/http';
import { HttpClientTestingModule, HttpTestingController }
    from '@angular/common/http/testing';
import { By } from '@angular/platform-browser';


describe('StockListComponent With Real Service', () => {
  let component: StockListComponent;
  let fixture: ComponentFixture<StockListComponent>;
  let httpBackend: HttpTestingController;          ❶

  beforeEach(async(() => {
    TestBed.configureTestingModule({
      declarations: [ StockListComponent, StockItemComponent ],
      providers: [ StockService ],
      imports: [
        HttpClientModule,
        HttpClientTestingModule                     ❷
      ]
    })
    .compileComponents();
  }));

  beforeEach(inject([HttpTestingController],
      (backend: HttpTestingController) => {
    httpBackend = backend;
    fixture = TestBed.createComponent(StockListComponent);
    component = fixture.componentInstance;
    fixture.detectChanges();
    httpBackend.expectOne({                         ❸
      url: '/api/stock',
      method: 'GET'
    }, 'Get list of stocks').flush([{              ❹
      name: 'Test Stock 1',
      code: 'TS1',
      price: 80,
      previousPrice: 90,
      exchange: 'NYSE'
    }, {
      name: 'Test Stock 2',
      code: 'TS2',
      price: 800,
      previousPrice: 900,
      exchange: 'NYSE'
    }]);
  }));

  it('should load stocks from real service on init',
      async(() => {
    expect(component).toBeTruthy();
```

```
    expect(component.stocks$).toBeTruthy();

    fixture.whenStable().then(() => {          ❺
      fixture.detectChanges();
      const stockItems = fixture.debugElement.queryAll(
        By.css('app-stock-item'));
      expect(stockItems.length).toEqual(2);
    });
  }));

  afterEach(() => {
    httpBackend.verify();                       ❻
  });
});
```

❶ Include the `HttpTestingController` as a local variable

❷ Import the `HttpClientModule` and the `HttpTestingController` in the module

❸ Set expectation that one call to */api/stock* will be made as part of the test

❹ Define a list of hardcoded stocks to return when the GET call is made

❺ Wait for the Angular task queue to get empty, and then proceed

❻ Verify that the GET call to */api/stock* was actually made as part of the test

While the test seems very long, the changes to support testing HTTP calls are actually pretty straightforward. The major change when it comes to writing tests for code that makes XHR calls is the use of the `HttpTestingController`. In our unit test, while we want to test the code flow that makes XHR calls, we don't really want to make the actual underlying call. Any network call in a test adds unreliable dependencies, and makes our tests brittle and possibly nondeterministic.

For this reason, we actually mock out the XHR calls in our tests, just check that the right XHR calls are made, and that if the response was a certain value, then it is handled correctly. Therefore, a lot of our tests would simply be setting up through the `HttpTestingController` what calls to expect and what responses to send when those calls are made. You even have control over whether the server responds with a 200 success response, or whether it is an error (a 400 or 500 response, which corresponds to a client- or server-side error, respectively).

With that context, let's walk through the points of interest in the preceding test:

1. The first and most important change is that we need to import the `HttpClient` `Module` so that our service can initialize with the injected `HttpClient`.

2. The second thing is that we include the `HttpClientTestingModule` from `@angu lar/common/http/testing`. This testing module helps automatically mock out the actual server calls, and replaces it with a `HttpTestingController` that can intercept and mock all server calls.

3. We hook these two modules up in the `imports` section of the `TestBed` module configuration.

4. Then in our test (or in this case, the `beforeEach`), we can inject an instance of the `HttpTestingController` to set our expectations and verify server calls.

5. After initializing the component instance as usual, we then start setting our expectations on the `HttpTestingController`. In this case, we expect that one GET call to the URL */api/stock*. We also pass it a human-readable text to print in the logs in case the test fails or that call is not made.

6. In addition to setting expectations on calls made, we can also define the response Angular should send when those calls are made. Here, we return an array of two stocks by calling the `flush` method. The first argument to `flush` is the response body.

7. The rest of the test is straightforward. We expect the component to be initialized. Then, we wait for the change detection to stabilize (by calling `fixture.whenSta ble()`), and then ensure that the response we returned is actually rendered in the template correctly.

8. In the `afterEach`, we call `httpBackend.verify()`. This ensures that all the expectations we set on the `HttpTestingController` were actually satisfied during the run of the test. It is generally good practice to do this in the `afterEach`, to ensure that our code doesn't make extra or fewer calls.

Let's quickly write one more test to see how to handle POST calls, and how to send non-200 responses from the server. We will create the *src/app/stock/create-stock/create-stock.component.spec.ts* file as follows:

```
/** Standard imports, skipping for brevity **/

describe('CreateStockComponent With Real Service', () => {
  let component: CreateStockComponent;
  let fixture: ComponentFixture<CreateStockComponent>;
  let httpBackend: HttpTestingController;

  beforeEach(async(() => {
    /** TestBed configuration similar to before, skipping for brevity **/
  }));

  beforeEach(inject([HttpTestingController],
      (backend: HttpTestingController) => {
    httpBackend = backend;
```

```
      fixture = TestBed.createComponent(CreateStockComponent);
      component = fixture.componentInstance;
      fixture.detectChanges();
   }));

   it('should make call to create stock and handle failure',
         async(() => {
      expect(component).toBeTruthy();
      fixture.detectChanges();

      component.stock = {
        name: 'Test Stock',
        price: 200,
        previousPrice: 500,
        code: 'TSS',
        exchange: 'NYSE',
        favorite: false
      };

      component.createStock({valid: true});

      let httpReq = httpBackend.expectOne({          ❶
        url: '/api/stock',
        method: 'POST'
      }, 'Create Stock with Failure');
      expect(httpReq.request.body).toEqual(component.stock);     ❷
      httpReq.flush({msg: 'Stock already exists.'},             ❸
          {status: 400, statusText: 'Failed!!'});

      fixture.whenStable().then(() => {
        fixture.detectChanges();
        const messageEl = fixture.debugElement.query(
            By.css('.message')).nativeElement;
        expect(messageEl.textContent).toEqual('Stock already exists.');     ❹
      });
   }));

   afterEach(() => {
     httpBackend.verify();          ❺
   });
});
```

❶ Expect a POST request to be made to */api/stock* during the test

❷ Ensure that the body of the POST request is the same as the stock we created in the component

❸ Define the response for the POST request, which is a failure 400 response

❹ Check that the server response is shown correctly by the component

---

❺ Ensure that the POST request happened during the test

Most of the preceding test should be very similar to the test we wrote for the Stock ListComponent. Let's talk about the major differences in detail:

- Instead of immediately flushing the response when we set the expectation on the httpBackend for the POST call, we save it to a local variable.

- We can then write expectations on the various parts of the HTTP request, like the method, URL, body, headers, and so on.

- We then ensure that the body of the request matches the stock in our component.

- Finally, we flush a response, but instead of just flushing the body, we pass a second options argument to configure the response further. We mark the response as a 400 response to trigger the error condition.

- The rest of the test doesn't change, from waiting for the fixture to stabilize, asserting on the elements, to verifying that the calls were made on the httpBackend.

 httpBackend.expectOne also takes an HttpRequest object instead of passing the URL and the method as a config object. In such a case, we can actually configure the HttpRequest object with the body of the POST request as well. Note that this does not enforce that the POST request is made with that body. You will still need to manually check it the way we did in the previous example. Do not assume that the body is automatically matched and forget to verify it.

The finished code is available in the *chapter10/simple-http* folder of the GitHub repository.

Conclusion

In this chapter, we dug deeper into testing services in Angular. We looked at how we could test services, as well as components that use services. We explored the various techniques and options to deal with services, from using the real service, to mocking it or stubbing it out. Then we moved onto seeing how we could handle async behavior when it came to unit tests, and then finally how to deal with XHR and HTTP in our tests.

In the next chapter, we will switch back to seeing how we can enhance our Angular applications with the ability to deep-link to certain pages and components. We will see how to start setting up our routes, as well as protect certain routes to be accessible under only certain conditions.

Exercise

Take the finished exercise from Chapter 9 (available in *chapter9/exercise/ecommerce*). Given this, now try to accomplish the following:

1. Update the `ProductListComponent` tests. Remove the isolated unit tests. Update the Angular tests to use the `HttpTestingController` to provide the list of stocks as well as handle quantity change.

2. Ensure that the list of stocks is reloaded when the quantity changes.

3. Add tests for the positive and negative cases of the `CreateProductComponent`. Check that the event is emitted when a product is successfully created as well.

Most of this can be accomplished using concepts covered in this chapter. You can check out the finished solution in *chapter10/exercise/ecommerce*.

CHAPTER 11

Routing in Angular

In the previous few chapters, we saw how to extend our application and make reusable services. We also saw how to integrate and deal with HTTP calls in our application using the `HttpClient` module, and deal with the asynchronous flows using observables and RxJS.

In this chapter, we will deal with another common requirement of web applications, which is to encapsulate various pages and pieces under different routes, and be able to deep-link to them when needed. We will implement Angular's built-in routing module. In addition, we will also dig into how to secure our application using `Auth Guards` and other features of the router.

Setting Up Angular Routing

For this chapter, we are going to build against a precoded server, as well as use a codebase that has most of the base components built so that we can focus only on the key aspects. We are going to continue extending our application that we have been working on across the chapters by adding routing capability to it. We are going to try to add four routes: one for the stock list, one to create a stock, one for registering, and one for logging in. Furthermore, we will protect the stock list route and the create stock route so that you can access them only if you are logged in. Finally, we will add protections to ensure that we don't lose our work by navigating away from a filled-in form.

Server Setup

As mentioned earlier, the server we will be working with is already developed and available in the repository in the *chapter11/server* folder. Before we start any web development, let's get our server up and running. Note that this server has more functionality than the previous ones, so please use this one instead of continuing to keep the previous server running.

Checkout and browse to the *chapter11/server* folder in the GitHub repository (*https://github.com/shyamseshadri/angular-up-and-running*). From within the folder, execute the following commands in your terminal:

```
npm i
node index.js
```

This installs all the necessary dependencies for our Node.js server, and then starts the server on port 3000. Keep this server running in the background. This will be what our application hits to fetch and save stocks, in addition to logging in and registering users.

 Note that this server is a very simplistic, dummy server with an in-memory data store. Anything you create/save will be reset if you restart the server. This includes any usernames you might register.

Starting Codebase

Similarly, instead of spending time building all the components for the remaining routes, and reviewing concepts we have already covered in previous chapters, we will instead use the precoded base Angular application that has a few more components. If you're planning to keep coding along, do note the following additions and make sure you add them to your application.

The code is available for you in the *chapter11/base-code-base* folder. The major additions are:

- A `LoginComponent` and `RegisterComponent`
- A `UserService` that makes HTTP calls to login and register a user
- A `UserStoreService` that stores whether a user is logged in or not, along with the token
- A `StockAppInterceptor` that will be used to send the authentication token if it exists with every request

All of these are also registered in the main `AppModule`.

Importing the Router Module

With all the set up done, we can now get into how to set up routing in our application. The very first thing is to set up our *index.html* to ensure that it is able to provide enough context to Angular on how to set up its navigation. We do this by using the base tag within the head element in *index.html*. If the application is being served from the root (like we are doing so far), then it is enough to add the following to your *index.html*:

```
<base href="/">
```

This is automatically done by the Angular CLI, so you only need to change it in case you are serving your application from a non-root location. The next thing to do is to import and set up the RouterModule, as routing is an optional module in Angular. Before we can add the RouterModule, we need to define the routes of our application. So we will first look at how to define the routes. We will then come back to seeing how to import and add the RouterModule.

We will define a separate routes module file, *app-routes.module.ts*, instead of defining it in the same *app.module.ts*. This is generally good practice, as you want to keep it separate and modular, even if you only have a few routes initially. While we are just defining a separate module for our routes, it would eventually make sense for us to define a separate module and routes for each feature. This would also allow us to lazy load feature modules and certain routes instead of loading all our code up front.

We could choose to manually create our new module and hook it up to the main AppModule, or let the Angular CLI do it for us, by running:

```
ng generate module app-routes --flat --module=app
```

This would generate an *app-routes.module.ts* file in the main *app* folder. We can drop the basic CommonModule import from it, as we won't be declaring any components as part of our routing module. Our final *app-routing.module.ts* might look something like the following:

```
import { NgModule } from '@angular/core';
import { RouterModule, Routes }  from '@angular/router';

import { CreateStockComponent }
    from './stock/create-stock/create-stock.component';
import { StockListComponent } from './stock/stock-list/stock-list.component';
import { LoginComponent } from './user/login/login.component';
import { RegisterComponent } from './user/register/register.component';

const appRoutes: Routes = [                        ❶
  { path: 'login', component: LoginComponent },
  { path: 'register', component: RegisterComponent },
  { path: 'stocks/list', component: StockListComponent },
  { path: 'stocks/create', component: CreateStockComponent },
];

@NgModule({
  imports: [
    RouterModule.forRoot(appRoutes),               ❷
```

```
  ],
  exports: [
    RouterModule                                    ❸
  ],
})
export class AppRoutesModule { }
```

❶ Declare the array of routes for our application

❷ Import and register the routes for the root application

❸ Export the `RouterModule` so that any module importing `AppRoutesModule` gets access to router directives

This is the first time we have created another module, separate from the auto-generated one of the Angular CLI. The `AppRoutesModule` (annotated with `@NgModule`) simply imports the `RouterModule` and then exports it so that all modules get access to router directives (which we will use in a bit). While importing the `RouterModule`, we mark it for the root module by calling the `forRoot` method on it, with the routes we are defining.

The routes we pass to the `forRoot` method are nothing but an array of `Routes`. Each route is simply a configuration that defines the `path` for the route, as well as the component to be loaded when the route is loaded. We define four routes, one for each of the components.

Next, we just need to hook up this module to our main module, by modifying the *app.module.ts* file as follows:

```
/** Other imports not changed, skipping for brevity **/
import { AppRoutesModule } from './app-routes.module';


@NgModule({
  declarations: [
    /** No change, skipping for brevity **/
  ],
  imports: [
    BrowserModule,
    FormsModule,
    HttpClientModule,
    AppRoutesModule,                    ❶
  ],
  providers: [
    /** No change, skipping for brevity **/
  ],
  bootstrap: [AppComponent]
})
export class AppModule { }
```

❶   Importing the newly created `AppRoutesModule`

There are a lot more components and services, but these were created before we started hooking up the routing. These were part of the base codebase we used to build on top of.

Displaying the Route Contents

The last thing we need to do to get our routing app up and running is to tell Angular where to load the components when a certain route or path is matched. If you consider what we have done so far, we have defined the base for our routing and set up the module and the routes.

The final thing we do is to mark out where Angular is to load the components, and we do that by using the `RouterOutlet` directive that is made available as part of the `RouterModule`. We will change the *src/app.component.html* file as follows:

```
<div>
  <span><a href="/login">Login</a></span>
  <span><a href="/register">Register</a></span>
  <span><a href="/stocks/list">Stock List</a></span>
  <span><a href="/stocks/create">Create Stock</a></span>
</div>
<router-outlet></router-outlet>
```

Previously, we used to have the `StockListComponent` and the `CreateStockComponent` as part of this HTML file. Instead, now we are telling Angular to load the relevant component based on the URL and path it matches. We have also added a bunch of links to the various pages we added.

We are at a point when we can now run the application, and see the various routes in action. Run it with the following command (making sure you proxy to the node server you have running):

```
ng serve --proxy proxy.conf.json
```

You should see something like Figure 11-1 when you browse to *http://localhost:4200* in your browser.

Clicking any of the links should open that particular component's page in your browser.

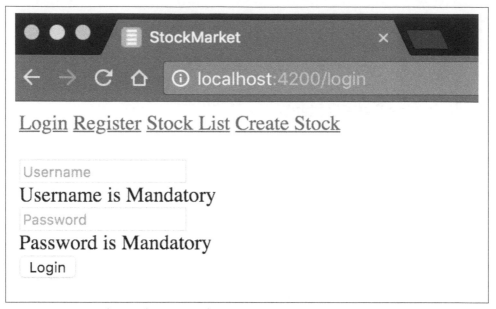

Figure 11-1. Angular application with routing

Navigating Within the Application

If you do click any of the links at the top, and open the network inspector simultaneously, you will see something interesting and unexpected. You will see that the entire page reloads, rather than behaving like how we might expect a Single-Page Application routing to work. What we would want and expect is that when the route changes, only the component is loaded, and its respective XHR calls (if any) are executed. So how do we accomplish this?

Angular provides a directive that allows us to navigate within the application. The modified *app.component.html* would look as follows:

```
<div class="links">
  <span>
      <a routerLink="/login" routerLinkActive="active">
          Login
      </a>
  </span>
  <span>
      <a routerLink="/register" routerLinkActive="active">
          Register
      </a>
  </span>
  <span>
      <a routerLink="/stocks/list" routerLinkActive="active">
          Stock List
      </a>
```

```
    </span>
    <span>
        <a routerLink="/stocks/create" routerLinkActive="active">
            Create Stock
        </a>
    </span>
</div>
<router-outlet></router-outlet>
```

We have slightly changed the content, and also added some styling to make it look nicer. From a functionality perspective, the major changes are as follows:

- We have replaced the href links with an Angular directive routerLink. This ensures that all navigation happens within Angular.

- We have also added another Angular directive, routerLinkActive, which adds the argument passed to it (active in our case) as a CSS class when the current link in the browser matches the routerLink directive. It is a simple way of adding a class when the current link is selected.

We also add some CSS to *app.component.css* as follows:

```
.links, .links a {
  padding: 10px;
}

.links a.active {
  background-color: grey;
}
```

We have added a background-color to the currently active link. This class will automatically get added to the link based on the current URL.

Now when you run the application, you should see the screen in Figure 11-2 in your browser.

By default, if you open *http://localhost:4200* in your browser, you will see an empty page with only the links at the top. If you click any of the links (say, Login), then the respective components will be loaded.

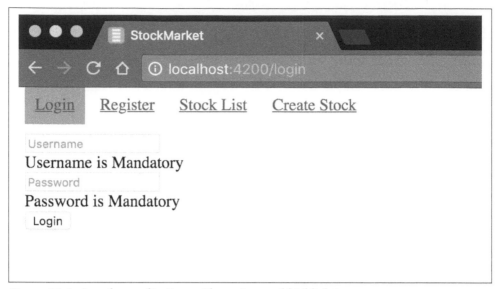

Figure 11-2. Angular application with routing and highlighting

Wildcards and Defaults

The one last thing we will take care of before we wrap up this example is handling the initial load. If we open up *http://localhost:4200* in our browser, we are treated with an empty page. Similarly, if we try to navigate to a URL that does not exist, it results in an error (in the developer console) and a redirect to the home page automatically. Let's see how we might tackle these in our application.

For both of these, we will go back to our AppRoutesModule. We will modify the *app-routes.module.ts* file as follows:

```
/** No change in imports, skipping for brevity **/

const appRoutes: Routes = [
  { path: '', redirectTo: '/login', pathMatch: 'full' },      ❶
  { path: 'login', component: LoginComponent },
  { path: 'register', component: RegisterComponent },
  { path: 'stocks/list', component: StockListComponent },
  { path: 'stocks/create', component: CreateStockComponent },
];

/** No change in remaining file, skipping for brevity **/
export class AppRoutesModule { }
```

❶ Add a default path to redirect to Login page

We have added one more entry to our routes array. Here, we match the empty path and ask Angular to redirect us to the login route. Note that for any path, instead of asking Angular to use a component, we can redirect to another already defined path as well. Also note the `pathMatch` key, which is set as `full`. This ensures that only if the remaining path matches the empty string do we redirect to the login route.

pathMatch

The default `pathMatch` is `prefix`, which would check if a URL starts with the given `path`. If we had the first route as the default matching one, and we forgot to add `pathMatch: full`, then every URL would match and redirect to the login path. Thus, both the ordering of routes as well as the `pathMatch` value is important.

You can check this out by changing the `pathMatch` to `prefix`. When you do this, all the links will end up linking to the Login page.

The final piece we will see is how to handle if the user types in a wrong URL, or we end up having bad links in our application. It is always useful to have a catch-all route that leads to a "Page not found" page or a redirect to some other page. Let's see how we can have such a capability in our application. Again, we will only modify the *app-routes.module.ts* file:

```
/** No change in imports, skipping for brevity **/

const appRoutes: Routes = [
  { path: '', redirectTo: '/login', pathMatch: 'full' },
  { path: 'login', component: LoginComponent },
  { path: 'register', component: RegisterComponent },
  { path: 'stocks/list', component: StockListComponent },
  { path: 'stocks/create', component: CreateStockComponent },
  { path: '**', redirectTo: '/register' }        ❶
];

/** No change in remaining file, skipping for brevity **/
export class AppRoutesModule { }
```

❶ Add a catch-all route that redirects to the Register page

Our catch-all route is added by matching the `path` `**`. On matching this route, we then have the option of loading a component (like the other routes). Alternatively, we can redirect again, as we have done here, to another route. We redirect to the `/regis ter` route in case we can't match the URL.

The end result of both of these changes is that if you just open *http://localhost:4200* in your browser, you will be automatically taken to the login route. In case we type in some random URL that doesn't exist, we will be redirected to the register route.

The entire finished example is available in the *chapter11/simple-routing* folder in the GitHub repository.

Common Routing Requirements

In this section, we will continue digging into Angular routing capabilities, and see how we might accomplish common tasks that are needed in the course of building a web application. In particular, we will focus on having and using routes with parameters (both required and optional), as well as understand the various ways we might navigate within our application, whether it be through the template or via our component code.

Required Route Params

Let's first see how we add a route where we might depend on the route to decide what to load. The simplest thing we can do within the context of our example is to build a details page for our stock.

For this section, we will use the previous section code as the base and build on top of it. In case you are not coding along, you can grab the codebase from the *chapter11/simple-routing* folder in the GitHub repository. Also, make sure you keep the Node server running in the background, and you proxy your requests to it when you serve your Angular application.

For the purpose of keeping our example focused on the routing, a completed (simplistic) `StockDetailsComponent` is already created in the *src/app/stocks* folder. It is already registered in the `AppModule`. All it shows is a repetition of the individual `StockItemComponent`, but without the favoriting logic. Before we look at it, let's first see how our routes definition would change to include this new route. We would modify the *app-routes.module.ts* file as follows:

```
/** No change in imports, skipping for brevity **/

const appRoutes: Routes = [
  { path: '', redirectTo: '/login', pathMatch: 'full' },
  { path: 'login', component: LoginComponent },
  { path: 'register', component: RegisterComponent },
  { path: 'stocks/list', component: StockListComponent },
  { path: 'stocks/create', component: CreateStockComponent },
  { path: 'stock/:code', component: StockDetailsComponent },    ❶
  { path: '**', redirectTo: '/register' }
];

/** No change in remaining file, skipping for brevity **/
export class AppRoutesModule { }
```

❶ A new route to load the details of a stock

There is only one addition to the route, which is a path to StockDetailsComponent. Note the path, which is stock/:code. This includes a variable in the URL, which can change based on which stock needs to be loaded. Our component in this case, the StockDetailsComponent, can then when it is loaded read the code from the route, and then load the corresponding stock from our server. Let's see how the Stock DetailsComponent looks:

```
import { Component, OnInit } from '@angular/core';
import { StockService } from '../../services/stock.service';
import { ActivatedRoute } from '@angular/router';
import { Stock } from '../../model/stock';

@Component({
  selector: 'app-stock-details',
  templateUrl: './stock-details.component.html',
  styleUrls: ['./stock-details.component.css']
})
export class StockDetailsComponent implements OnInit {

  public stock: Stock;
  constructor(private stockService: StockService,
              private route: ActivatedRoute) { }      ❶

  ngOnInit() {
    const stockCode = this.route.snapshot.paramMap.get('code');      ❷
    this.stockService.getStock(stockCode).subscribe(stock => this.stock = stock);
  }
}
```

❶ Injecting the activated route into the constructor

❷ Using the activated route to read the code from the URL

Most of the component is similar to the remaining components we have seen so far, except for two differences:

- We inject what we call an ActivatedRoute into the constructor. The Activated Route is a context-specific service that holds the information about the currently activated route, and knows how to parse and retrieve information from it.

- We then use the ActivatedRoute to read the stock code (code) from the URL. Note that we read it from a snapshot. The paramMap in the snapshot is a map of all the URL parameters. We will talk about what that implies in just a bit.

Then we use the code to make a service call, and store the return value in a variable. This is then used to display information in the UI, like we have done so far.

The StockService.getStock code is a trivial addition to the *src/app/services/stock.service.ts* file as follows:

```
import { Injectable } from '@angular/core';
import { HttpClient, HttpHeaders, HttpResponse } from '@angular/common/http';

import { Observable } from 'rxjs/Observable';

import { Stock } from 'app/model/stock';
import { HttpEvent } from '@angular/common/http/src/response';
import { UserStoreService } from './user-store.service';

@Injectable()
export class StockService {

  /** Skipped for brevity **/

  getStock(code: string): Observable<Stock> {
    return this.http.get<Stock>('/api/stock/' + code);
  }

  /** Skipped for brevity **/
}
```

The preceding code skips most of the implementation, other than the new addition. Make sure you add it to the existing service. `getStock` simply makes a GET request with the provided `code` to the server and returns the relevant stock.

At this point, if we run the application, we would have a route that corresponds the stock details. But if you navigate via URL to it (say *http://localhost:4200/stock/TSC*), you would see an empty page with just the $ sign. Inspect the Network tab in developer tools, and you will actually see a request to get the stock details, but it is responding with a `403` at this point because the user is not logged in right now. A `403` status response is usually sent when the access is forbidden to a certain resource, usually because the user is not logged in or doesn't have access to the data. We will see how to deal with it in the section "Route Guards" on page 247.

Navigating in Your Application

Now that we have the route for details of a stock, let's hook up the navigation within the application. These are the few activities we want to enable:

- Navigate to the login page on successful registration
- Navigate to the stock list page on successful login
- Navigate to the stock detail page when we click any stock item in the stock list

Of these, two need to be handled in the TypeScript code, while the other is handled in the template HTML. Let's see how we can achieve this.

First, we'll modify the `RegisterComponent` by changing *src/app/user/register/register.component.ts* as follows:

```
import { Component } from '@angular/core';
import { UserService } from '../../services/user.service';
import { Router } from '@angular/router';

@Component({
  selector: 'app-register',
  templateUrl: './register.component.html',
  styleUrls: ['./register.component.css']
})
export class RegisterComponent {

  public username: string = '';
  public password: string = '';

  public message: string = '';
  constructor(private userService: UserService,
              private router: Router) { }          ❶

  register() {
    this.userService.register(this.username, this.password)
      .subscribe((resp) => {
        console.log('Successfully registered');
        this.message = resp.msg;
        this.router.navigate(['login']);           ❷
      }, (err) => {
        console.error('Error registering', err);
        this.message = err.error.msg;
      });
  }
}
```

❶ Inject the Router into the component

❷ Navigate to a path using the Router

We have made some minor changes in the `RegisterComponent`. Primarly, we have now injected an instance of the Angular Router into our constructor, which gives us the capabilities to navigate within our application. Then, when we make a successful register call, at that point, we use the `router.navigate` call to navigate to the login page. The `navigate` method takes an array of commands, which together will resolve to a particular route.

There are more intricacies to the `router.navigate` method. By default, any array of commands that we pass to it result in an absolute URL that Angular navigates to. So if we use `router.navigate(['stocks', 'list'])`, it would navigate to `stocks/list` route. But we can also specify the route it is relative to (for example, the current route, which we can obtain by injecting the current `ActivatedRoute` in the constructor). So if we wanted to navigate to the parent of the current route, we could execute `router.navigate(['../'], {relativeTo: this.route})`.

We also have the capability to preserve the URL, skip changing the location, and so on. You can read up more on the other capabilities in the official Angular Docs (*https://angular.io/api/router/Router#navigate*).

We can make a similar change to the `LoginComponent` as follows:

```
import { Component } from '@angular/core';
import { UserService } from '../../services/user.service';
import { Router } from '@angular/router';

@Component({
  selector: 'app-login',
  templateUrl: './login.component.html',
  styleUrls: ['./login.component.css']
})
export class LoginComponent {

  public username: string = '';
  public password: string = '';

  public message: string = '';
  constructor(private userService: UserService,
              private router: Router) { }              ❶

  login() {
    this.userService.login(this.username, this.password)
      .subscribe((resp) => {
        console.log('Successfully logged in');
        this.message = resp.msg;
        this.router.navigate(['stocks', 'list']);    ❷
      }, (err) => {
        console.error('Error logging in', err);
        this.message = err.error.msg;
      });
  }
}
```

❶ Inject the `Router` into the component

❷ Navigate to a path using the `Router`

Just like the `RegisterComponent`, we again inject the `Router`, and then use it on successful login to redirect to the stocks list page. Notice here that we use an array of commands to redirect to the correct stocks list page.

Finally, let's see how we might ensure that clicking a stock takes us to the details page for that stock. We have already created and hooked up the route for the `Stock DetailsComponent`, which is at `stock/:code`. Let's modify *src/app/stock/stock-item/ stock-item.component.html* as follows:

```
<div class="stock-container" routerLink="/stock/{{stock.code}}">
  <div class="name">{{stock.name + ' (' + stock.code + ')'}}</div>
  <div class="exchange">{{stock.exchange}}</div>
  <div class="price"
      [class.positive]="stock.price > stock.previousPrice"
      [class.negative]="stock.price <= stock.previousPrice">
      $ {{stock.price}}
  </div>
  <button (click)="onToggleFavorite($event)"
          *ngIf="!stock.favorite">Add to Favorite</button>
  <button (click)="onToggleFavorite($event)"
          *ngIf="stock.favorite">Remove from Favorite</button>
</div>
```

The only change is on the first line, where we use the `routerLink` directive on the container `div` element itself. Note that unlike the links we had in the navigation bar, here we combine the `routerLink` directive with a binding. Thus, depending on the stock, the value of `routerLink` will change to have the correct code in it.

Now run the application, and perform the following steps in order:

1. Open *http://localhost:4200* in your browser. It should redirect you to the login page.

2. You can try entering a username and password, and it should update the UI with a message that the username and password is incorrect.

3. Click the Register link at the top. It should redirect you to the Register page, and also highlight the Register link at the top (this is using the `routerLinkActive` directive if you remember).

4. Enter a username and password, and click Register. It should redirect you to the Login page if successful.

5. Enter the same username and password. It should now redirect you to the stocks list page, with three stocks present.

6. Click any of the stocks. It should open a page with only that stock (no new details though, we were lazy!). Notice that the URL has also changed.

A few things to note and keep in mind:

- We have not added any local storage capabilities in our application yet. Refreshing the page means you will have to login again!

- Restarting the node server will mean that you have to register again, as the Node server also keeps all data in memory.

- If you try to open the stocks list page or the stock details page directly via URL, expect to see a page with empty data, as the authentication token gets reset (between reloads of the page) and you have to go through login again.

Optional Route Params

Before we wrap up this section and example, we will look at one last thing. There are routes where we might want additional params that may or may not be optional. These could be things like the current page number, the page size, or any filtering data that might be passed around, and we want to ensure that they can be book-marked. First we will cover how to handle those cases, and then quickly look at another way in Angular to read both defined parameters and query parameters.

Let's assume that we wanted to pass a page number to the StockListComponent so that it can display the corresponding page. Now this parameter would be optional, so we want to pass it as a query parameter.

First, let's modify the LoginComponent to pass in a page number to the route:

```
/** Imports and Decorator unchanged, skipping for brevity **/
export class LoginComponent {

  /** Code unchanged, skipping for brevity **/

  login() {
    this.userService.login(this.username, this.password)
      .subscribe((resp) => {
        console.log('Successfully logged in');
        this.message = resp.msg;
        this.router.navigate(['stocks', 'list'], {
          queryParams: {page: 1}                    ❶
        });
      }, (err) => {
        console.error('Error logging in', err);
        this.message = err.error.msg;
      });
  }
}
```

❶ Passing query params as part of navigation request

We have made a slight change to the router.navigate in the subscribe, in that we pass a queryParams object as part of the second argument to the call. This will trans-late to query parameters in the route.

Now let's see how we might read the query params when necessary in our compo-nent. We would modify the StockListComponent as follows:

```
/** Imports unchanged, skipping for brevity **/
import { ActivatedRoute } from '@angular/router';

@Component({
  selector: 'app-stock-list',
  templateUrl: './stock-list.component.html',
  styleUrls: ['./stock-list.component.css']
})
export class StockListComponent implements OnInit {

  public stocks$: Observable<Stock[]>;
  constructor(private stockService: StockService,
              private userStore: UserStoreService,
              private route: ActivatedRoute) { }        ❶

  ngOnInit() {
    console.log('Page No. : ',
        this.route.snapshot.queryParamMap.get('page'));   ❷
    this.stocks$ = this.stockService.getStocks();
  }
}
```

❶ Inject the current `ActivatedRoute` into the constructor

❷ Read the query parameter from the route `snapshot`

Very similar to how we read the defined parameters, we can also read the query parameters from the `ActivatedRoute` snapshot. In this case, when we run the application, when we successfully login, we would see that our route in the browser becomes *http://localhost:4200/stocks/list?page=1*, and we get the page number printed in the console.

Before we wrap up this topic, there is one additional thing to note or be wary of when working with routes and route parameters (whether mandatory or query parameters). So far, we used the `snapshot` from the `ActivatedRoute` to read our parameters in the `ngOnInit` of our components. This is OK if the component is loaded only once, and we navigate from it to another component and route. But if there is a chance that the same component might need to be loaded with different parameters, then it is recommended that we do not rely on the `snapshot`.

Instead, we can treat the parameters and query parameters as an observable, just like service calls and HTTP requests. This way, the subscription will get triggered each time the URL changes, allowing us to reload the data rather than relying on the `snapshot`.

Let's change our `StockListComponent` slightly to see it action. First we will add a button to our template to simulate moving to the next page, by modifying the *src/app/stock/stock-list/stock-list.component.html* file as follows:

```
<app-stock-item *ngFor="let stock of stocks$ | async"
                [stock]="stock">
</app-stock-item>
<div>
  <button type="button" (click)="nextPage()">Next page</button>
</div>
```

We simply added a button, which on click triggers the `nextPage()` method that we will create. Next, let's modify the component code to use a subscription to an observable, instead of relying on the `snapshot`. Our finished *src/app/stock/stock-list/stock-list.component.ts* would look like this:

```
/** Imports unchanged, skipping for brevity **/
import { ActivatedRoute, Router } from '@angular/router';

@Component({
  selector: 'app-stock-list',
  templateUrl: './stock-list.component.html',
  styleUrls: ['./stock-list.component.css']
})
export class StockListComponent implements OnInit {

  public stocks$: Observable<Stock[]>;
  private page = 1;
  constructor(private stockService: StockService,
              private userStore: UserStoreService,
              private router: Router,                        ❶
              private route: ActivatedRoute) { }            ❷

  ngOnInit() {
    console.log('Page No. : ',
        this.route.snapshot.queryParamMap.get('page'));      ❸
    this.route.queryParams.subscribe((params) => {           ❹
      console.log('Page : ', params.page);
      this.stocks$ = this.stockService.getStocks();
    });
  }

  nextPage() {
    this.router.navigate([], {
      queryParams: {
        page: ++this.page                                    ❺
      }
    })
  }
}
```

❶ Inject router into the constructor

❷ Inject `ActivatedRoute` into the constructor

❸ Read page from query params `snapshot`

❹ Subscribe to `queryParams` for any changes

❺ Navigate to the same page while increasing the page number

There are a few changes, so let's go over them one by one:

- We added a local variable `page`, and initialized it to 1.
- We added a `nextPage()` method, which on click navigates (using `router.navi gate`) to the next page. Note that we don't provide any commands, to keep it at the same page, but just change the query params.
- In the `ngOnInit`, we left the old `console.log` as it is reading from the `snapshot`. In addition, we subscribe to the `queryParams` observable. This subscription will trigger each time the `page` changes, while we remain on the same component.

Now, you can try the following:

- Login (or register again, in case you restarted the server).
- Note the developer tools console to see the initial page number in the `snapshot` as well as the observable subscription getting triggered.
- Click the "Next page" button a few times, to see the subscription getting triggered.

Whether we subscribe to the `queryParams` or to `params`, the code doesn't change by much. This is a super useful approach in case you have a component where the data will get loaded for various parameters without the component getting reloaded.

The entire completed example (including parameters, navigation, and query parameters including the subscription-based approach) can be found in the *chapter11/ navigation-and-params* folder in the GitHub repository.

Route Guards

The next thing we will cover is the concept of route guards. Route guards in Angular are a way of protecting the loading or unloading of a route based on your own conditions. Route guards give you a lot of flexibility in the kinds of checks you want to add before a route opens or closes. In this section, we will deal with three in particular: a guard to prevent a route from opening, a guard to prevent a route from closing, and a guard that loads necessary data before a route is opened. We will keep the examples very simple, but these could be extended to do whatever is needed in your use case.

For this entire section, we will use the codebase from the previous section as a base to build on. In case you are not coding along, you can find the starter code in the *chapter11/navigation-and-params* folder in the GitHub repository.

Authenticated-Only Routes

The first thing we will tackle is the issue we saw in the previous section, where if we tried to navigate to the Stock List component without logging in, we would end up seeing an empty page. What we would ideally want in this case is a message or error, and a redirection to the login page so that we can prompt the user to login.

For this, we will rely on the UserStoreService to figure out if the user is currently logged in or not. Using this service, we will then create an authentication guard, which will kick in before we open a protected route. The authentication guard will then decide whether we can continue on to the route, or if we need to redirect to a different route.

To accomplish this, the first thing we will do is create an AuthGuard. To get it kickstarted, you can of course use the Angular CLI (remember, ng g guard guards/auth will do the trick). Replace the content of the generated file (*src/app/guards/auth.guard.ts*) with the following:

```
import { Injectable }    from '@angular/core';
import { CanActivate, Router }    from '@angular/router';
import { UserStoreService } from '../services/user-store.service';
import { Observable } from 'rxjs/Observable';

@Injectable()
export class AuthGuard implements CanActivate {

  constructor(private userStore: UserStoreService,
              private router: Router) {}

  canActivate(): boolean {
    console.log('AuthGuard#canActivate called');

    if (this.userStore.isLoggedIn()) { return true };

    console.log('AuthGuard#canActivate not authorized to access page');
    // Can store current route and redirect back to it
    // Store it in a service, add it to a query param
    this.router.navigate(['login']);

    return false;
  }
}
```

The AuthGuard class is straightforward, and looks and behaves just like an Angular service. The service looks pretty simple, but let's walk through the changes one by one:

- We implement an interface called CanActivate from the Angular router module.

- We inject both the UserStoreService and the Router as part of the constructor.

- We then implement the canActivate method. The canActivate method can return either a boolean or an Observable<boolean>. If it resolves to true, then the route will activate. If not, the route will not open.

- In the canActivate, we check the UserStoreService to see if the user is logged in. If he's not, we redirect the user to the Login page, and return false as well.

In the last step is where we can add our custom logic, if needed. For example, we could preserve the URL we were trying to open. Once the user successfully logs in, we can then redirect to the saved URL rather than the default.

We also can access the newly activated route as well as the router snapshot as arguments to the canActivate method, in case we need to access any route or URL-specific values to make our decision.

Another thing to note is that in our example, we are actually relying on synchronous state to decide whether to proceed or not. But as mentioned, canActivate can also return an observable or a promise, thus allowing you to make server calls to decide whether or not to proceed. Angular will wait for the service to return before making a decision on whether or not the route should activate.

Make sure that you hook up the service in the AppModule before you proceed further. This might be required even if you use the Angular CLI, as we have multiple modules in our application.

Now, let's hook up our AuthGuard to the routing. We will modify the *src/app-routes.module.ts* file as follows:

```
/** Imports unchanged, skipping for brevity **/
import { AuthGuard } from './guards/auth.guard';

const appRoutes: Routes = [
  { path: '', redirectTo: '/login', pathMatch: 'full' },
  { path: 'login', component: LoginComponent },
  { path: 'register', component: RegisterComponent },
  { path: 'stocks/list', component: StockListComponent,
    canActivate: [AuthGuard] },                          ❶
  { path: 'stocks/create', component: CreateStockComponent,
    canActivate: [AuthGuard] },                          ❷
  { path: 'stock/:code', component: StockDetailsComponent,
    canActivate: [AuthGuard] },                          ❸
```

```
    { path: '**', redirectTo: '/register' }
];

/** Code unchanged, skipping for brevity **/
export class AppRoutesModule { }
```

❶ Add the AuthGuard to the StockListComponent

❷ Add the AuthGuard to the CreateStockComponent

❸ Add the AuthGuard to the StockDetailsComponent

To the three stock routes, we have added another key to the route definition. We have added a canActivate key, which takes an array of guards. We only have the Auth Guard, so we pass that as the only element of the array. Thus, only the routes we add to the canActivate guard will use the guard, and the others will continue to work as normal.

Before we run this application, ensure that the AuthGuard is hooked up as a provider in the AppModule, which the ng generate guard does not do by default. Your *src/app.module.ts* file should have the following in it:

```
/** Other imports unchanged, skipping for brevity **/
import { AuthGuard } from './guards/auth.guard';

@NgModule({
  /** No changes to imports and declarations **/
  providers: [
    /** No changes to other services **/
    AuthGuard,                          ❶
    {
      provide: HTTP_INTERCEPTORS,
      useClass: StockAppInterceptor,
      multi: true,
    }
  ],
  bootstrap: [AppComponent]
})
export class AppModule { }
```

❶ Add AuthGuard to the providers list

If you run the application at this point, you should see that trying to navigate directly to the stock list or create stock page will end up redirecting you to the Login page. You can confirm that the guard is working by checking the web development console logs.

Preventing Unload

Similar to how we can prevent loading of a route, we can also prevent deactivation of a route using guards. The canDeactivate guard is most commonly used to prevent the user from losing data by navigating away unintentionally from a form page, or to autosave the data when the user navigates away from a page. Other creative uses for the canDeactivate guard could be logging and analytics.

In this example, we will again keep it very simple to just demonstrate the point, but you can extend it for your purpose. We will simply always prompt the user when navigating away from the CreateStockComponent. But you could make it smarter by looking at the form state, and whether there are any changes before prompting.

Create a CreateStockDeactivateGuard (again, your choice, either create it manually or using the Angular CLI). Don't forget to register it in the providers array in the AppModule, and then replace the contents of the service with the following:

```
import { Injectable } from '@angular/core';
import { CanDeactivate, ActivatedRouteSnapshot, RouterStateSnapshot }
    from '@angular/router';
import { CreateStockComponent }
    from '../stock/create-stock/create-stock.component';
import { Observable } from 'rxjs/Observable';

@Injectable()
export class CreateStockDeactivateGuard
        implements CanDeactivate<CreateStockComponent> {        ❶

  constructor() { }

  canDeactivate(component: CreateStockComponent,               ❷
                currentRoute: ActivatedRouteSnapshot,          ❸
                currentState: RouterStateSnapshot,             ❹
                nextState?: RouterStateSnapshot):              ❺
                    boolean | Observable<boolean> | Promise<boolean> {
    return window.confirm('Do you want to navigate away from this page?');
  }
}
```

❶ Implement the CanDeactivate interface, specific for our CreateStockComponent

❷ Instance of the CreateStockComponent passed to the canDeactivate method

❸ The currently ActivatedRoute snapshot passed to the canDeactivate method

❹ The current router state snapshot passed to the canDeactivate method

❺ The next state that is being navigated to from the current state

Our `CanDeactivate` guard is slightly different from the `CanActivate` guard, and for a few reasons. The most important reason is that usually, the deactivation is in context of an existing component, and so the state of that component is usually important in deciding whether or not the router can deactivate the component and route.

Here, we implement a `CanDeactivate` guard that is specific to our `CreateStockCompo nent`. The advantage is that we can access state and methods from our component to make the decision (not that we are doing it in our example!). If we had the form state available in the component, this would be a great place to access it and check if the form was `dirty` or not. You can also refer to the current route and state, as well as what the transition is going to and factor all of these into your decision.

You can return a simple `boolean` (like we are), or return an observable or a promise that translates to a `boolean`, and Angular will wait for the asynchronous behavior to finish before making a decision.

Now, let's hook up this guard to the `AppRoutesModule`:

```
/** Imports unchanged, skipping for brevity **/
import { CreateStockDeactivateGuard }
    from './guards/create-stock-deactivate.guard';

const appRoutes: Routes = [
  { path: '', redirectTo: '/login', pathMatch: 'full' },
  { path: 'login', component: LoginComponent },
  { path: 'register', component: RegisterComponent },
  { path: 'stocks/list', component: StockListComponent,
    canActivate: [AuthGuardService] },
  { path: 'stocks/create', component: CreateStockComponent,
    canActivate: [AuthGuardService],
    canDeactivate: [CreateStockDeactivateGuard] },    ❶
  { path: 'stock/:code', component: StockDetailsComponent,
    canActivate: [AuthGuardService] },
  { path: '**', redirectTo: '/register' }
];

/** Code unchanged, skipping for brevity **/
export class AppRoutesModule { }
```

❶ Add the `CreateStockDeactivateGuard` to the create stock route

We have only added another guard (`canDeactivate`) on the `stocks/create` route, and hooked up the `CreateStockDeactivateGuardService` as the only item in the array.

Make sure you hook up the new guard to the `AppModule` and register it with the `providers` array like the other guard. Don't forget to do this for any new service or guard if it is not automatically added by the Angular CLI.

Once you do this, you can run your application. Log in and navigate to the create stock page, and then try clicking any of the links at the top. At that point, you should see the confirmation asking whether you really want to navigate away. Clicking "No" should leave you on the same page, while clicking "Yes" would allow you to navigate away.

Again, remember that you are free to make the logic as complex as needed. You need to make a call to server to persist the data and then only navigate away? Feel free to change the guard around. The only thing to note is that this will not detect if you change the URL manually yourself. It will only detect navigation within the application context.

A Generic CanDeactivate Guard?

We just saw that the `CanDeactivate` guard was specific to a component, and we get an instance of that component in the `canDeacti vate` method. Then is it possible for us to create a generic guard?

The answer is yes. One common technique is to create an interface (say, `DeactivateableComponent`), with a method (say, `canDeacti vate`) that returns a `boolean`, a `Promise<boolean>`, or an `Observa ble<boolean>`.

We can then create a `CanDeactivate<DeactivateableComponent>` that relies on the return value of `canDeactivate` to decide whether to deactivate or not. Each component that needs this guard simply needs to implement this interface, and you can then reuse the guard as needed.

Again, this is only useful for a select handful of cases, primarily if you have multiple components that need to decide whether they can deactivate or not, but all in different ways.

Preloading Data Using Resolve

The last thing we will see in this section is how to preload data before a route is activated. There might be cases where we want to make the service call to fetch its data before the component loads. Similarly, we might want to check if the data exists before even opening up the component. In these cases, it might make sense for us to try to prefetch the data before the component itself. In Angular, we do this using a `Resolver`.

Let's take an example to demonstrate how a `Resolver` works and how you might implement one. Say we wanted to resolve the stock data even before we open up the details of a stock. This would also in some sense allow us to check if the stock with a particular code exists even before opening the stock details component.

To accomplish this, we would use a `Resolver`. Use the Angular CLI or manually create a `StockLoadResolver`, with the following content:

```
import { Injectable } from '@angular/core';
import { StockService } from './stock.service';
import { Resolve, ActivatedRouteSnapshot, RouterStateSnapshot }
  from '@angular/router';
import { Stock } from '../model/stock';
import { Observable } from 'rxjs/Observable';

@Injectable()
export class StockLoadResolverService implements Resolve<Stock> {

  constructor(private stockService: StockService) { }

  resolve(route: ActivatedRouteSnapshot,
          state: RouterStateSnapshot):
            Stock | Observable<Stock> | Promise<Stock> {
    const stockCode = route.paramMap.get('code');
    return this.stockService.getStock(stockCode);
  }
}
```

A `Resolver` implements the `Resolve` interface, and is typed. In this case, we are building a `Resolver` that returns one individual stock. We inject the `StockService` into the constructor, and then implement the `resolve` method. Here we have access to the route and state, which allows us to fetch the parameter information from the URL.

In the `resolve`, we load the `stockCode` from the URL, and then return an `Observable<Stock>` by making the service call to `getStock` for the given `stockCode`. That is all there is to the `Resolver`.

Make sure you hook this up to the `AppModule` and register it with the `providers` array like the other guards.

Now we can hook this up to the `AppRoutesModule` as follows:

```
/** Imports unchanged, skipping for brevity **/
import { StockLoadResolverService } from './resolver/stock-load-resolver.service';

const appRoutes: Routes = [
  { path: '', redirectTo: '/login', pathMatch: 'full' },
  { path: 'login', component: LoginComponent },
  { path: 'register', component: RegisterComponent },
  { path: 'stocks/list', component: StockListComponent,
```

```
      canActivate: [AuthGuardService] },
    { path: 'stocks/create', component: CreateStockComponent,
      canActivate: [AuthGuardService],
      canDeactivate: [CreateStockDeactivateGuardService] },
    { path: 'stock/:code', component: StockDetailsComponent,
      canActivate: [AuthGuardService],
      resolve: { stock: StockLoadResolverService } },    ❶
    { path: '**', redirectTo: '/register' }
];

/** Code unchanged, skipping for brevity **/
export class AppRoutesModule { }
```

❶   Add a resolver to the stock details route

Again, this file has only changed in one line. To the `stock/:code` route, we have now added a `resolve` key, which is an object. For each key of the object, we map a `Resolver` implementation. In this case, we only have the `stock` that needs to be resolved using the `StockLoadResolverService`. This is one part of the work that needs to be done, which ensures that the stock with the given code (based on the URL) is prefetched.

Next, let's see how to modify the `StockDetailsComponent` to use the prefetched information instead of making the service call itself:

```
import { Component, OnInit } from '@angular/core';
import { StockService } from '../../services/stock.service';
import { ActivatedRoute } from '@angular/router';
import { Stock } from '../../model/stock';

@Component({
  selector: 'app-stock-details',
  templateUrl: './stock-details.component.html',
  styleUrls: ['./stock-details.component.css']
})
export class StockDetailsComponent implements OnInit {

  public stock: Stock;
  constructor(private route: ActivatedRoute) { }

  ngOnInit() {
    this.route.data.subscribe((data: {stock: Stock}) => {
      this.stock = data.stock;
    });
  }
}
```

The major change in the component is that we have now gotten rid of our dependency on the `StockService`. Instead, we just use the `ActivatedRoute`. In the `ngOnInit`, we subscribe to changes on the `data` element on the `ActivatedRoute`. The resolved data would be made available in the data with the key that we used in the route (`stock` for us). We simply read the key and store the data for use.

You could easily extend the resolve to any data and any number of data items that you want to prefetch. The completed example is available in the *chapter11/route-guards* folder in the GitHub repository.

Conclusion

In this chapter, we took a deep dive into Angular routing. In particular, we saw how to start setting up the Angular router for any Angular application. We then dealt with handling different kinds of routes, and handling required and optional parameters in routing. We also dealt with handling protected routes, as well as ensuring that we don't lose data by navigating away from a filled-out form.

In the next chapter, we will bring together all the topics we have covered, and then talk about what it takes to build a performant Angular application, and how to think about deploying it in production.

Exercise

Take the base exercise from *chapter11/exercise/starter*. Install and run the server in the *chapter11/exercise/server* folder by running:

```
npm i
node index.js
```

from within the folder. This will start a local Node.js server which can work with products (similar to one we had for stocks). It exposes the following APIs:

- GET on */api/product* to get a list of products. It can also take an optional query param q, which is the product name to search for.

- GET on */api/product/:id* to get an individual product with an ID.

- POST on */api/product* with a product information in the body to create a product on the server (in-memory of course; restarting the server would lose all created products).

- PATCH on */api/product/:id* with the product ID in the URL and a field `changeIn Quantity` in the body would change the quantity in the cart of the product by that amount.

Given this, now try to accomplish the following:

- Hook up routing in the application. We want a login route, a register route, the product list route, a create product route, and a product details route. The components for the route are already created, as are the extra services you might need.

- Only the create product route should be protected and accessible after login.
- In the product list and product details route, the add to cart should only be visible after login.
- See if you can adapt the login flow to remember that the user has logged in even through page refreshes.

Most of this can be accomplished using concepts covered in this chapter. The only new thing might be trying to remember that you have logged in across page refreshes, for which you need to extend the service using localStorage or something similar. You can check out the finished solution in *chapter11/exercise/ecommerce*.

CHAPTER 12

Productionizing an Angular App

In all the chapters so far, we have talked about the various bits and pieces that add up to an Angular application. We started at the very basic, and went to the more detailed and complex, from simple components to routing and server calls. But through all this, we focused on functionality and getting different bits to interact and play well together. At this point, you as a developer are ready to tackle 90% of most Angular application needs.

In this chapter, we will focus on what it takes to get that application you have built out into production in a performant manner. We will cover all the things you will have to keep in mind when deploying your Angular applications to production, as well as some other concerns that you may not have thought of. We will cover how to build an Angular app for production, how to reduce the size of the build, how to improve the performance, and even briefly cover other concerns like SEO.

Building for Production

So far, whenever we run our application, we usually ask the Angular CLI to serve our application, by running:

```
ng serve
```

This runs the Angular compiler, and builds and serves your Angular application using the internal server that the Angular CLI has. You could use the `build` command to generate the files to serve it for production as well. The command would simply be:

```
ng build
```

This would by default generate all your compiled files in a folder called *dist/*. You can then simply copy everything from this folder, put it on an HTTP server, and be off and running. But it is not what you should be doing! The build that gets generated by default is a suboptimal, overweight build that would make your production application slow to load and slow to run (comparatively, that is!). Angular allows you to build an optimized version of your application, so let's see how we might do that.

Production Build

The simplest thing we can do to create a better build for production is to use the `prod` flag with the `ng build` command. Simply, you can run:

```
ng build --prod
```

This does a few things of note:

Bundling
> When we write our code, we like to keep it in nice, disparate files to make it easier to read, manage, and update. But for the end browser, loading 1,000 files is not as efficient as loading, say, 4 or 5 files. Angular CLI bundles all the application and library files into a few bundles to make it faster to load in the browser. Note that bundling happens both with and without the `--prod` flag.

Minification
> Spaces, indentation, and the like are useful for us developers, but the browser and systems running the code don't care. Minification is the process of removing all unneeded spaces. The `--prod` does this for us, thus saving a few bytes of space in the final build.

Uglification
> The `--prod` flag uglifies the code as well, which is the process of replacing all nice, readable variable and function names with a smaller, two or three character name to save a few bytes. The overall code is much more efficient and smaller to load.

AOT
> We will talk about Ahead-of-Time (AOT) compilation in a little bit more detail in the following section, but in a nutshell, AOT compilation allows us to further reduce the size of code by dropping unused paths.

Run Angular in production mode
> When we run Angular using `ng serve` (or build and run it without the `prod` flag), the Angular library performs some checks each time it renders in the UI. Think of these as training wheels, to ensure that the developer doesn't end up developing something that invalidates or goes against Angular's patterns. These checks can add up to a few precious milliseconds during each render, and thus it is recommended that we turn these off in the final production build. The `--prod` does this for you.

Dead code elimination

There are times when you erroneously leave a module imported, or you haven't ended up using all of the functionality from a module. The build process removes all unused code and unreferenced modules, thus dropping the bundle size further.

At the end of this, you should have the files you need to deploy in the *dist* folder, each with an individual hash based on the contents. This would be a pretty optimal build that should be good in a majority of cases.

Ahead-of-Time (AOT) Compilation and Build Optimizer

We briefly mentioned Ahead-of-Time compilation in the previous section. This mode has become enabled by default in any production build since the 1.5 version of the Angular CLI.

Angular applications use what we call Just-in-Time (JIT) compilation, where the application is compiled at runtime in the browser before running. This is also the default when you run the Angular application using ng serve or ng build.

In production mode, Angular uses AOT for compilation, which means that Angular compiles as much of the application as possible upfront. Thus, when the application is served to the browser, it is already precompiled and optimal, thus allowing the browser to quickly render and execute the application.

Furthermore, as part of the compilation process, all HTML templates and CSS are inlined within the application bundle, thus saving asynchronous requests to load them later.

There is also a significant reduction in the size of the built bundle, as the Angular compiler, which constitutes almost half of the Angular library, can be omitted. The compiler's work, of checking templates, bindings, and the like, can now be done at compile time, thus catching them earlier rather than after deploying the application.

Build Optimizer is a webpack plug-in that was introduced by the Angular team to further optimize the bundle beyond what webpack is capable of. In particular, it focuses on removing some of the decorators and other code that is not relevant for the final build. It only works with AOT, so you shouldn't end up using it with non-AOT builds. Since Angular CLI 1.5, this has been enabled by default whenever you do a production build in Angular along with AOT.

There is a lot more to the AOT compiler, and the options it provides and how we can modify and play around with it. You can read up on it in more detail in the official Angular docs (*https://angular.io/guide/aot-compiler*).

Thus, unless there is a very strong reason (and there usually isn't), leave the AOT enabled when you generate the final build, which should give you as close to an optimal build with minimal additional work.

Base Href

One additional concern when building and deploying any Single-Page Application is where it is served from. In cases where your application is served from the root domain (say, *www.mytestpage.com*), the default should work.

In other cases though, where your application is served not from the root domain (say, *www.mytestpage.com/app* or something similar), then it is important that we update our `<base>` tag in the *index.html*.

The HTML `base` tag is responsible for setting the base path for all relative URLs in our application. These include, but are not limited to, CSS/style files, our JavaScript application and library files, images, and more.

Let's take the case of serving an application from *www.mytestpage.com/app*, and see how the `base` tag would impact this:

1. Let's assume that we didn't have a `<base>` tag, or the tag was `<base href="/">`. In this case, when we have the script tag `<script src="js/main.js">`, then the browser will make a request to *www.mytestpage.com/js/main.js*.

2. Now let's assume that we had the following base tag: `<base href="/app">`. In this case, when we have the script tag `<script src="js/main.js">`, then the browser will make a request to *www.mytestpage.com/app/js/main.js*.

As you can clearly see, the second request is the correct one, and ensures that the necessary images and scripts are loaded correctly.

How does this play into our Angular application? When we build our Angular application using the Angular CLI, we can specify or overwrite the `base href` value. Continuing our example from earlier, we could build our application as follows:

```
ng build --base-href /app/
```

This would ensure that the generated *index.html* has the correct base tag for your deployment.

Deploying an Angular Application

There are a ton more options when building your Angular application for deployment, and you can read up on all the options and their uses at the Angular CLI build wiki (*https://github.com/angular/angular-cli/wiki/build*).

But for the purpose of deploying a mostly performant Angular application, the options we just reviewed cover the majority of the use cases. At this point, you would have a *dist/* folder (unless you have overriden the default) with generated files. Each generated file would also have a hash representing the contents.

At this point, you should be able to take the entire folder, drop it in to your frontend server (be it nginx, Apache, or whatever), and start serving your Angular application. As long as you serve the entire folder, and your base path (as we saw in the preceding section) is set correctly, you should be off to the races. There are a few more concerns that we will cover in the next section, from handling caching, deep-linking, and others, but this would be the base you will build off of.

Other Concerns

In the previous section, we saw the bare minimum it would take to drop a mostly optimal build into our frontend server and have it start serving traffic. In this section, we will go slightly deeper into specific concerns that we need to think about to ensure better performance or proper functionality.

Caching

The first topic we will start with is caching. And in this section, we are particularly talking about frontend code caching, not the API response caching. That is, how and when should we cache our *index.html*, our JS files and CSS files, and how long should they remain cached.

When we create our production builds, notice that our generated files (other than the *index.html*) have a hash in the filename (like *inline.62ca64ed6c08f96e698b.bundle.js*). This hash is generated based on the contents of the file, so if the content of the file changes, the hash in the filename also changes! Also, our generated *index.html* explicitly refers to these generated files and loads them as scripts or as styles.

This gives us a great mechanism now for caching these files on the browser. Our simple rule of thumb for caching now becomes:

- We *never* cache our *index.html* file on the browser. This would mean setting the `Cache-Control` header on your server just for the *index.html* to be set to `no-cache`, `no-store`, `must-revalidate`. Note that this is only for the *index.html* file, and not for all other files from your frontend server. The *index.html* file is tiny anyway, and we can quickly revalidate it if needed.

- We *always* cache all other asset files, like our JavaScript bundles and our CSS files, as long as possible. Again, because the asset filenames themselves will change, we can be guaranteed that our noncached *index.html* will always load the correct asset files. And those files can remain cached indefinitely. This ensures a great second load performance, where all asset files can be served from the cache.

Now, let's talk through a few potential user scenarios to make it clear how this caching strategy handles them:

First load, new user

For the very first request from a fresh user, the browser first requests the *index.html* from the server. The server returns it, after which the browser processes the *index.html*. Based on the files it then asks for, the browser makes request for the styles and scripts from the server. Since it is the first request, none of the data is cached, and all the required files are served by the server. Finally, the app is up and running after all the files are loaded.

Second load, repeat user

The second time the user comes back to our application, the browser again requests the *index.html* from the frontend server. This is because the *index.html* has not been cached according to our `Cache-Control` headers. The frontend server responds with the latest content for *index.html*, which has not changed. Now, the browser looks at the script and style files it has to load, which has also not changed. But these files are perpetually cached on the browser. Thus, the browser doesn't need to make server requests to load them, and instead loads them from the local cache. Our app is now up and running immediately almost as soon as the *index.html* finishes loading.

First load, new user, website updated

In case a new user visits after we have updated our website source code, the flow followed is exactly the same as the first load case for a new user.

Second load, repeat user, website updated

In this case, the user had visited our website in the past, and has a cached version of the styles and scripts on his browser. Now when we visit the website, after we have pushed out a new update, the very first thing that happens will not change. The browser will make a request for *index.html* from the frontend server. The server will return the new version of the *index.html* that points to the new script and style tags. Now when the browser tries to load these, it will realize that it doesn't have a cached version of the script and style tags (because the content-hash in the filename has changed). It will again make a request to the server to load all these files, and thus the flow becomes very similar to the first flow where the user is visiting for the first time.

Thus, we can see that with this kind of caching mechanism, we get the best of both worlds, which is ensuring that we cache as much as possible, without breaking the user experience in case of pushing out updates to our web application.

API/Server Calls and CORS

The second topic worth covering is how to set up your web application so that it can make server calls successfully. The browser, for security reasons, prevents your web application from making asynchronous calls outside of its domain (this includes sub-domains as well). That is, your web application running on *www.mytestpage.com* cannot make an AJAX call to *www.mytestapi.com*, or even to *api.mytestpage.com*.

We get around this during development by using a proxy as part of the Angular CLI (remember `ng serve --proxy proxy.config.json`?). The proxy ensured that our requests were made to the same frontend server (and domain) serving our static files, and it then was responsible to proxy the calls to the actual API server.

When we deploy our web application in production, you will also need to set up something similar to this. That is, your frontend server will be the one getting the initial API calls, and it then has to proxy those requests forward to the actual API server.

Your frontend server would end up behaving something like shown in Figure 12-1.

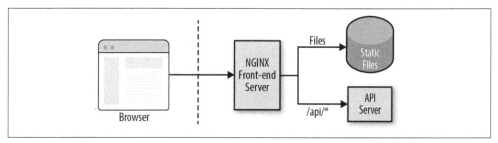

Figure 12-1. Simple end-to-end architecture for a web application

We have used NGINX as an example, but you could easily replace it with Apache or IIS configuration, which does exactly the same. We simply route all requests to our API server (*/api/*), and all others to our static files, which is our Angular application.

If you really can't do this (for whatever reason), then there is a second option, which again requires changes on your server. We can enable Cross-Origin Resource Sharing (CORS) on our server, which can allow pages from different origins (read domains or subdomains) to make requests, bypassing the browser security restrictions. It simply requires the API server to respond with an additional header:

```
Access-Control-Allow-Origin: *
```

You can also restrict this header to allow only requests from certain origins, instead of all origins like we have done here. Once you do this, then you can allow your web application to directly make requests to the API server. You can learn more about CORS here (*https://en.wikipedia.org/wiki/Cross-origin_resource_sharing*), and see how to configure it for your particular server here (*https://enable-cors.org/server.html*).

Different Environments

Another common requirement when building an application is having different configuration for different environments. For example, you might have different API keys for your client-side tracking libraries, or you might even have different server URLs to configure for test versus production.

In such cases, you can use the concept of *environments* in Angular. By default, when you create a new Angular application using the Angular CLI, it creates an *src/environments* folder, with one file per environment. By default, the Angular CLI makes the properties available in the *environment.ts* file available across your application. But you can override it by running Angular with:

```
ng serve --env=prod
```

When you run it like this, it uses the value passed to --env flag, and loads and makes available the corresponding environments file. In this case, it would make the *environment.prod.ts* file available.

In your application, you can simply import the main *environment* file like so, and Angular will ensure you get the correct properties based on the flag:

```
import { environment } from './environments/environment';
```

Handling Deep-Linking

The last thing to have a really complete web application is to support deep-linking. We already saw how to enable routing for your Angular application in Chapter 11. Once you deployed your Angular application, you might notice something weird or annoying. When you navigate to the base route of your application, your frontend server serves the *index.html*, and your application works. Any routes from that point on work as you would expect it to. But if you try to directly link to a route within your application, it might not.

This is due to how we have set up our frontend server to serve the static files necessary for the Angular application. Let's take a closer look at what is happening here:

1. If you request for the base route, your frontend server translates that to serve the *index.html* file. This also loads all the relevant scripts and CSS, and bootstraps your Angular application.

2. After this, any link within your application is intercepted by Angular within the browser, and Angular serves the relevant content for that route. So while the route in your browser changes, it is actually not making a request to the server for that new route. It behaves like a Single-Page Application should.

3. Now in the case that we want to directly open a certain route, when we enter that route in the browser, the browser makes that request to our frontend server.

Unless you have set up your frontend server configuration correctly, it is not going to find any match for this URL (which is a frontend only route). Thus it fails to serve and most often ends up serving the 404 page (or whatever you might have configured).

To work around this, we need to set up our frontend server to serve requests as follows, in order of priority:

1. Recognize all API requests, and proxy that to the actual backend server to serve those requests. Keep API requests under a common path, so that you can proxy all of them consistently and first (for example, always beginning API requests with /api).

2. Match and serve any request that translates to a static file (say, a JS, CSS file, or something like those).

3. Either serve all remaining requests with the *index.html* file, or match all frontend routes (in addition to the base / route) with the *index.html*.

An easy way to do this with an NGINX server would be to use the `try_files` directive to serve the *index.html* as a fallback in case a file with the path is not found.

Once you have set up your frontend server as described, then a deep-linked route will end up matching the last category of requests, and the *index.html* will be served. Once the *index.html* loads and Angular is bootstrapped, Angular then takes over for all further routing and loading necessary content based on the route in the browser.

 Make sure your `base` tag is set up correctly so that the web page knows where to load the static files and relative paths from. Otherwise, your Angular application will not work even if you have set up your frontend server correctly.

You can look at the official Angular docs (*https://angular.io/guide/deployment#routed-apps-must-fallback-to-indexhtml*) for an updated set of configurations that works for different frontend servers. Configurations for NGINX, Apache, IIS, and more are available there.

Lazy Loading

One more technique for a highly performant app, which we very briefly touched upon in Chapter 11 when we were talking about routing in Angular, is lazy loading. Once we introduced the concept of routing into our Angular applications, you might have realized that not all of the routes are really necessary or need to be loaded.

So one common trick that we use to increase the performance and reduce the initial load time is to try to load the bare minimum up front in the initial request, and defer loading everything else to as and when it's needed. We accomplish this by leveraging the Angular routing and using what we call child routes.

The technique in a nutshell is as follows:

1. Instead of defining all our routes up front, we break up our application into smaller modules, each with their routes defined in self-contained units.

2. The respective components are now registered at these submodule level only, and not at the main application-level module.

3. We register all these routes as child routes in each individual module.

4. At the application level, we change our routing to instead point certain subpaths at the new module, rather than the individual routes.

Now, when we run our application, Angular will load the bare minimal code up front, and load the remaining modules as and when we navigate to those routes.

Let's take our application from the previous chapter, and see how to convert it into a lazy-loading application. You can use the code from *chapter11/route-guards* as the base to convert into the lazy-loading application. Before we get into the nitty gritties, let's talk through the changes we will make:

- We will create two new modules, a `UserModule` and a `StockModule`. The `UserModule` will hold the Login and Register components, and the routes for them. The `StockModule` would hold the routes and components related to showing and creating stocks. Note that for now, we will leave the services registered at the parent level, though you could optimize further and split them into related modules only.

- We will redefine our routes to have a nice parent path for all related and grouped routes. So our login and register routes will move under a `user` parent path, and the stock routes will move under a `stock` parent path. This also means that all our redirects and navigation within the app will have to change to refer to the new URLs.

- Finally, we will change the main `AppModule` and the routes to use lazy routing and register only relevant components and services.

Let's walk through these changes step by step, along with the respective code.

First, we will generate two new modules, along with their corresponding routing module:

```
ng generate module stock --routing
ng generate module user --routing
```

This will generate the following four files:

- *src/app/stock/stock.module.ts*
- *src/app/stock/stock-routing.module.ts*
- *src/app/user/user.module.ts*
- *src/app/user/user-routing.module.ts*

Now let's see how we will modify each one to set up our application for lazy loading. First, we'll start with the *user-routing.module.ts* file:

```
import { NgModule } from '@angular/core';
import { Routes, RouterModule } from '@angular/router';
import { LoginComponent } from './login/login.component';
import { RegisterComponent } from './register/register.component';

const routes: Routes = [
  { path: 'login', component: LoginComponent },
  { path: 'register', component: RegisterComponent },
];

@NgModule({
  imports: [RouterModule.forChild(routes)],
  exports: [RouterModule]
})
export class UserRoutingModule { }
```

We simply add our two routes for login and register to the `routes` array. These have been moved from the *app-routes.module.ts* file. Also, note one major difference. Previously, whenever we registered our routes, we registered them as `RouterModule.for Root`. Now we have started registering them as child routes. This is how Angular differentiates between parent/root routes and child routes.

Our *user.module.ts* will also change as follows:

```
import { NgModule } from '@angular/core';
import { CommonModule } from '@angular/common';

import { LoginComponent } from './login/login.component';
import { RegisterComponent } from './register/register.component';


import { UserRoutingModule } from './user-routing.module';
import { FormsModule } from '@angular/forms';

@NgModule({
  imports: [
    CommonModule,
    FormsModule,
    UserRoutingModule
  ],
```

```
    declarations: [
      LoginComponent,
      RegisterComponent,
    ]
  })
  export class UserModule { }
```

We end up with a very simple `UserModule`, which just declares the two components: `LoginComponent` and the `RegisterComponent`. Also note that we have imported the `FormsModule`, because we use `ngModel` binding in the forms. We don't define the services here, because we rely on them from the main `AppModule` instead.

Our changes to the *stock-routing.module.ts* file are also similar:

```
import { NgModule } from '@angular/core';
import { Routes, RouterModule } from '@angular/router';
import { StockListComponent } from './stock-list/stock-list.component';
import { AuthGuardService } from 'app/services/auth-guard.service';
import { CreateStockComponent }
    from './create-stock/create-stock.component';
import { CreateStockDeactivateGuardService }
    from 'app/services/create-stock-deactivate-guard.service';
import { StockDetailsComponent }
    from './stock-details/stock-details.component';
import { StockLoadResolverService }
    from 'app/services/stock-load-resolver.service';

const routes: Routes = [
  { path: 'list', component: StockListComponent,
    canActivate: [AuthGuardService] },
  { path: 'create', component: CreateStockComponent,
    canActivate: [AuthGuardService],
    canDeactivate: [CreateStockDeactivateGuardService] },
  { path: ':code', component: StockDetailsComponent,
    canActivate: [AuthGuardService],
    resolve: { stock: StockLoadResolverService } },
];

@NgModule({
  imports: [RouterModule.forChild(routes)],
  exports: [RouterModule]
})
export class StockRoutingModule { }
```

Very similar to the `UserRoutingModule`, we have simply moved the stock list, create, and details routes to the `StockRoutingModule`. Do note that we dropped the prefix from the paths and just kept it relative to the current module. Other than prefilling the `routes` array, everything else is just the autogenerated code.

Our `StockModule` change is also trivial and straightforward:

```
import { NgModule } from '@angular/core';
import { CommonModule } from '@angular/common';

import { StockItemComponent } from './stock-item/stock-item.component';
import { CreateStockComponent } from './create-stock/create-stock.component';
import { StockListComponent } from './stock-list/stock-list.component';
import { StockDetailsComponent } from './stock-details/stock-details.component';


import { StockRoutingModule } from './stock-routing.module';
import { FormsModule } from '@angular/forms';

@NgModule({
  imports: [
    CommonModule,
    FormsModule,
    StockRoutingModule
  ],
  declarations: [
    StockDetailsComponent,
    StockItemComponent,
    StockListComponent,
    CreateStockComponent,
  ]
})
export class StockModule { }
```

We import the FormsModule along with declaring all the stock-related components. Now let's take a look at the modified AppModule first before we go redefine the routes:

```
/** No major changes in imports, skipping for brevity **/

@NgModule({
  declarations: [
    AppComponent,
  ],
  imports: [
    BrowserModule,
    HttpClientModule,
    AppRoutesModule,
  ],
  providers: [
    StockService,
    UserService,
    UserStoreService,
    AuthGuardService,
    CreateStockDeactivateGuardService,
    StockLoadResolverService,
    {
      provide: HTTP_INTERCEPTORS,
      useClass: StockAppInterceptor,
      multi: true,
    }
```

```
    ],
    bootstrap: [AppComponent]
})
export class AppModule { }
```

The major change is the declarations array of the NgModule. All the components that we moved into the child modules have been removed from the declarations in the AppModule now. These components will now be loaded if necessary based on the route.

Now we can finally move to the *app-routes.module.ts* file, which changes as follows:

```
/** Imports omitted for brevity **/

const appRoutes: Routes = [
  { path: '', redirectTo: 'user/login', pathMatch: 'full' },
  { path: 'stock', loadChildren: 'app/stock/stock.module#StockModule' },
  { path: 'user', loadChildren: 'app/user/user.module#UserModule' },
  { path: '**', redirectTo: 'user/register' }
];

@NgModule({
  imports: [
    RouterModule.forRoot(appRoutes),
  ],
  exports: [
    RouterModule
  ],
})
export class AppRoutesModule { }
```

The major change is again only restricted to the appRoutes array. Previously, we defined all our routes in this one file. Now, we use the loadChildren key to tell Angular that these routes are defined as part of a child module. This also means that our login and register routes have changed from /login to /user/login and so on, and similar for the stock routes. Make sure you make a pass through the entire application to fix all the routes changed, in particular the following files:

- *register.component.ts* to redirect after registering
- *login.component.ts* to redirect after login
- *app.component.html* to fix all the navigation links

Now, we can run our application (after making sure you start the Node.js server and proxy to it). When you run it, open up the network inspector of your browser, and see the requests getting made. Create/register a user, and then try logging in. Now if you have the network inspector open, you should see something like Figure 12-2.

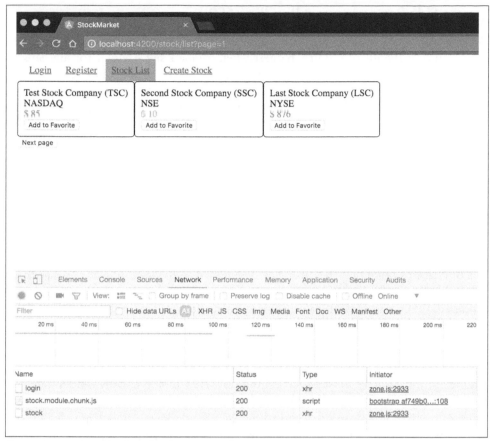

Figure 12-2. Angular lazy loading at work

Notice the additional request to load *stock.module.chunk.js* when a login happens. This is lazy loading the `StockModule` chunk once we log in.

You could extend this and configure it to your liking. You might choose to lazy load only the `StockModule`, and always load the `UserModule`, or vice versa. It just adds one more item in your toolbox to use to your liking.

The finished example that we created is available in the *chapter12/lazy-loading* folder in the GitHub repository.

Lazy loading can really impact performance and speed up the initial load for a very large application with lots of routes and code flows. It also makes a lot of sense when there are routes you know most users will not load or open. And as we saw, it is pretty straightforward to implement and add to your application.

Server-Side Rendering and Handling SEO

We will look at one last thing in terms of performance before we wrap up this section. If we consider the life of the first request when we load any Angular (or any Single-Page Application in general) app in our browser, it looks something like this:

1. A request is made with the base path to the server (say *www.mytestpage.com*).

2. The server serves the *index.html* file for that path.

3. The browser starts loading the *index.html*, and then for every static file it needs (CSS, JS, etc.), it will make another request to the server for them.

4. Once all the content has been loaded, Angular will bootstrap, parse the route, and load the necessary components.

5. The components will then make necessary server calls to fetch the data, and then render them.

It is only at this point that the final view is rendered to the user. As you can see, there are multiple hops back-and-forth between the client and the server before this view is rendered. Of course, for future routes and navigation, it is only the component and its calls that happen, so the first few hops are skipped in a Single-Page Application for further routes.

This back-and-forth nature also makes it difficult to handle when it comes to search engine optimization, as most search engine crawlers will not actually render and execute JavaScript when they try to crawl web pages (for various security reasons). Thus, more often than not, deep links and routes in a Single-Page Application also do not get indexed properly. One option to solve this is to use something like Pre-render (*https://github.com/prerender/prerender*), which can render the web application in PhantomJS on the server, and serve the fully rendered HTML for search engines to index.

But with Angular, there is another option: rendering the application server-side. We accomplish this using something known as Angular Universal (*https://angular.io/guide/universal#angular-universal-server-side-rendering*). With this approach, we render the Angular application for serving the initial request on the server itself, and then let Angular bootstrap and take over for the remaining application on the client-side. Thus, we get the best of both worlds, where the initial request does not have the usual back-and-forth, and future requests behave like a Single-Page Application. It also helps in reducing the perceived latency, as the user immediately gets the information he needs while the remaining libraries and framework load.

In this section, we won't go too much into the details of exactly how Angular accomplishes this, but rather focus on what it takes for us to integrate and get it working. Let's see how we might take the Angular application we have been working on so far and make it into an Angular Universal application that can seamlessly run on both client and server.

 Angular Universal is in its infancy, so expect to face lots of trouble as you go about integrating it, especially when it comes to working with third-party libraries and components. Even the online guides and tutorials will often be out-of-date, incomplete, or not working as the work is still in progress and prone to sudden changes.

We will again use the codebase from *chapter11/routing-guard* as the base, and add server-side rendering capability to it. There are fundamentally five new files we will need to add to get Angular Universal working:

- A bootstrapper for the server app (*main.server.ts*)
- TypeScript configuration for our server (*tsconfig.server.json*)
- An application module for our server-side app (*app.server.module.ts*)
- An express web server to serve our application code (*server.ts*)
- Webpack server configuration to define how the build happens (*webpack.server.config.js*)

In addition, we will be making changes to a few other files as we go along.

Dependencies

To get started, we will rely on a few Angular platform libraries and frameworks. We will need to install the following npm packages:

@angular/platform-server
These provide the Angular server-side components to run and render our application code on the server.

@nguniversal/module-map-ngfactory-loader
In case we use lazy loading for routes, we use the factory loader to lazy load routes in the context of a server-side render.

@nguniversal/express-engine
An express engine to integrate with Angular Universal and render our application.

ts-loader
TypeScript loader to transpile our server-side application into JavaScript and run it using Node.js.

You can install all of these using the following command:

```
npm install --save @angular/platform-server
                   @nguniversal/module-map-ngfactory-loader
                   ts-loader@3.5.0 @nguniversal/express-engine
```

This will install and save all of these dependencies to your *package.json*. Note that we have installed a specific version of the `ts-loader`, because of a bug (*https://github.com/angular/angular-cli/issues/9783*) with the library and how it interacts with our Angular Universal application.

Making the changes

The first thing we will do is modify the `AppModule` to have the capability to hook into a rendered server-side Angular application. We accomplish this by replacing the `BrowserModule` import in *src/app/app.module.ts* with the following line:

```
BrowserModule.withServerTransition({ appId: 'stock-app' }),
```

The `appId` is just for reference and a keyword for Angular to use when it renders server-side styles and the like. You can replace it with anything of your choice. We can also get runtime information about the current platform (whether Angular is running on the server or the client) and the `appId` through Angular as well. We can add the following constructor to the `AppModule`:

```
import { NgModule, Inject, PLATFORM_ID, APP_ID } from '@angular/core';
import { isPlatformBrowser, APP_BASE_HREF } from '@angular/common';

@NgModule({
/** Skipped for brevity */
  providers: [
     /* Skipping common ones for brevity */
     {provide: APP_BASE_HREF, useValue: ''}
  ]
})
export class AppModule {

  constructor(
     @Inject(PLATFORM_ID) private platformId: Object,
     @Inject(APP_ID) private appId: string) {
    const platform = isPlatformBrowser(platformId) ?
       'in the browser' : 'on the server';
    console.log(`Running ${platform} with appId=${appId}`);
  }
}
```

`isPlatformBrowser` is a useful check that you can use in other contexts as well, to selectively enable/disable certain flows and features in your application. There might be preloading, caching, and other flows you might want to keep only for the browser, and you can use `isPlatformBrowser` for this.

The next major change is to the URLs to which we make HTTP calls. In the browser, relative URLs are fine. But in a Universal app, especially on the server side, the HTTP URLs must be absolute for Angular Universal to be able to resolve them correctly. One trick (which we will do here) is to use the APP_BASE_HREF token, which we can inject into our services. In the context of our browser, this will be what we have defined it to be, and in the server, it will have the entire URL. Another way to do it might be to again use isPlatformBrowser to check and change the URL. So in our browser-specific flow, we set the value of APP_BASE_HREF in the main module to be an empty string.

We will use the APP_BASE_HREF trick in the *stock.service.ts* file as follows:

```
import { Injectable, Optional, Inject } from '@angular/core';
import { APP_BASE_HREF } from '@angular/common';

/** Remaining imports skipped for brevity */

@Injectable()
export class StockService {

  private baseUrl: string;

  constructor(private http: HttpClient,
              private userStore: UserStoreService,
              @Optional() @Inject(APP_BASE_HREF) origin: string) {
    this.baseUrl = `${origin}/api/stock`;
  }

  getStocks() : Observable<Stock[]> {
    return this.http.get<Stock[]>(this.baseUrl);
  }

  /** Remaining skipped for brevity */
}
```

We would make the same change in the *user.service.ts* file as well, which we are skipping for brevity. You can always look up the changes in the finished example if you are unsure.

Additions for the server side

Next, we will look at some of the additions we need to do on the server side for the application to actually run. We will first start with a parallel AppServerModule (created as *src/app/app.server.module.ts*) to the AppModule, which will be used by the server:

```
import { NgModule } from '@angular/core';
import { ServerModule } from '@angular/platform-server';
import { ModuleMapLoaderModule } from '@nguniversal/module-map-ngfactory-loader';
```

```
import { AppModule } from './app.module';
import { AppComponent } from './app.component';
import { APP_BASE_HREF } from '@angular/common';

@NgModule({
  imports: [
    AppModule,
    ServerModule,
    ModuleMapLoaderModule
  ],
  providers: [
    // Add universal-only providers here
    {provide: APP_BASE_HREF, useValue: 'http://localhost:4000/'}
  ],
  bootstrap: [ AppComponent ],
})
export class AppServerModule {}
```

Notice that we import the original `AppModule` into our `AppServerModule`, and then add the `ServerModule` from Angular along with the `ModuleMapLoaderModule` to handle any lazy-loaded routes. We still bootstrap the `AppComponent`. We would set up any Universal-specific providers in the `providers` section, which would be for services that are only server-specific. In this case, we ensure that the value of `APP_BASE_HREF` is provided with an absolute path so that our server can actually make the correct requests.

We would also create a parallel *main.server.ts* that will be responsible as the entry point for our server-side Angular application, which would be very straightforward. Create it as *src/main.server.ts* with the following content:

```
export { AppServerModule } from './app/app.server.module';
```

Now we are ready to create our server. For the purpose of this example, we will use a Node.js express server, for which Angular Universal has out-of-the-box integration support. It is not necessary to understand the depths of this server code. Create a *server.ts* file in the main root folder of the application with the following content:

```
// These are important and needed before anything else
import 'zone.js/dist/zone-node';
import 'reflect-metadata';

import { enableProdMode } from '@angular/core';

import * as express from 'express';
import { join } from 'path';

import * as proxy from 'http-proxy-middleware';


// Faster server renders w/ Prod mode (dev mode never needed)
enableProdMode();
```

```
// Express server
const app = express();

const PORT = process.env.PORT || 4000;
const DIST_FOLDER = join(process.cwd(), 'dist');

// * NOTE :: leave this as require() since this file
// is built Dynamically from webpack
const { AppServerModuleNgFactory, LAZY_MODULE_MAP } =
    require('./dist/server/main.bundle');

// Express Engine
import { ngExpressEngine } from '@nguniversal/express-engine';
// Import module map for lazy loading
import { provideModuleMap } from '@nguniversal/module-map-ngfactory-loader';

app.engine('html', ngExpressEngine({
  bootstrap: AppServerModuleNgFactory,
  providers: [
    provideModuleMap(LAZY_MODULE_MAP)
  ]
}));

app.set('view engine', 'html');
app.set('views', join(DIST_FOLDER, 'browser'));

app.use('/api', proxy({
  target: 'http://localhost:3000',
  changeOrigin: true
}));


// Server static files from /browser
app.get('*.*', express.static(join(DIST_FOLDER, 'browser')));

// All regular routes use the Universal engine
app.get('*', (req, res) => {
  res.render(join(DIST_FOLDER, 'browser', 'index.html'), { req });
});

// Start up the Node server
app.listen(PORT, () => {
  console.log(`Node server listening on http://localhost:${PORT}`);
});
```

The preceding server is a very simplistic, insecure web server that serves your Angular application, but after rendering it on the server side. Again, *add your security and authorization checks* before you take it to production.

We make a few assumptions so that the whole process is easier for us. Primarily:

- The server uses the `ngExpressEngine` to convert all client requests into a server-rendered page. We pass it the `AppServerModule` that we wrote, which acts as the bridge between the server-side rendered application and our web application.

- We need to figure out what requests are for data, which are for static files, and which are Angular routes.

- We expect all */api/** routes to be API/data routes, and the work to handle that if left incomplete.

- We also expect that any request with an extension (say, *.js* or *.css*) will be for a static file, and serve that as a static file from a predefined folder.

- Finally, any request without an extension is then treated as an Angular route, and uses the `ngExpressEngine` to render the Angular server-side rendered page.

Configuration

Finally, we get to the configuration that pulls all of these together. The first thing is to write a configuration for TypeScript, which we can add as *src/tsconfig.server.json* with the following content:

```
{
  "extends": "../tsconfig.json",
  "compilerOptions": {
    "outDir": "../out-tsc/app",
    "baseUrl": "./",
    "module": "commonjs",
    "types": []
  },
  "exclude": [
    "test.ts",
    "**/*.spec.ts"
  ],
  "angularCompilerOptions": {
    "entryModule": "app/app.server.module#AppServerModule"
  }
}
```

We extend the existing *tsconfig.json*, and point it to our new `AppServerModule` as the entry module. Also, the module *must* be set to `commonjs` for the Angular Universal application to work.

Next, we need the Webpack configuration for our server to compile and work. We add it as *webpack.server.config.js* at the root folder level, with the following content:

```
const path = require('path');
const webpack = require('webpack');
```

```
module.exports = {
  entry: { server: './server.ts' },
  resolve: { extensions: ['.js', '.ts'] },
  target: 'node',
  // this makes sure we include node_modules and other third-party libraries
  externals: [/(node_modules|main\..*\.js)/],
  output: {
    path: path.join(__dirname, 'dist'),
    filename: '[name].js'
  },
  module: {
    rules: [{ test: /\.ts$/, loader: 'ts-loader' }]
  },
  plugins: [
    new webpack.ContextReplacementPlugin(
      /(.+)?angular(\\|\/)core(.+)?/,
      path.join(__dirname, 'src'), // location of your src
      {} // a map of your routes
    ),
    new webpack.ContextReplacementPlugin(
      /(.+)?express(\\|\/)(.+)?/,
      path.join(__dirname, 'src'),
      {}
    )
  ]
};
```

This is mainly so that our Node.js *server.ts* compiles into executable JavaScript code, with some fixes for some bugs in the Angular CLI. It also hooks up the ts-loader plug-in we installed so that it can convert our TypeScript into JavaScript correctly.

We also need to make a small change to the Angular CLI configuration JSON file (*.angular-cli.json*) to make sure it outputs our application code correctly based on the platform. Add the following configuration as another entry into the apps array:

```
{
  "platform": "server",
  "root": "src",
  "outDir": "dist/server",
  "assets": [],
  "index": "index.html",
  "main": "main.server.ts",
  "polyfills": "polyfills.ts",
  "test": "test.ts",
  "tsconfig": "tsconfig.server.json",
  "testTsconfig": "tsconfig.spec.json",
  "prefix": "app",
  "styles": [
    "styles.css"
  ],
  "scripts": [],
  "environmentSource": "environments/environment.ts",
```

```
    "environments": {
      "dev": "environments/environment.ts",
      "prod": "environments/environment.prod.ts"
    }
  }
}
```

While you are at it, also change the existing entry and change the `outDir` from `dist`
to `dist/browser`. Your combined `apps` array in *.angular-cli.json* should look something like this:

```
"apps": [
  {
    "root": "src",
    "outDir": "dist/browser",
    "assets": [
      "assets",
      "favicon.ico"
    ],
    "index": "index.html",
    "main": "main.ts",
    "polyfills": "polyfills.ts",
    "test": "test.ts",
    "tsconfig": "tsconfig.app.json",
    "testTsconfig": "tsconfig.spec.json",
    "prefix": "app",
    "styles": [
      "styles.css"
    ],
    "scripts": [],
    "environmentSource": "environments/environment.ts",
    "environments": {
      "dev": "environments/environment.ts",
      "prod": "environments/environment.prod.ts"
    }
  }, {
    "platform": "server",
    "root": "src",
    "outDir": "dist/server",
    "assets": [],
    "index": "index.html",
    "main": "main.server.ts",
    "polyfills": "polyfills.ts",
    "test": "test.ts",
    "tsconfig": "tsconfig.server.json",
    "testTsconfig": "tsconfig.spec.json",
    "prefix": "app",
    "styles": [
      "styles.css"
    ],
    "scripts": [],
    "environmentSource": "environments/environment.ts",
    "environments": {
```

```
        "dev": "environments/environment.ts",
        "prod": "environments/environment.prod.ts"
      }
    }
  ],
```

Once we do this, we can now finally add the executable scripts to our *package.json*. Add the following commands to the scripts section in your *package.json*.

```
"build:universal":
    "npm run build:client-and-server-bundles && npm run webpack:server",
"serve:universal": "node dist/server.js",
"webpack:server": "webpack --config webpack.server.config.js --progress --colors"
```

At this point, we should now be ready to run our Angular Universal application.

Running Angular Universal

Building our Angular Universal application is now as simple as executing:

`npm run build:universal`

This runs and generates the build for both our server- and browser-side Angular applications. It creates two folders in our *dist* folder, one each for *browser* and for *server*.

Now we can run our Angular application as:

`npm run serve:universal`

This should now start your application, and allow you to hit the application at *http://localhost:4000*.

When you open the URL in your browser, open the Network Inspector and look at the requests being made and the responses. In particular, notice the very first request. With a normal Angular application, you would see the barebones *index.html* being served, which would then load all the relevant source code and trigger Angular.

In this case though, you would see that the very first request itself comes with the route content preloaded, and the template HTML also loaded. It is then that the rest of Angular triggers and starts working in the background. This becomes even more apparent if you throttle the speed to 3G or below, to see the difference in perceived latency in an Angular Universal application versus a normal Angular application.

The finished code for this application is available in the *chapter12/server-side-rendering* folder in the GitHub repository.

Conclusion

This brings us to the end of our journey of learning Angular, step by step. In this chapter in particular, we covered what it takes to bring the Angular application you

---

have been building so far to production. We covered all the steps from building to deploying, and then went in-depth into various concerns for performance, from caching to prerendering. We also touched upon lazy loading and saw how simple it is to take an Angular application and move it to lazy load certain sections of your application.

That said, we have just begun to scratch the surface of Angular. There are tons of things in Angular itself that we didn't cover in this book, from creating directives and pipes, to advanced concepts. But what we have done is build a solid base for you to build from, and covered about 80%–90% of the common tasks you will have in building any application. From here, you should be able to build pretty complex things, and leverage the official documentation to see you the rest of the way through.

Index

Symbols

(pound sign), prefacing template reference variables, 113

$event variable, 100, 102

() (parentheses), event binding syntax, 27, 30

* (asterisk), beginning structural directives, 42

@Component decorator, 54

@Injectable decorator, 151

@NgModule TypeScript annotation, 13

[(ngModel)] banana-in-a-box syntax, 103

[] (square brackets), property binding syntax, 24, 30

{{ }} (double curly braces), interpolation syntax, 16, 21

    replacing in components, 60

A

Access-Control-Allow-Origin: header, 265

ActivatedRoute, 239, 241

    snapshot, 245

    subscribing to changes on data element, 255

AfterContentChecked interface, 73

AfterContentInit interface, 73

AfterViewChecked interface, 73

AfterViewInit interface, 73

ahead-of-time (AOT) compilation, 260

    and Build Optimizer, 261

Angular

    advantages of, 2

    and AngularJS, 1

    core fundamentals, xi

    shift to property and event binding, 30

    starting a project, 7

    testing utilities, 83

    versioning and upgrades, 2

Angular services, 147-173

    about, 147

    creating, 148-166

        Angular and dependency injection, 160-166

        examining the code, 148-158

        introduction to dependency injection, 158

    moving to asynchronous operation, 167-172

    service dependencies and interceptors, 199

    unit testing, 209-228

        async services, 219-222

        HTTP calls, 222-227

        testing components with a service dependency, 213-218

Angular Universal, 274

    caveats, 275

    files needed to make it work, 275

    running, 283

animations, controlling for components, 60

annotations, 14

API/server calls, 265

AppComponent (example), 14

applications (Angular)

    basics of, 11-16

    creating on the CLI, 7

AppRoutesModule, 231

APP_BASE_HREF, setting value, 277, 278

as operator, 202

async utility function, 91, 220

    fakeAsync function vs., 221

asynchronous operations in services, 167-172

    testing, 219-222

onSubmit method, 126, 139
options object, HTTP headers and parameters, 184-185
options parameter, observe/response type, 186-191
Output decorator, 64

P

packages, naming convention for, 4
parameters (HTTP queries), sending, 184
paramMap, 239
parent/root routes and child routes, 269
PATCH call (HTTP), making, 178
path (for routes), 232, 236
pathMatch key, 237
Pipe, using in ngFor expression, 172
POST calls (HTTP), making, 177-183
Pre-render, 274
prefix value (pathMatch), 237
prefixing components, 8
preserveWhitespaces attribute, 59
production mode
    running Angular in, 260
    running application in, 9
productionizing Angular apps, 259-283
    API/server calls and CORS, 265
    building for production, 259-263
        ahead-of-time compilation and Build Optimizer, 261
        base href tag, 262
        deploying applications, 262
        ng build --prod command on CLI, 260
    caching, 263
    configurations for different environments, 266
    handling deep-linking, 266
    lazy loading, 267-273
    server-side rendering and handling SEO, 274-283
        additions for the server side, 277
        configuration, 280
        dependencies, 275
        making changes to the code, 276
        running Angular Universal, 283
promises, converting observables to, 201
property binding, 22-25
    Angular shift to, 30
    class property (example), 32
    using in template-driven forms, 99

value property of input element, 100
Protractor, 83
providers, 218
    providers array in Angular modules, 153
    Universal-specific, 278
proxy server, setting up, 183, 265

Q

queryParams object, 244, 247

R

reactive forms, 123-145
    differences from template-driven forms, 124
    form controls, 124-128
    FormArrays, 139-145
    FormBuilders, 131
    handling form data, 132-139
        control state, validity, and error messages, 133-135
        form and data model, 135-139
reactive programming, 123
ReactiveFormsModule, importing, 125
RegisterComponent, 240
resolve method, 254
Resolver, preloading data with, 253-256
responseType property, options parameter, 186
root component, 12
    AppComponent (example), 14
Router object, 241
    injecting into LoginComponent and using for redirect, 242
    navigate method, 241, 244
routerLink directive, 235, 243
routerLinkActive directive, 235, 243
RouterModule, importing and setting up, 231
RouterOutlet directive, 233
routing, 229-257
    common tasks in, 238-247
        navigating in your application, 240
        optional route params, 244
        required route params, 238
    directly linking to routes within an application, 266
    in lazy loading applications, 268-273, 278
    route guards, 247-256
        authenticated-only routes, 248-250
        preloading data using Resolver, 253-256
        preventing unload, 251-253
    setting up Angular routing, 229-238

About the Author

Shyam Seshadri is the CTO at ReStok Ordering Solutions based out of India. He has previously worked at both Amazon and Google as a software engineer, and headed the engineering for Hopscotch, an ecommerce startup based out of Mumbai. He has written two books on Angular, is a polyglot when it comes to programming languages, and enjoys working full stack and developing innovative solutions.

Colophon

The animal on the cover of *Angular: Up and Running* is a tub gurnard (*Chelidonichthys lucerna*). This fish is a bottom-dweller found around the Mediterranean and Atlantic coasts of Europe and Africa. Gurnards are also known as sea robins because the swimming motion of their fins resembles that of a flying bird (and one species, *Prionotus carolinus*, has an orange belly). The gurnard makes a unique croaking or grunting noise, generated by squeezing a muscle against its swim bladder—this sound is commonly heard when they are caught by fishermen.

The tub gurnard is the largest gurnard species. It is primarily red in color, with a bony armored head and large blue pectoral fins. These fins contain sensitive feeler-like spines that help the fish explore the seabed for food, such as smaller fish, crustaceans, and carrion.

In the past, the bony gurnards were often considered bycatch and discarded (or used to bait lobster and crab traps). But as other marine species have become overfished, gurnards are becoming more popular in the seafood industry. Their flesh is firm and holds together well in soups and stews, such as the French bouillabaisse.

Many of the animals on O'Reilly covers are endangered; all of them are important to the world. To learn more about how you can help, go to *animals.oreilly.com*.

The cover image is from *Meyers Kleines Lexicon*. The cover fonts are URW Typewriter and Guardian Sans. The text font is Adobe Minion Pro; the heading font is Adobe Myriad Condensed; and the code font is Dalton Maag's Ubuntu Mono.

Learn from experts.
Find the answers you need.

Sign up for a **10-day free trial** to get **unlimited access** to all of the content on Safari, including Learning Paths, interactive tutorials, and curated playlists that draw from thousands of ebooks and training videos on a wide range of topics, including data, design, DevOps, management, business—and much more.

Start your free trial at:

oreilly.com/safari

(No credit card required.)